WE SHALL OVERCOME

WE
SHALL
OVERCOME

MARTIN LUTHER KING, JR., AND

THE BLACK FREEDOM STRUGGLE

EDITED BY PETER J. ALBERT
AND RONALD HOFFMAN

Published by Pantheon Books in cooperation with the
United States Capitol Historical Society

All rights reserved under International and Pan-American Copyright
Conventions. Published in the United States by Pantheon Books, a division of
Random House, Inc., New York, and simultaneously in Canada
by Random House of Canada Limited, Toronto.

Grateful acknowledgment is made to UPI/Bettmann Newsphotos and AP/Wide
World Photos for permission to reprint the photographs in this work.

Photograph on page 249 courtesy Leonard Freed/Magnum

Library of Congress Cataloging-in-Publication Data
We shall overcome: Martin Luther King, Jr., and the Black freedom struggle/
Peter J. Albert and Ronald Hoffman, editors.
p.   cm.
ISBN 0-394-58399-X
1. King, Martin Luther, Jr.,1929–1968.   2. Afro-Americans—
Biography.   3. Civil rights workers—United States—Biography.   4. Baptists
—United States—Clergy—Biography.   5. Afro-Americans—Civil
rights.   6. Civil rights movements—United States—History—20th
century.   7. United States—Race relations.   I. Albert, Peter J.   II. Hoffman,
Ronald, 1941–   .
E185.97.K5W4   1990
323'.092—dc20
[B]   89-71016

Book Design by Tim O'Keeffe

Manufactured in the United States of America

First Edition

Contents

CONCLUSION

THOUGHTS AND REFLECTIONS

Preface

Earlier versions of the essays and commentaries in this volume were given at the symposium " 'We Shall Overcome': Martin Luther King, Jr.—The Leader and the Legacy," held in October 1986 in Washington. The papers presented by Clayborne Carson, James H. Cone, John Hope Franklin, David J. Garrow, Louis R. Harlan, George M. Houser, Richard H. King, and Aldon D. Morris have been substantially revised for publication here. Those of Shun P. Govender, Coretta Scott King, and Cornel West, and the commentaries of Mary Frances Berry, Vincent Harding, Nathan I. Huggins, Robert Parris Moses, and Howard Zinn were transcribed from audio tapes of the symposium sessions; they have been revised and edited with an eye to retaining, as much as possible, the flavor of their original delivery, as well as the intellectual excitement and the extemporaneous interplay of ideas that were the hallmarks of this conference.

This volume—and the symposium that preceded it—began with the vision of Fred Schwengel, the president of the United States Capitol Historical Society. Throughout his public career, first in the Iowa state legislature and later as a member of the United States House of Representatives, Mr. Schwengel has aggressively championed the cause of racial and social justice so that all citizens might share equally in the promise of the nation.

Once active planning for the meeting commenced, the editors consulted extensively with their colleague Ira Berlin, and the quality of both the conference and the book owe a major debt to his sage advice.

The editors also wish to thank the Martin Luther King, Jr., Center for Nonviolent Social Change and the United States Congress for their cooperation and assistance which contributed so vitally to the success of this undertaking. In addition, we are grateful for the contributions made at the conference by the Honorable Julian Bond, Dr. Arthur S. Flemming, Senator Charles McC. Mathias, Jr., and Diane Nash.

We would like to express our appreciation for the financial support of the symposium provided by the following corporate sponsors: AT&T Foundation, C&P Telephone Company, Federal Express Corporation, General Foods Corporation, Phillip Morris Corporation, Reader's Digest, and the Ford Foundation.

We also want to thank the following for providing us with audiotapes of conference sessions: C-SPAN, particularly its executive vice president, Mike Michaelson; the Voice of America, especially its public affairs officer, Patricia A. Seaman; and Frank van der Linden.

Finally, we gratefully acknowledge the work of the following individuals: Mary C. Jeske, who transcribed, from the audiotapes of the conference sessions, several of the papers and all of the commentaries presented at the symposium; Alice Cole, Marla J. Hughes, Sally Mason, Katherine A. Morin, and David Muir, who provided editorial assistance; and Aileen Arnold and Megan Albert, who typed the manuscript.

WE SHALL OVERCOME

Introduction

This book had its genesis in the symposium " 'We Shall Overcome':
Martin Luther King, Jr.—The Leader and the Legacy," held in the
Caucus Room of the Russell Senate Office Building in Washington in
October 1986. The meeting was jointly sponsored by Congress and the
United States Capitol Historical Society with the cooperation of the
Martin Luther King, Jr., Center for Nonviolent Social Change, and an
extraordinary group of civil rights scholars and activists presented pa-
pers and commentaries to a large and intensely enthusiastic audience.
The inspiration and climax of the conference was the permanent instal-
lation in the Capitol of sculptor John Wilson's magnificent bust of Dr.
King—the *only* sculpture of an African-American in a building that,
more than any other, symbolizes this country's founding commitment
to freedom and equality.

From the first stages of organizing the conference, it was apparent
that Martin Luther King was as vulnerable as any other dead hero to the
processes of co-option, canonization, and commercialization that con-
spire to replace with a more comfortable legend the stark truth of a
courageous life cut short by an act of cowardice and bigotry. Un-
checked, these insidious tendencies to lionization do more than distort
the past—they rob us of the future by muting the clarity of King's
ringing call for justice and for individual responsibility in the ongoing
struggle to achieve it. The conference therefore became not simply an
event to honor King but rather a forum to bring together men and
women who had walked the mean streets and dusty backroads of the
unreconstructed South in behalf of human dignity and civil rights, as

well as scholars who have begun to examine the movement and its leadership from history's ever-lengthening perspective. And, once assembled, they would be asked to "tell it like it was."

The candor and passion with which they did so gave the audience, many of whom had also participated in the movement, an unforgettable experience, full of the tension and excitement that spring from confrontations among individuals who believe deeply in the views they espouse. The papers and commentaries given at the symposium, and the responses from the audience, focused on a wide range of issues. At the most fundamental level, the conference participants struggled to move beyond the simplistic figure of legend and popular myth, the hallowed image of the martyred national hero that now so profoundly shapes the memory of Martin Luther King, Jr. They sought instead to portray in a more accurate and balanced way the real, dynamic personality of King, to assess his relationship to the civil rights movement, and to evaluate both his accomplishments and his failures.

Louis Harlan and Clayborne Carson addressed the problem of de-mythologizing King most explicitly, but the issue was implicit in many of the other papers as well, as was the shared conviction that to focus exclusively on either King's accomplishments or his failures, to deify him or to debunk him, makes him inaccessible and irrelevant for our time. Consequently, the King that emerged from the presentations at the conference was, to be sure, a successful strategist, a cogent thinker, a persuasive speaker, and a skillful conciliator among the movement's leaders—a man who could mobilize the black community as well as speak persuasively to the white world. Nevertheless, Carson argued, he was only one of the many capable grass-roots leaders who emerged from black communities in the 1950s and 1960s. He did not create the civil rights movement, set its course, or control its destiny. Far from fitting the now-popular image of the authoritative, infallible, and charismatic leader, King repeatedly experienced the frustrating limitations of his influence and effectiveness; he neither wanted nor received unquestioning support from other activists in the movement. He was a highly self-critical man who was keenly aware of his own human limitations and weaknesses, who experienced discouragement and self-doubt, disillusionment and exhaustion.

As they grappled with the problem of demythologizing King, some of the conference participants focused on his career and his impact on the national and world stage. Aldon Morris, John Hope Franklin, and, to some extent, Louis Harlan evaluated the historical and sociological forces that influenced him and gave momentum to the black freedom struggle of the 1950s and 1960s. Morris reviewed racism, black urbanization, the growth of black institutions, the impact of events in the

Third World, technological developments in the mass media, and the black protest tradition, and then explored the interplay of these socio-historical forces with King's personality—strongly influenced as it was by his family, his church, and his education. Focusing specifically on the history of the African-American protest tradition, Franklin examined its two principal manifestations: one a "quiet, nonviolent protest against slavery, against disfranchisement, against discrimination, against degredation," and the other a pattern of individual or collective violence. While Franklin traced these patterns of resistance through American history since the 1770s, Harlan restricted his scope to the twentieth century, enumerating such developments as the Niagara Movement, the activities of the NAACP in the 1920s and 1930s, A. Philip Randolph's March on Washington Movement, the founding of CORE, and the developments in the years immediately following World War II.

David Garrow and Louis Harlan then dealt more explicitly with King's career itself, providing both an overview of its major phases and, particularly in Garrow's case, chronicling its course. George M. Houser, James H. Cone, and Shun P. Govender explored international dimensions of King's activities. Houser discussed the interconnections of the American civil rights movement and the revolt against colonialism and imperialism in Africa, while Cone examined both the impact of the Third World liberation movements on King's ideas and tactics and, conversely, King's influence on these movements in Africa, Asia, and Latin America. Shun Govender reflected on the situation in South Africa at the time of the conference.

Complementing these studies of King's public career and its impact, a number of the program participants dealt with emotional, religious, and intellectual aspects of his inner life. For example, Garrow traced the difficult interior journey that paralleled King's public one between 1955 and 1968. He recounted in moving and sensitive detail the "mountain-top experience" in early 1956 during the Montgomery bus boycott, a central moment of spiritual crisis and transformation that left King with an assurance of divine companionship, a feeling of self-confidence, and a growing sense of mission. Nathan Huggins emphasized the importance of King's religious faith and maintained that the power of his charismatic leadership was grounded in his conversion experience and in the faith that empowered him, his belief in a personal, Christian God. Richard King and Cornel West explored the content and sources of King's thought. Professor King examined the paradoxical interplay between freedom and destiny—a tension exemplified by the contrast between King's choice to accept his calling and risk his life, and his sense of being chosen, a paradox captured in the phrase the "choice to be chosen." He went on to explicate the various political meanings for King of the concept of freedom. In his address, which was, to a large extent, extemporaneous, West studied four major sources of Martin Luther King's thought—the black church, liberal Christianity, the Gandhian philosophy of nonviolent resistance, and American civil religion.

Besides analyzing and evaluating Martin Luther King as an historical figure, the conference was concerned with establishing the nature of King's relationship to the civil rights movement. This issue surfaced repeatedly in papers, commentaries, and remarks from the audience, though in the end, it remained unresolved. Exemplifying one point of view were Robert Moses and Howard Zinn, who approached the problem metaphorically and described King as a mighty wave on the ocean that was the civil rights movement. They maintained that he emerged from the movement, that he neither created it nor could be understood apart from it. To perceive King as a superman, they argued, makes us dependent on the appearance of a great leader to save us and limits our grasp of the potential that ordinary individuals have to work as catalysts for change. In a similar vein, Clay Carson pointed out that the black freedom struggle was in reality "a locally based mass movement rather than . . . a reform movement led by national civil rights leaders," and said therefore that even "if King had never lived, the black struggle would have followed a course of development similar to the one it did." Louis Harlan, on the other hand, maintained that King, through "his example, his personal style of leadership, and his dream altered the direction and accelerated the timetable of the civil rights movement." Nathan Huggins agreed. While admitting the difficulty of dealing with the individual in history, the danger of idolizing or deifying a figure from the past, he argued that people are "not interchangeable parts. You cannot remove Martin Luther King from that picture and have the story happen more or less the same way. . . . We know that there are movements, that there are convergent forces, and that there are historical processes that shape history at a given moment. But at the same time we also know that individuals are important."

A related focus of the symposium was an attempt to define the objectives and contributions of Martin Luther King and to underscore the areas where his program and methods are relevant to our own time and can be applied them. Conference participants agreed that, up to 1965, King focused on traditional civil rights goals; then, in the remaining years before his death, he increasingly emphasized the issues of poverty and the war in Vietnam. This shift in program, which represented a radical break from the traditional concerns of black leaders and a call, in Vincent Harding's words, for "a fundamental transformation of the values, the institutions, the life, and the direction of society," strained King's relationship with the political establishment and with other civil rights leaders.

However, while the conference reached a consensus on the nature of King's goals, assessments of his achievements varied somewhat—for the most part because of differences of emphasis or semantics—from one speaker to another. Mary Frances Berry, for example, highlighted three: his demonstration that nonviolent social change is an effective tactic for achieving justice, that "protest is an essential ingredient of political activity," and that love is fundamental in bringing about nonviolent social change. In Coretta Scott King's view, he enabled "black people in this country" to stand up "as a united force" and linked the "nonviolent civil rights revolution" with "the whole human rights struggle."

But however they defined the nature of King's accomplishments, the conference participants agreed on the importance of learning from King and applying these lessons in our day. Vincent Harding opened his commentary by quoting Rabbi Abraham Heschel, who said that King represented "a voice, a vision, and a way," and who warned that "the whole future of America depends upon how seriously we take this voice, this vision, and this way." Harding spoke for many conference participants when he raised a challenging question for our time: How are we today to follow this voice, this vision, this way?

ONE

Martin Luther King, Jr., and the Civil Rights Movement

David J. Garrow

Martin Luther King, Jr., and the Spirit of

Leadership

I FIRST BEGAN STUDYING THE southern civil rights struggle and Dr. King during the summer of 1974, when I was starting work on my undergraduate senior honors thesis at Wesleyan University. A thesis was mandatory, and I had written a junior-year paper that had critiqued a prominent political science argument about the central role of political parties in bringing excluded groups into political participation (Samuel P. Huntington's *Political Order in Changing Societies*); I examined how no southern Democratic or Republican state party (with the possible exception of Winthrop Rockefeller's Arkansas Republicans), had, up through the mid-1960s, manifested the slightest interest in actively enfranchising black voters. Hence I chose to focus my senior thesis on what *had* allowed southern black citizens to join the electoral process in significant numbers, the Voting Rights Act of 1965.

In the course of the ensuing nine months I quickly came to realize that the emergence and congressional passage of the Voting Rights Act were inseparable from the protest campaign in Selma, Alabama, in early 1965 which had sparked national—and presidential —interest in southern blacks' electoral exclusion. In turn, the Selma demonstrations were inseparable from the conscious strategic plan that Dr. King and SCLC had employed in sponsoring those protests. Hence, the resulting 475-page thesis, "Federalizing a Political Conflict: The Violence of Selma and the Voting Rights Act of 1965," focused as much on Dr. King and SCLC's efforts in Selma as it did on the Voting Rights Act itself.

I enjoyed the library research for the thesis sufficiently that even by the fall of 1974 I had decided to attend graduate school in political science. Believing it preferable to go to graduate school in the South, rather than New England, if I was to write on southern politics and civil rights, I chose Duke University where one of my three principal advisors, James David Barber, was kind enough to interest Yale University Press in my Wesleyan thesis manuscript. After taking off a semester to expand its research and to rewrite it, *Protest at Selma: Martin Luther King, Jr., and the Voting Rights Act of 1965* was published in the fall of 1978.

In the immediate wake of *Protest at Selma*'s publication, I was undecided as to which of its two main figures, King or Lyndon Johnson, I would write something more about. By December 1978 I had settled on King, and I began my research for what eventually became *Bearing the Cross* with a painstaking reading of the very first King biography, L. D. Reddick's extremely useful *Crusader without Violence*. In April 1979, as I continued and expanded my research, I filed my initial Freedom of Information Act (FOIA) request, for all documents concerning Dr. King and SCLC, with the FBI. Early that fall, shortly after moving from Durham to spend a year at the Institute for Advanced Study at Princeton, I interviewed former Johnson Administration Attorney General Nicholas Katzenbach. In discussing the attitudes of the Kennedy and Johnson administrations toward Dr. King, Katzenbach emphasized in very strong terms that one of the greatest influences during those years had been the negative materials on King that the FBI had sent to both administrations in an unceasing flow, and most importantly the exceptionally serious and tremendously sensitive allegations that the FBI's top informant in the communist world had made concerning one of King's closest friends and advisors, New York lawyer Stanley Levison.

Levison was already a familiar name to me, and his legendary closeness to King, along with his extremely low visibility through the years, had led me to write him in late 1978 as one of the very first steps in my King project. He had been kind enough to write me his appreciation of *Protest at Selma,* but his rapidly declining health—he died just a month prior to my conversation with Katzenbach—had precluded us ever meeting. Now Katzenbach's emphasis upon Levison's centrality to the greatest unplumbed mystery of King's career persuaded me to focus initially on the many complicated strands of this story, and I spent much of the balance of the academic year 1979–80 tracking down the many loose ends of Levison's life and of the FBI's pursuit of King. Three major groups of sources emerged—former agents of the FBI who had worked on either the Levison and/or King probes, individuals who had been close friends of Levison wholly apart from his relationship with King, and SCLC aides with whom I wanted to speak for the larger project but who could also shed light on Levison and, potentially, on the FBI's unnamed informant within SCLC in the years after 1964.

By August 1980 I had, with considerable good luck, solved the Levison mystery and also identified the FBI's informant within SCLC. The Bureau's FOIA releases of the SCLC and King files were also beginning to arrive, and that fall, just after moving to Chapel Hill to join the faculty at the University of North Carolina, I wrote what became *The FBI and Martin Luther King, Jr.: From "Solo" to Memphis*. It was published in September 1981, and also served as my doctoral dissertation at Duke.

With the FBI book complete I returned to intensive research on my larger King and SCLC project, research which had continued at a fairly solid pace even while the FBI book proceeded to publication. In that 1980–81 period, two developments, each more significant than the particulars of my FBI-world research, fundamentally enlarged and enriched my appreciation of King. The first was my rapidly growing interest in interviewing virtually everyone who still survived who had been in any way close to King between 1955 and 1968. Earlier, both in *Protest at Selma* and in my initial 1978–79 work, my presupposition had been that oral history was an inessential luxury. By 1981, however, and even more pronouncedly by 1983 and 1984, I had become quite committed to the belief that it was imperative to meet and talk with as many movement veterans as possible, not so much because of the specific information they could provide but rather for the emotional texture and sense of personalities that the conversations conveyed.

Second, in mid-1980 I had been lucky enough to obtain, from a West Coast speech professor who once had worked as a transcriptionist in one of SCLC's New York offices, copies of the transcripts of several score of King's unpublished and otherwise totally unavailable sermons. More than any of King's other writings or statements, this trove of sermons (which I subsequently gave to the King Center Library in Atlanta) brought home to me in a very powerful—and almost totally new —fashion how central King's religious faith and spiritual orientation were to any complete understanding of the man. Perhaps nothing else in all the years of my research on King and the movement had as significant and important an impact on me, and my exposure to those sermons determined my focus upon the main theme—one conveyed by the title—that I then explored in *Bearing the Cross*.

The actual writing of *Bearing the Cross* took place during 1983, while I was still teaching at North Carolina, but between 1983 and 1985, while I prepared the footnotes for the manuscript, I continued to enlarge the book's research, mainly by means of more oral interviews. Out of one of those interviews, with Ms. Jo Ann Robinson in Los Angeles in April 1984, came one of the things that I am most proud of, namely my midwifing, at Ms. Robinson's very fervent request, of the University of Tennessee Press's publication of her important but long-unpublished memoir of the origins of the Montgomery bus boycott.

Following my move to City College and CUNY Graduate Center in 1984–85, I completed the final work on *Bearing the Cross;* the book was published in December 1986, at much the same time that the important PBS documentary series "Eyes on the Prize" was coming to fruition and broadcast. The success of those shows, for which I along with other colleagues such as Vincent Harding served as principal advisors, helped draw a tremendous amount of attention to *Bearing the Cross.* One would be hard-pressed to envision a kinder reception for a book than what *Bearing the Cross* received, and its receipt of both the Pulitzer Prize in biography and the Robert F. Kennedy Book Award capped a period for me, reaching back to 1974 at Wesleyan, that was as pleasant as it was productive.

Martin Luther King, Jr., began his public career as a reluctant leader, drafted, without any foreknowledge on his part, by his colleagues to serve as president of the newly created Montgomery Improvement Association (MIA). The organization was set up by Montgomery's black ministers and civic activists to direct the boycott of the city's segregated buses, which had been called by the Women's Political Council (WPC) immediately after the December 1, 1955, arrest of Mrs. Rosa Parks.[1] King was only twenty-six years of age at the time, a newly minted Boston University Ph.D. who had passed up possible academic jobs to return to his native deep South as pastor of an upper-middle-class Baptist church. Devoted to his church responsibilities and excited by the mid-November birth of his first child, a daughter, he had declined nomination as president of the Montgomery branch of the NAACP on the grounds that his church and family obligations precluded yet another commitment.

Late in the afternoon of Monday, December 5, at the formative meeting of the MIA executive board in the pastor's study at the Mt. Zion AME Church, longtime Montgomery civic activist Rufus A. Lewis, a member of King's own Dexter Avenue Baptist Church, nominated his young pastor as a candidate—the only candidate—for the MIA's presidency. King's best friend, Rev. Ralph D. Abernathy of Montgomery's First Baptist Church, who knew of his NAACP refusal, fully expected King to decline. Instead, after a pause, King told his colleagues, "Well, if you think I can render some service, I will," and his selection was ratified. After other MIA officers were chosen, the group turned its attention to planning a mass meeting for that evening. There, community sentiment and enthusiasm would determine whether the fabulously successful one-day boycott of Montgomery's buses would be extended, a strategy, it was hoped, that would put additional pressure on white officials to change the racially discriminatory seating practices in the buses.[2]

Two years later, in a now long-obscure interview focusing upon his leadership of the Montgomery boycott, King told a young questioner that "I was surprised to be elected . . . both from the standpoint of my age, but more from the fact that I was a newcomer to Montgomery." That afternoon, however, King was as much anxious as surprised, for it would be his remarks, as the MIA's newly chosen leader, that would be the centerpiece of the evening's crucial rally. As he sought to gather his thoughts, King later wrote, he became "possessed by fear" that he would not be able to carry it off and "obsessed by a feeling of inadequacy." He turned to prayer to overcome his uncertainties of the moment.[3]

King betrayed none of his self-doubts or fears at that evening's mass meeting. "First and foremost we are American citizens," he told the huge crowd that overflowed the sizable Holt Street Baptist Church. As citizens, they would protest relentlessly for racial justice. As Christians, they would protest in a spirit of love, not one of hate. "Love is one of the pinnacle parts of the Christian faith," King told his listeners, but he gave equal emphasis to a parallel theme, that of justice. "We must keep God in the forefront. Let us be Christian in all of our action." Action, however—protest, not passivity—was King's principal message. "Not only are we using the tools of persuasion, but we've got to use tools of coercion. Not only is this thing a process of education, but it is also a process of legislation."[4]

At first, King and his MIA colleagues mistakenly assumed that a longer boycott would be a relatively brief matter, that white city and bus company officials would be eager to negotiate a quick solution to the dispute. The enthusiastic, overflow crowd at the mass meeting had immediately and affirmatively resolved the question of whether to extend the protest, and what the MIA was demanding from Montgomery City Lines and the elected, three-member City Commission that controlled the bus franchise was very modest indeed. First, the black community insisted that bus drivers begin displaying at least a modicum of courtesy toward black riders and that the heretofore regular use of racial epithets and other insults be terminated. Second, and most important, the MIA demanded the elimination of two extremely troublesome bus seating practices that the WPC had been protesting for several years prior to Mrs. Parks's arrest. One of these was the reservation of the first ten seats on each bus for whites only, even if it meant that black riders had to stand over fully empty seats; the other was that black riders seated to the rear of that reserved section had to surrender their seats to any newly boarding white riders for whom seats were not available in the front. Instead, the MIA proposed that black riders seat themselves starting at the rear of each bus, and work their way forward, while whites would start from the front, and work their way back. People of different races would not ever share parallel seats, but would sit on a "first come, first served basis," with no reserved seats and no surrendering of seats. Third, and perhaps put forth largely as a bargaining tool, the MIA also asked that blacks, who comprised upwards of 70 percent of Montgomery City Lines' ridership, be allowed to apply for jobs as bus drivers, positions that until then had been reserved for whites.

The MIA leadership initially anticipated little difficulty in achieving its two major demands. Hence, throughout the first few days of his presidency of the new organization, Martin Luther King, Jr., went out of his way to emphasize to the press that the MIA was *not* seeking to end segregation on the city's buses, only alterations in the way that segregation was implemented. Indeed, the MIA argued that its proposals fit well within the strictures of Alabama's existing segregation statutes. "We are not asking for an end to segregation," King told reporters on December 6. "That's a matter for the legislature and the courts. We feel that we have a plan within the law. All we are seeking is justice and fair treatment in riding the buses. We don't like the idea of Negroes having to stand when there are vacant seats. We are demanding justice on that point." [5]

Only on Thursday afternoon, December 8, after the first negotiating session with the city commissioners and bus company officials had ended with the whites evincing absolutely no willingness to compromise with the MIA's requests, did King and his colleagues begin to realize that they had fundamentally misjudged the situation. "We thought that this would all be over in three or four days," Ralph Abernathy explained. Since "our demands were moderate," King admitted, "I had assumed that they would be granted with little question." Jo Ann Robinson, the WPC president and Alabama State professor who actually initiated the boycott in the wake of Mrs. Parks's arrest, soon grasped why the MIA's calculated moderation nonetheless had been greeted by total white obstinacy. "They feared that anything they gave us would be viewed by us as just a start." King soon realized the same fact. [6]

As the MIA began organizing its own car pool system of transportation and digging in for a boycott of more than just a few days, a second and then a third negotiating session produced only continued white obduracy. At that third meeting, King objected strenuously to the addition of a leader of the White Citizens Council, an aggressively segregationist group, to the white delegation. His objection angered several of the whites, who in return accused King himself, the MIA's principal spokesperson, of acting in bad faith. King, still anxious about his role, was taken aback and was left temporarily speechless. At first, none of his MIA colleagues spoke up in his defense. "For a moment," King later wrote, "it appeared that I was alone. Nobody came to my rescue" until Ralph Abernathy, who was fast becoming an even closer friend of King's, began to rebut the whites' claims. Thanks to Abernathy's crucial assistance, King's first moment of particular anxiety since the afternoon of his election passed quickly.[7]

In the aftermath of that tense session, however, King's doubts about his ability to serve as the boycott's principal leader increased. He later said he felt "a terrible sense of guilt" over the angry exchanges that had occurred at the meeting, and he became painfully aware that white Montgomery, hoping to break the strength of the ongoing boycott, had launched a negative whispering campaign against him personally. Why should older black ministers, including many who had pastored in Montgomery for decades more than King, take a backseat and cede leadership of the Negro community to this brand new, twenty-six-year-old, northern-educated whippersnapper? "I almost broke down under the continuing battering of this argument," King confessed two years later. His MIA colleagues, however, rallied around him and made clear their full support, both to King and to whites who were attempting to practice this divide-and-conquer strategy.[8]

By mid-January 1956, as the boycott entered its seventh week and began to receive increased press coverage, King for the first time became the focal point of substantial public attention. He realized that the MIA's initial strategy had been faulty. "We began with a compromise when we didn't ask for complete integration," he told one questioner. "Frankly, I am for immediate integration. Segregation is evil, and I cannot, as a minister, condone evil." Further, he had come to understand that much more than bus seating practices were at issue in the Montgomery movement. Indeed, King now saw the boycott as "part of a world-wide movement. Look at just about any place in the world and the exploited people are rising up against their exploiters. This seems to be the outstanding characteristic of our generation."[9]

King's increased visibility also made him one of the first targets when Montgomery's city commissioners adopted new, "get tough" tactics against the MIA during the latter part of January. On Thursday, January 26, while giving several people a lift as part of the MIA's extremely successful car pool transportation system, King was pulled over by two policemen and taken to the city jail on the fallacious charge of going thirty miles per hour in a twenty-five-mile-per-hour zone. For the first time since the protest had begun, King feared for his immediate physical safety. Initially, he was uncertain as to where the officers were taking him. "When I was first arrested," he admitted later, "I thought I was going to be lynched." Instead, King was fingerprinted, jailed for the first time in his life, and thrown into a filthy group cell with a variety of black criminals. In just a few moments' time, however, Ralph Abernathy and other MIA colleagues began arriving at the jail, and white officials agreed to King's release. His trial was to be on Saturday.[10]

That arrest and jailing focused all the personal tensions and anxieties King had been struggling with since the afternoon of his election. The increased news coverage had brought with it a rising tide of anonymous, threatening phone calls to his home and office, and King had begun to wonder whether his leadership of the boycott would eventually cost him and his young family much more than he could initially have imagined. The next evening, Friday, January 27, King's crisis of confidence peaked. He returned home late, received yet another threatening phone call, and went to bed, but found himself unable to sleep. He went to the kitchen, made some coffee, and sat down at the kitchen table. "I started thinking about many things," he later explained. He thought about the obstacles the boycott was confronting and the increasing threats of physical harm. "I was ready to give up," he remembered. "With my cup of coffee sitting untouched before me I tried to think of a way to move out of the picture without appearing a coward" —to hand over the leadership of the MIA to someone else.

He thought about his life up until that time. "The first twenty-five years of my life were very comfortable years, very happy years," King later recalled.

> I didn't have to worry about anything. I have a marvelous mother and father. They went out of their way to provide everything for their children. . . . I went right on through school; I never had to drop out to work or anything. And you know, I was about to conclude that life had been wrapped up for me in a Christmas package.
>
> Now of course I was religious, I grew up in the church. I'm the son of a preacher . . . my grandfather was a preacher, my great-grandfather was a preacher

. . . my daddy's brother is a preacher, so I didn't have much choice, I guess. But I had grown up in the church, and the church meant something very real to me, but it was a kind of inherited religion and I had never felt an experience with God in the way that you must . . . if you're going to walk the lonely paths of this life.

That night, for the first time in his life, King felt such an experience as he thought about how his leadership of the MIA was fundamentally altering what up until then had been an almost completely trouble-free life.

If I had a problem, I could always call Daddy—my earthly father. Things were solved. But one day after finishing school, I was called to a little church down in Montgomery, Alabama, and I started preaching there. Things were going well in that church, it was a marvelous experience. But one day a year later, a lady by the name of Rosa Parks decided that she wasn't going to take it any longer. . . . It was the beginning of a movement, . . . and the people of Montgomery asked me to serve them as a spokesman, and as the president of the new organization . . . that came into being to lead the boycott. I couldn't say no.

And then we started our struggle together. Things were going well for the first few days, but then, . . . after the white people in Montgomery knew that we meant business, they started doing some nasty things. They started making some nasty telephone calls, and it came to the point that some days more than forty telephone calls would come in, threatening my life, the life of my family, the life of my child. I took it for a while, in a strong manner.

That night, however, in the wake of his arrest and jailing and the continuing telephone threats, King's strength was depleted. Then, in what would forever be, in his mind, the most central and formative event in his life, Martin Luther King's basic understanding of his role underwent a profoundly spiritual transformation.

"It was around midnight," he explained years later in describing what occurred. "You can have some strange experiences at midnight." That last threatening phone call had gotten to him. "Nigger, we are tired of you and your mess now, and if you aren't out of this town in three days, we're going to blow your brains out and blow up your house."

> I sat there and thought about a beautiful little daughter who had just been born. . . . She was the darling of my life. I'd come in night after night and see that little gentle smile. And I sat at that table thinking about that little girl and thinking about the fact that she could be taken from me any minute.
>
> And I started thinking about a dedicated, devoted and loyal wife who was over there asleep. And she could be taken from me, or I could be taken from her. And I got to the point that I couldn't take it any longer. I was weak. Something said to me, you can't call on Daddy now, he's up in Atlanta a hundred and seventy-five miles away. You can't even call on Mama now. You've got to call on that something in that person that your Daddy used to tell you about, that power that can make a way out of no way.
>
> And I discovered then that religion had to become real to me, and I had to know God for myself. And I bowed down over that cup of coffee. I never will forget it. . . . I prayed a prayer, and I prayed out loud that night. I said, "Lord, I'm down here trying to do what's right. I think I'm right. I think the cause that we represent is right. But Lord, I must confess that I'm weak now. I'm faltering. I'm losing my courage. And I can't let the people see me like this because if they see me weak and losing my courage, they will begin to get weak."

Then it happened. "And it seemed at that moment that I could hear an inner voice saying to me, 'Martin Luther, stand up for righteousness. Stand up for justice. Stand up for truth. And lo I will be with you, even until the end of the world.' . . . I heard the voice of Jesus saying still to fight on. He promised never to leave me, never to leave me alone. No never alone, no never alone. He promised never to leave me, never to leave me alone." That experience, that vision in the kitchen, gave King a new strength and courage to go on. "Almost at once my fears began to go. My uncertainty disappeared."[11]

Three nights later, when a bomb went off on the front porch of King's parsonage, that strength and courage allowed King, with a calmness that astounded some onlookers, to reassure the large crowd of angry black citizens that gathered. "I want you to love our enemies. Be good to them. Love them and let them know you love them," King told several hundred onlookers. "I did not start this boycott," he reminded his listeners. "I was asked by you to serve as your spokesman. I want it to be known the length and breadth of this land that if I am stopped, this movement will not stop. If I am stopped, our work will not stop, for what we are doing is right, what we are doing is just. . . . If anything happens to me," he concluded, "there will be others to take my place." [12]

The vision in the kitchen allowed King to go forward with feelings of companionship, self-assurance, and a growing sense of mission that were vastly greater spiritual resources than anything he had been able to draw upon during the boycott's first eight weeks. It also allowed him to begin appreciating that his leadership role was not just a matter of accident or chance, but was first and foremost an opportunity for service. It was not one King would have sought, but it was an opportunity he could not forsake. His new strength also enabled him to conquer, in a most thorough and permanent fashion, the fear that had gripped him that Friday night in his kitchen. At the same time, it allowed him to appreciate that although his calling might indeed be a unique one, it was that calling, and not he himself, which was the spiritual centerpiece of his developing role. King's emerging understanding of himself came through quite clearly in a late March interview, just after a Montgomery judge formally had convicted him of violating a long-obscure Alabama antiboycotting statute. The reporter asked if he was sometimes afraid. King's answer was clear and firm.

> No, I'm not. My attitude is that this is a great cause. This is a great issue that we are confronted with and the consequences for my personal life are not particularly important. It is the triumph for the cause that I am concerned about, and I have always felt that ultimately along the way of life an individual must stand up and be counted and be willing to face the consequences, whatever they are. If he is filled with fear, he cannot do it. And my great prayer is always that God will save me from the paralysis of crippling fear, because I think when a person lives with the fear of the consequences for his personal life, he can never do anything in terms of lifting the whole of humanity and solving many of the social problems that we confront. [13]

That strength and dedication remained with King throughout the duration of the Montgomery protest, which ended successfully with the integration of the city's buses just prior to Christmas 1956—381 days after the boycott had begun. In the wake of that achievement, however, some whites repeatedly directed acts of violence against the newly de-segregated buses, and, in mid–January 1957, a series of bombings struck several black churches and the homes of MIA leaders. The violence weighed heavily on an already exhausted King, for whom the success of the Montgomery protest had resulted in an avalanche of speaking invitations from across the country, opportunities for spreading Mont-gomery's message that King felt he could not ignore. Then, on Sunday morning, January 27—the first anniversary of King's kitchen experience —twelve sticks of dynamite, along with a fuse that had smoldered and died, were found on the porch of King's parsonage.

The murder attempt deeply affected King. Later that morning, in his sermon to his Dexter Avenue Baptist Church congregation, he ex-plained how his experience a year earlier had allowed him to resolve his fears about his role and his fate. "I realize that there were moments when I wanted to give up and I was afraid but You gave me a vision in the kitchen of my house and I am thankful for it." King told his listeners how, early in the boycott, "I went to bed many nights scared to death." Then,

> early on a sleepless morning in January, 1956, rational-ity left me. . . . Almost out of nowhere I heard a voice that morning saying to me, "Preach the gospel, stand up for truth, stand up for righteousness." Since that morning I can stand up without fear.
>
> So I'm not afraid of anybody this morning. Tell Montgomery they can keep shooting and I'm going to stand up to them; tell Montgomery they can keep bombing and I'm going to stand up to them. If I had to die tomorrow morning I would die happy because I've been to the mountaintop and I've seen the promised land and it's going to be here in Montgomery.[14]

Those remarks, uttered in January 1957 and so clearly presaging the very similar and much more widely known comments that King made in Memphis, Tennessee, on the evening of April 3, 1968, bring home a very simple but extremely crucial point: that King's mountaintop ex-perience did not occur in April 1968, nor even in August 1963, but took place in the kitchen at 309 South Jackson St. in Montgomery on January 27, 1956. King's understanding of his role, his mission, and his fate, then, was essentially *not* something that developed only or largely in the latter stages of his public career, but was present in a rather complete form even before the end of the Montgomery boycott—indeed as early as its second month.

Appreciating King's own understanding of his role and responsibilities is as crucial as anything—and really more crucial than anything else, I would contend—for comprehending the leadership contribution that Martin Luther King, Jr., made to the American black freedom struggle of the 1950s and 1960s. Throughout the late 1950s, and the very slow, gradual effort to build SCLC into what its creators initially had envisioned—a region-wide organization for stimulating and coordinating mass direct action protests in cities and towns all across the South—King continually struggled with his reluctant and ambivalent realization that he was not, in a very fundamental way, in full charge of his own life, and that his increasing obligations to the movement were such that he could not escape from those responsibilities even though the thought often occurred to him.

Several times during those years King, as he himself put it, "reluctantly" turned down offers of professorships or deanships at well-known seminaries. But his tension and his feeling of obligation to a mission far more important than his own life or happiness came through most starkly in late 1959 when, in response to repeated proddings from colleagues such as Fred Shuttlesworth that he devote considerably greater time to building SCLC, King decided to leave Dexter Avenue Church and Montgomery for Atlanta, where he could serve with his father as copastor of Ebenezer Baptist Church. One of his explanations for that move captured King's tensions poignantly:

> For almost four years now I have been faced with the responsibility of trying to do as one man what five or six people ought to be doing. . . . I found myself in a position which I could not get out of. This thrust new and unexpected responsibilities my way. . . .
>
> What I have been doing is giving, giving, giving and not stopping to retreat and meditate like I should—to come back. . . .
>
> I have a sort of nagging conscience that someone will interpret my leaving Montgomery as a retreat from the civil rights struggle. Actually, I will be involved in it on a larger scale. I can't stop now. History has thrust something upon me from which I cannot turn away.[15]

King's move to Atlanta took place on February 1, 1960—by chance the same day that the sit-in movement was launched when four black students from North Carolina A&T College refused to leave the segregated lunch counter of a Greensboro F. W. Woolworth's store when they were denied service. The rapid spread of the student movement and the mid-April founding of SNCC quickly guaranteed that King would not have the increased opportunities for rest and reflection that he had hoped his move to Atlanta would provide. The sit-ins, the Atlanta student movement of 1960–61, the Freedom Rides of May 1961, and the protest campaign of the Albany, Georgia, movement during the winter of 1961 and the summer of 1962 all served to draw Martin King deeper and deeper into a struggle that was spreading across the South. Then, in January 1963, in response to repeated requests from Fred Shuttlesworth, King and his SCLC staff agreed to undertake for the first time a protest campaign initiated largely by themselves, rather than by the students of SNCC, by CORE—the originators of the Freedom Ride—or by local activists such as those in Albany.

The Birmingham protests of May 1963 marked a fundamentally new level of achievement for the black freedom struggle in the South; for the first time, the movement and "Bull" Connor's attempted repression of it succeeded in presenting black demands to a nationwide audience in so dramatically powerful a way that neither the American people nor the Kennedy administration could any longer ignore or avoid them. For Martin King, Birmingham and the March on Washington, which followed closely in its wake, represented a fundamental shift as well, a shift toward an even larger and more demanding leadership role in a movement whose expanding size and scope made increasingly unlikely any chance that King at some future time would be able to retreat to a quieter and less burdensome life. "My notion of it," Andrew Young has explained, "is that it was almost Birmingham . . . before he took up the mantle of leadership, that from '57 to '63 he was being dragged into one situation after another that he didn't want to be in. . . . He didn't see himself as being the leader of everything black people wanted to do. He resisted as long as he could the responsibilities and burdens of taking on a whole movement for social change."[16]

After the 1963 March, however, King increasingly came to accept the destiny that accompanied his growing role, though that destiny, like the role, was not something with which he was at all fully comfortable. King thought regularly about what he once termed "this challenge to be loyal to something that transcends our immediate lives." "We have," he explained to one audience, "a responsibility to set out to discover what we are made for, to discover our life's work, to discover what we are called to do. And after we discover that, we should set out to do it with all of the strength and all of the power that we can muster." As Young later expressed it, "I think that Martin always felt that he had a special purpose in life and that that purpose in life was something that was given to him by God, that he was the son and grandson of Baptist preachers, and he understood, I think, the scriptural notion of men of destiny. That came from his family and his church, and basically the Bible."

The revelation in the kitchen seven years earlier had given King not only the ability to understand his role and destiny, but also the spiritual strength necessary for accepting and coping with his personal mission and fate. It was also, of course, much more profoundly an ongoing sense of companionship and reassurance than simply a seven-year-old memory of a one-time sensation. "There are certain spiritual experiences that we continue to have," King stated, "that cannot be explained with materialistic notions." One "knows deep down within there is something in the very structure of the cosmos that will ultimately bring about fulfillment and the triumph of that which is right. And this is the only thing that can keep one going in difficult periods." [17]

King's understanding of his life underwent a significant deepening when he was awarded the 1964 Nobel Peace Prize. A man who belittled most honors, including even his own 1963 *Time* magazine "Man of the Year" designation, King welcomed the Nobel award as a recognition of the international status that the movement, rather than he himself, had attained. At the same time, however, the prize signaled the beginning of a fundamental growth in King's own sense of mission and willingness to accept a prophetic role. "History has thrust me into this position," he told reporters the day the award was announced. "It would both be immoral and a sign of ingratitude if I did not face my moral responsibility to do what I can in this struggle." [18]

Following the landmark 1965 SCLC right-to-vote campaign in Selma, Alabama, which stimulated prompt congressional passage of the powerful Voting Rights Act, King's expanding sense of duty and mission led him to take on two issues that he had always been cognizant of, but which had never previously been prominent in his public political agenda—the economic aspects of racial discrimination in non-southern and urban parts of the United States, and the increasingly immoral role of American foreign policy in fostering international violence, especially in Vietnam and Southeast Asia. More and more, a harsh edge crept into King's public comments about the state of American society, the nature of the American economy, the meaning of America's role in the world, and the basic orientation of most white Americans. The 1966 Meredith March, the advent of the phrase "Black Power," and SCLC's protracted and ultimately frustrating 1966 urban organizing campaign in Chicago further magnified King's growing concern about both the state of the movement and the likely future course of American life.

At a mid-August rally in Chicago, King gave voice to just how drained he felt. "I'm tired of marching," he told the crowd, "I'm tired of the tensions surrounding our days. . . . I'm tired of living every day under the threat of death. I have no martyr complex; I want to live as long as anybody in this building tonight, and sometimes I begin to doubt whether I'm going to make it through. I must confess I'm tired. . . . I don't march because I like it, I march because I must."[19]

More and more King thought of his own life in terms of the cross. It was an image he had invoked repeatedly over the years, beginning as early as his 1960 imprisonment in Georgia's Reidsville State Prison. He particularly focused upon it, and upon the memory of his vision in the kitchen, at times of unusual tension and stress. In mid-September of 1966, following a deluge of harsh comments criticizing SCLC's half-a-loaf negotiated settlement halting the Chicago protests, and amidst a deteriorating intramovement debate about the desirability or harmfulness of the "Black Power" slogan, King talked in a remarkably revealing fashion to a church convention about how his sense of mission was increasingly also becoming a sense of burden. "We are gravely mistaken to think that religion protects us from the pain and agony of moral existence. Life is not a euphoria of unalloyed comfort and untroubled ease. Christianity has always insisted that the cross we bear precedes the crown we wear. To be a Christian one must take up his cross, with all its difficulties and agonizing and tension-packed content, and carry it until that very cross leaves its mark upon us and redeems us to that more excellent way which comes only through suffering."[20]

More than anything else, the Vietnam War brought King face-to-face with what was becoming a consciously self-sacrificial understanding of his role and fate. He had spoken out publicly against America's conduct of the war as early as March 1965, and had stepped up his comments during July and August of that year, but had drawn back from further extended public remarks in the face of harsh, Johnson administration–inspired criticism of his foreign policy views. Throughout all of 1966, despite a deepening self-reproach for not publicly criticizing a war whose harmful domestic economic effects were becoming increasingly obvious, King largely kept his peace; he was reluctant to reignite a public debate about the political propriety of the nation's leading civil rights spokesman becoming a head-on critic of one of the incumbent administration's most prominent policies. Then, during a long and peaceful January 1967 vacation in Jamaica, King was particularly affected by some graphic color photos in *Ramparts* magazine showing young Vietnamese children who had suffered severe napalm burns as the result of American bombing, and he vowed to take on Lyndon Johnson's war publicly as never before.[21]

King knew full well that his new, aggressive stance on the war would harm him politically and might well damage SCLC financially. Those considerations, however, were not enough to shake him from his resolve. "At times you do things to satisfy your conscience, and they may be altogether unrealistic or wrong, but you feel better," King explained over wiretapped phone lines to his long-time friend and counselor, Stanley Levison. America's involvement in Vietnam was so evil, King explained, that "I can no longer be cautious about this matter. I feel so deep in my heart that we are so wrong in this country and the time has come for a real prophecy and I'm willing to go that road." [22]

Many of King's SCLC colleagues, especially some on the board of directors, as well as other civil rights spokespersons such as NAACP Executive Secretary Roy Wilkins, actively opposed King's new stance. King admitted to his board that in 1965 he "went through a lot of bitter and certainly vicious criticism by the press for taking that stand," but popularity was not a consideration for him anymore. He reminded the board about "those little Vietnamese children who have been burned with napalm" and he prepared to deliver what would be his harshest condemnation of America's Southeast Asia war policies, an April 4 address at New York's Riverside Church. [23]

King's statements in that speech, and particularly his denunciation of the United States government as "the greatest purveyor of violence in the world today," brought down a flood of public criticism upon his head. Black newspapers such as the *Pittsburgh Courier* joined liberal white ones such as the *Washington Post* and *New York Times* in rebuking King for his comments, and even some of King's most trusted advisors, including Levison, reproached him for the tone of the speech. King, however, rejected these complaints. "I was politically unwise but morally wise. I think I have a role to play which may be unpopular," he insisted to Levison. "I really feel that someone of influence has to say that the United States is wrong, and everybody is afraid to say it." [24]

King privately considered, and then publicly rejected, overtures from some opponents of the war to run as an independent, third-party anti-Vietnam candidate in the upcoming 1968 presidential election. "Being a peace candidate is not my role," he told one questioner. "I feel I should serve as a conscience of all the parties and all of the people, rather than be a candidate myself." He explained to his Ebenezer congregation that his evolving role was in part a response to the Nobel Prize, which he termed "a commission to work harder than I had ever worked before for the brotherhood of man." The burden of that role was substantial, however; public opinion polls told King that 73 percent of Americans disagreed with his opposition to the Vietnam War and 60 percent believed it would hurt the civil rights movement. Even among black respondents, only 25 percent agreed with King's criticisms; 48 percent said he was wrong. [25]

The Vietnam issue helped lead King toward an increasingly radical critique of American politics and society. "We are called upon to raise certain basic questions about the whole society," he told SCLC's staff during a May 1967 retreat in Frogmore, South Carolina. "We must recognize that we can't solve our problem now until there is a radical redistribution of economic and political power" in America. The Vietnam War was "symptomatic of a deeper malaise of the American spirit." The nation required "a revolution of values and of other things. . . . We must see now that the evils of racism, economic exploitation, and militarism are all tied together, and you really can't get rid of one without getting rid of the others." In short, "the whole structure of American life must be changed." [26]

As his closest colleagues always knew, King privately was as harsh a critic of himself as he was of the war and the ills of American society. "He criticized himself more severely than anyone else ever did," Coretta Scott King later recalled. "He was always the first to say, 'Maybe I was wrong, maybe I made a mistake.' . . . He would go through this agonizing process of self-analysis many times." Vietnam was only one example of this inclination, as King made clear at the Frogmore retreat when he told his staff how much he now regretted not having continued to publicly condemn the war after 1965. "I had my own vacillations and I asked questions whether on the one hand I should do it or whether I shouldn't." Then, King explained, recalling his *Ramparts* experience, "I picked up an article entitled 'The Children of Vietnam,' and I read it, and after reading that article I said to myself, 'Never again will I be silent on an issue that is destroying the soul of our nation and destroying thousands and thousands of little children in Vietnam.' "

At that retreat King also spoke to his staff about how he had come to see the war issue in terms of his own understanding of the cross. "When I took up the cross, I recognized its meaning. . . . The cross is something that you bear and ultimately that you die on. The cross may mean the death of your popularity. It may mean the death of a foundation grant. It may cut down your budget a little, but take up your cross, and just bear it. And that's the way I've decided to go." No longer did he suffer from any indecision on the question of the war. "I want you to know that my mind is made up. I backed up a little when I came out in 1965. My name then wouldn't have been written in any book called *Profiles in Courage*. But now I have decided that I will not be intimidated. I will not be harassed. I will not be silent, and I will be heard." [27]

King's view of American society became increasingly critical in 1967 and early 1968. "America has been, and she continues to be, largely a racist society," he told a July conference in Chicago. "Maybe something is wrong with our economic system the way it's presently going. . . . There comes a time when any system must be re-evaluated," and

America's time was at hand. "The movement must address itself to restructuring the whole of American society. The problems that we are dealing with . . . are not going to be solved until there is a radical redistribution of economic and political power."

King's harsher critique developed hand-in-hand with a more negative attitude toward his own ability, and the ability of the broader movement, to bring about any truly significant alterations in the basic character of American society and governmental policies. Up until 1965 and 1966, King wistfully observed, "We really thought we were making great progress. . . . We somehow felt that we were going to win the total victory, before we analyzed the depths and dimensions of the problem." Then, in the wake of the Civil Rights Act of 1964 and the Voting Rights Act of 1965, King had begun to realize more and more that the fundamental obstacles confronting the movement and black America were economic rather than legal, and tied much more closely to questions of class than to issues of race.[28]

King's awareness that he and the movement were less and less likely to be able to bring about significant changes in American life, with regard to either Vietnam or domestic economic problems, was a difficult and painful realization to accept. Although he was a fundamentally humble man, in no way overawed by his own gifts and influence, his understanding of the public role into which he had grown over the course of the period from 1956 to 1967 left him with a deep-seated belief that he had to do all that he could, regardless of personal cost. This attitude manifested itself both in his decision in early 1967 to speak out on Vietnam and in his beginning, during the summer of that year, to plan a radical economic movement, which by late that fall he had named the Poor People's Campaign. In part, as Stanley Levison later explained, King's growing inclination to sacrifice himself to his larger mission stemmed from his own discomfiture over the role that he played. King believed, Levison stressed, that he "was an actor in history at a particular moment that called for a personality, and he had simply been selected as that personality." However, King felt that

> he had not done enough to deserve it. He felt keenly
> that people who had done as much as he had or *more*
> got no such tribute. This troubled him deeply, and he
> could find no way of dealing with it because there's no
> way of sharing that kind of tribute with anyone else:
> you can't give it away, you have to accept it. But when
> you don't feel you're worthy of it and you're an honest,
> principled man, it tortures you. . . . If he had been less
> humble, he could have lived with this kind of acclaim,

but because he was genuinely a man of humility, he really couldn't live with it. He always thought of ways in which he could somehow live up to it.[29]

Coretta Scott King understood this aspect of her husband, terming him "a guilt-ridden man" who "never felt he was adequate to his positions." In the late summer of 1967, she remembered, "he got very depressed," a depression that "was greater than I had ever seen it before. . . . He said, 'People expect me to have answers and I don't have any answers.' He said, 'I don't feel like speaking to people. I don't have anything to tell them.' " One August day King was supposed to fly to Louisville for an address, but failed to make his airplane and called his wife from the airport. " 'I know why I missed my flight; I really don't want to go. I get tired of going and not having any answers.' He had begun to take this very personally," Coretta later explained. " 'People feel that nonviolence is failing,' " King had told her. "I said, 'But this is not so. You mustn't believe that people are losing faith in you; there are millions of people who have faith in you and believe in you and feel that you are our best hope. . . . Somehow you've just got to pull yourself out of this and go on. Too many people believe in you and you're going to have to believe that you're right.' He said, 'I don't have any answers.' I said, 'Well, somehow the answers will come. I'm sure they will.' " Seven hours late, Martin King did indeed arrive in Louisville.[30]

King's depression continued throughout the fall and winter of 1967. "These have been very difficult days for me personally," he told one audience. "I'm tired now. I've been in this thing thirteen [sic] years now and I'm really tired." Nonetheless, even at his darkest moments, faith in God gave King the inner equilibrium to face life's problems and "conquer fear," as he explained to his Ebenezer congregation. "I know this. I know it from my own personal experience."[31]

King's increased focus on organizing the Poor People's Campaign became his principal means to avoid despondency. "The decade of 1955 to 1965, with its constructive elements, misled us," he told the SCLC staff at a late November retreat that marked the actual beginning of work on the campaign. True, the movement had won many battles, "but we must admit that there was a limitation to our achievement," he declared. "The white power structure is still seeking to keep the ways of segregation and inequality substantially intact," and was deflecting the movement's efforts. However, King stressed, "I am not ready to accept defeat. . . . We must formulate a program, and we must fashion new tactics which do not count on government good will. . . . The movement for social change has entered a time of temptation to despair, because it is clear now how deep and how systematic are the evils it confronts." Thus, "we in SCLC must work out programs to bring the social change movements through from their early and now inadequate protest phase to a stage of massive, active, nonviolent resistance to the evils of the modern system. . . . Let us therefore not think of our movement as one that seeks to integrate the Negro into all the existing values of American society," but as one that would alter those values.[32]

King's mixture of determination and depression appeared repeatedly throughout early 1968. The upcoming Poor People's Campaign protests in Washington would have to be "dislocative and even disruptive" because "pressureless persuasion does not move the power structure" and rioting "doesn't pay off," King told one audience. "I wish we could have it a different way because I'm frankly tired of marching. I'm tired of going to jail." In one Sunday sermon he spoke even more plaintively. "Living every day under the threat of death, I feel discouraged every now and then and feel my work's in vain, but then the Holy Spirit revives my soul again." In Washington, trying to drum up support for a campaign that was drawing very little enthusiasm, even from some of SCLC's own staff members, King gave voice openly to his growing despair. "I can't lose hope. I can't lose hope because when you lose hope, you die."[33]

During February and March of 1968 many colleagues and observers saw a wistful and melancholic attitude in King. Long-time friend and companion Ralph Abernathy, back from a lengthy trip to Asia, found him "sad and depressed." King told his Ebenezer congregation that "life is a continual story of shattered dreams," and even when Abernathy talked King into going to Acapulco for a quick, three-day vacation, King remained "troubled and worried" about the future in general and the uncertain prospects of the Poor People's Campaign in particular.[34]

"In our low moments, when the pressures build, you look for a graceful way out; you have periods when you feel overwhelmed and want to retreat," Jesse Jackson has said in characterizing King's last several months of life. Andrew Young made a similar point: "Fatigue was not so much physical with him as it was emotional. He had the constitution of a bull. He could go on and on and on when things were going well. It was when he didn't have a clear sense of direction that he got very tired."[35]

In early 1968 it was clear to everyone around him that King was very tired indeed. Those who knew him best, in reflecting back upon the changes they had witnessed in him, identified the onset of those changes with King's early 1967 decision to tackle the Vietnam war issue. Long-time SCLC staff member Dorothy Cotton, who understood him as well as anyone, saw April 1967 as the beginning of a new and different "exhaustion," how King "was just really *emotionally* weary, as well as physically tired." "That whole last year I felt his weariness, just weariness of the struggle, that he had done all that he could do."[36]

King's despair and worries came to a peak on Thursday, March 28, 1968, when he made his second visit of the month to Memphis, Tennessee, to help boost community support for striking black sanitation men whose demand for recognition of their nascent union had been rejected out of hand by conservative Memphis Mayor Henry Loeb. That Thursday's march, organized by local strike supporters rather than by any of SCLC's experienced staff, ended in considerable turmoil and some looting when young adults, feeling excluded from the movement by the Rev. James M. Lawson, chairperson of the strike support committee, started breaking windows as the procession headed into downtown Memphis.

King and his SCLC colleagues Ralph Abernathy and Bernard Lee left the scene speedily, but King was deeply agitated over the turmoil, angry at Lawson, and extremely fearful of the harm that negative, hostile news media accounts of the Memphis violence could do to the Poor People's Campaign. "I had never seen him so depressed," Abernathy recalled. King phoned Coretta in Atlanta, and told her, too, how upset he was that a march he had been leading had ended violently, with one suspected looter fatally shot by a police officer. "He was very depressed about it and I kept trying to tell him, 'You mustn't hold yourself responsible, because you know you aren't,' " Mrs. King later remembered, but King remained extremely anguished. The next day, after a private meeting with some of the youths and a press conference at which reporters peppered King with hostile questions, he poured out his feelings to Levison in a long phone conversation. Levison refused to accept King's assertions that the Memphis violence was an all-but-fatal blow to his own public status as a nonviolent civil rights leader. King demurred. "All I'm saying is that Roy Wilkins, that Bayard Rustin and that stripe, and there are many of them, and the Negroes who are influenced by what they read in the newspapers, Adam Clayton Powell, for another reason . . . their point is, 'I'm right. Martin Luther King is dead. He's finished. His nonviolence is nothing, no one is listening to it.' Let's face it, we do have a great public relations setback where my image and my leadership are concerned." Levison disagreed, reminding King that the Memphis disruption had been caused by less than 1 percent of the participants, and that he should not accept any media portrayal of himself as a failure if 99 percent of his followers remained totally nonviolent. King acknowledged that, but insisted that the media reaction nonetheless would be extremely damaging, and explained how SCLC would have to stage a second, completely successful Memphis march in order to negate or overcome the damage from the first one.

King went on to tell Levison he was now deeply pessimistic about his own future and that of the Poor People's Campaign. "I think our Washington campaign is doomed." Even though he had long been "a symbol of nonviolence" to millions, in the press coverage of Thursday's disruption "everything will come out weakening the symbol. It will put many Negroes in doubt. It will put many Negroes in the position of saying, 'Well, that's true, Martin Luther King is at the end of his rope.' " Levison again responded that King ought not to accept the media's assumptions and parameters. "You can't keep them from imposing it," King answered. "You watch your newspapers. . . . I think it will be the most negative thing about Martin Luther King that you have ever seen."[37]

King's expectations proved largely correct. The *New York Times,* terming the Memphis violence "a powerful embarrassment to Dr. King," recommended he call off the Poor People's Campaign since it likely would prove counterproductive to his cause. "None of the precautions he and his aides are taking to keep the capital demonstration peaceful can provide any dependable insurance against another eruption of the kind that rocked Memphis."

King's frustration and despair manifested themselves at a tense and emotional Saturday meeting of SCLC's executive staff in Atlanta, where, after some difficulty, he succeeded in convincing his aides as to the necessity of both a second, completely peaceful march in Memphis and their fundamental rededication to going ahead with the Poor People's Campaign, come what may.[38]

On Wednesday, April 3, King returned to Memphis to aid in the preparations for that upcoming second march. That evening, at the cavernous Mason Temple church, before a modestly sized but emotionally enthusiastic crowd, King vowed that both the Memphis movement and the Poor People's Campaign would go forward. Then he turned to an emotional recapitulation of his own involvement in the preceding thirteen years of the black freedom struggle, expressing how happy and thankful he was that he had been given the opportunity to contribute to and live through the Montgomery boycott, the sit-ins, the Freedom Rides, the Albany campaign, the Birmingham demonstrations, the March on Washington, and the Selma protests. He closed with the same ending he had used more than eleven years earlier in Montgomery when he had first explained how the vision in the kitchen had given him the strength and the courage to keep going forward.

> I don't know what will happen now. We've got some difficult days ahead. But it really doesn't matter with me now, because I've been to the mountaintop.

And I don't mind. Like anybody, I would like to live a long life. Longevity has its place. But I'm not concerned with that now. I just want to do God's will. And He's allowed me to go up to the mountain, and I've looked over, and I've seen the promised land. I may not get there with you. But I want you to know tonight that we, as a people, will get to the promised land. And so I'm happy tonight. I'm not worried about anything. I'm not fearing any man. Mine eyes have seen the glory of the coming of the Lord.[39]

In sum, then, the most important thing to grasp and appreciate in seeking to comprehend Martin Luther King's own understanding of his life, his role, his burden, and his mission lies in that spiritual experience that began for him in the kitchen of 309 South Jackson St. on January 27, 1956. Martin King's awareness that his calling was to devote and ultimately to sacrifice his own individual life in the service of a great and just cause ennobled him as a human being, strengthened him as a leader, and allowed him to accept the symbolic role and accompanying fate that helped propel a struggle that the mature Martin King rightly recognized would be neverending.

Aldon D. Morris

A Man Prepared for the Times:
A Sociological Analysis of the Leadership of
Martin Luther King, Jr.

IT IS NO ACCIDENT THAT I have devoted considerable time to studying and writing about the civil rights movement and Dr. Martin Luther King, Jr. I was born in Mississippi and spent my early childhood there. I vividly remember the oppression, exploitation, and pain that I, and all black people, had to endure in the South of the 1950s. I knew firsthand how it felt to have yourself and adult role models called niggers and treated like slaves. I heard the low voices of adults crying with grief and fear when young Emmett Till was murdered in Mississippi. I attended a resource-starved segregated colored school, but was well aware of the superior schools that my white counterparts enjoyed simply because of their skin color. I knew the grinding poverty of the black sharecropper and the feudal-like system committed to black subjugation. Although I was not sure exactly why, I knew as a young child that a great injustice engulfed black people from birth to death.

By the time the civil rights movement exploded upon the national scene I, like many other blacks, had moved North seeking the promised land of equality. In the midst of pursuing this elusive goal, I was stunned and electrified by developments in the South as, day after day, television coverage showed black people were openly confronting white racism with determination, dignity, and courage. I identified with each of their triumphs and shared in their setbacks, pain, and noble suffering. My attention was riveted on Dr. Martin Luther King, Jr., for his voice, eloquence, and deeds articulated the oppression of blacks to the world in such clear terms. It became clear to me that Dr. King was a genius at communicating the yearnings for freedom rooted in the very souls of black folks. At last I was secure in the knowledge that change was possible.

I study and write about the civil rights movement and Dr. Martin Luther King, Jr., because they directly affected my life, the nation, and the world. Dr. King and the movement opened my eyes to social oppression more generally and to the courageous social movements throughout history that have attempted to extend human liberation across the globe and throughout all economic and social groupings. As a professional sociologist I study such movements so that I can understand them, and I write about them in the hope that others will understand them. The real hope is that as others grow to understand they will create and lead progressive movements and, in so doing, create a better world. Dr. King and the civil rights movement proved that at times such hopes can be realized.

It is clear that Dr. Martin Luther King, Jr., was one of the greatest leaders ever produced by America. Indeed, his importance to this country was recently acknowledged when the United States government formally recognized his birthday as a national holiday. The impact of his leadership on the world is equally clear, and was underscored when he was awarded the Nobel Peace Prize in 1964. By the end of 1983 at least thirty-three nations had honored him by issuing commemorative postage stamps bearing his picture.[1] King was an extraordinary leader who helped shape the destiny of the United States and many parts of the world.

How is the emergence and success of such a leader to be explained? Was the man a prophet preordained by God to reach heights undreamt of by ordinary mortals? Can his phenomenal leadership be attributed solely to his unusually charismatic personality? Or is it possible that the convergence of large, impersonal social forces were responsible for his brilliant leadership?

The argument of this essay is that the quality and success of King's leadership stemmed from the interaction of large social and historical factors with the unique combination of qualities that were deeply rooted in his own personality. It should be stated at the outset, however, that neither these social forces nor King's personality should be viewed as static; rather, both were relatively fluid and underwent changes over time. The strategy of this essay will be first to describe and analyze the major historical and social forces that made King's leadership possible, and then to connect his personal experiences and personality to these forces with the aim of demonstrating how the sociological and personal converged, producing a dynamic leadership.

HISTORICAL AND SOCIOLOGICAL CONTEXT OF KING'S LEADERSHIP

The sociohistorical factors central to the emergence of the civil rights movement and King's leadership were a comprehensive system of domination imposed on blacks, the urbanization of the black population, institution-building within the black community, the changing nature of international relations, the technological development and expansion of the media, and the black protest tradition. Each of these factors merits discussion.

Oppression has always been—and continues to be—one of the defining characteristics of black life in the United States. Indeed, throughout American history, blacks have struggled against a comprehensive system of domination imposed on them by whites. Powerful whites— landowners, politicians, business elites, and others—have been the architects of this system. Throughout more than two hundred years of slavery and subsequent slave-like conditions, racial domination has enabled whites to build one of the most powerful empires ever known to human civilization. Racial domination in America was constructed in such a manner as to benefit all whites, at least in the short run. Poor and middle class whites benefited because the segregated labor force prevented blacks from competing with them for better-paying jobs. The white ruling class benefited because blacks supplied them with cheap labor and a weapon against the labor movement, the threat to use unemployed blacks as strikebreakers in labor disputes. Finally, most whites benefited from the system's implicit assurance that no matter how poor or uneducated, they were always better than the niggers.[2]

In the 1950s southern blacks experienced this system of domination most acutely. Like their northern counterparts, they found themselves at the bottom of the economic ladder and without any substantial political power, but for them the economic and political oppression was compounded by a legal system of racial segregation that denied them personal freedoms routinely enjoyed by whites. Segregation was an arrangement that set blacks off from the rest of humanity and stigmatized them as an inferior race. Forced to use different toilets, drinking fountains, waiting rooms, parks, schools, and the like, facilities contrasting sharply with the well-kept ones reserved for whites only, blacks were forever reminded of their low status. The "colored" and "white only" signs that dotted the buildings and public places of a typical southern city expressed the reality of a social system committed to the subjugation of blacks and the denial of their human dignity and self-respect.

This perplexing problem of economic, political, and social domination has absorbed the creative energies of black leadership since the days of slavery. Great black leaders, including Frederick Douglass, Booker T. Washington, W. E. B. Du Bois, Marcus Garvey, and A. Philip Randolph, have had to tackle this problem, each in his own way, depending on the resources and changing conditions of the black masses and the larger society at the time. Black leadership, therefore, can be assessed in terms of its response to this tripartite system of domination; any aspiring black leader has had to confront racism with creative strategies and methodologies. It was this system of domination, well entrenched in the South of the 1950s and crippling to the black masses, that confronted Martin Luther King, Jr., and his generation. To understand King's leadership one has to situate it within this social context of domination.

The rapid urbanization of the black population during the first half of the twentieth century was an advantage to King that was not available to the black leaders who preceded him. The quality of the leadership of any oppressed group is directly proportionate to the group's collective strength. The phenomenal migration of rural blacks to southern and northern cities during the first and second world wars enhanced the collective strength of the black community tremendously. Life in the cities contrasted sharply with that found in southern rural settings. The sociologist E. Franklin Frazier described rural black communities as follows: "The cabins are scattered in the open country so that the development of village communities has been impossible. Consequently, communication between rural families as well as the development of rural institutions has been limited by the wide dispersion of the population."[3] Black urbanization created densely populated black communities where blacks could interact freely among themselves. In an urban setting rich social networks flourished, embedded in kinship, religious, and community ties. New political and social organizations, as well as economic enterprises, sprang up, and existing ones were strengthened. In the urban milieu sophisticated communication networks that crisscrossed within and between black communities proliferated and hardened. Although money was scarce and unemployment high, blacks fared slightly better economically in the cities than they had on the farms.

Recent research has demonstrated that social movements are likely to emerge from groups characterized by solid communication networks, organizational strength, and a variety of resources, of which financial capital is extremely important.[4] By the 1950s, southern black urban communities were fast becoming such sources of emerging movements; it was from these communities that Martin Luther King, Jr., would derive his leadership. Indeed, King's organizational documents reveal that he was acutely aware of these structural developments.

"Social and economic forces are bringing about great changes in the South. Urbanization, industrialization, scientific agriculture and mass education are making it possible to remove the barriers to a prosperous, free and creative life for all southerners."[5]

Black urbanization also increased the political strength of the black community, especially in the urban North. As blacks concentrated there, they began to form voting blocs that could not be ignored by the two main political parties. This created a weapon for the black community because the Democratic party in particular had to give lip service to black equality in order to attract the black vote; in effect it had to go on record as supporting the aspirations of the black masses. This stance, coupled with the 1954 Supreme Court ruling declaring segregated schools to be unconstitutional, went far toward legitimizing the black struggle.

Institution-building within the black community following black urbanization was also important to the rise of the modern civil rights movement and King's leadership. In cities, this institutional development was evident on a number of fronts. The black press, political organizations, barber and beauty shops, and a host of other groups all experienced growth, thanks to black migration. In particular, the institution-building that occurred in the black church, colleges, and the family was crucial to the development of the civil rights movement.

The strength of the black community parallels that of the black church to a considerable degree, and this was especially true in the 1950s. A unique institution, the black church was organized and developed by an oppressed group shut off from the institutional life of the larger society. As a result, it provided the organizational framework for most activities of the community: economic, political, and educational, as well as religious.[6] The church furnished outlets for social and artistic expression, a forum for the discussion of important issues, a social environment that developed, trained, and disciplined potential leaders from all walks of life, and an arena that lent itself to the development of charisma and meaningful symbols to engender hope, enthusiasm, and a resilient group spirit. The church was also a platform where group interests could be collectively articulated and defended.

Two other factors made the church important to the black movement and to King's leadership. First, its principal human resource was its organizational base—the congregation. The black community has always contributed the voluntary labor and financial capital necessary to meet the church's considerable needs in its role as the main community center. Accordingly, it was the church that provided the movement and King with the work force and the money capable of challenging white domination. Second, the black church was the only popularly based institution within the black community that was, for the most part, economically and politically independent of the white community. This independence allowed it to serve as a staging ground for the black protest movement. This, of course, is one of the reasons why a dispro-portionate number of prominent protest leaders were ministers: their activities could not be derailed by white economic reprisals. Thus, the black church functioned as the institutional bedrock of black resistance.

The urbanization of the black population during the first half of the twentieth century rapidly increased the strength of the black church.[7] For one thing, the membership of the urban church was much larger than that of the rural church. For example, Doug McAdam found that the average membership of southern urban churches was three times greater than that of rural churches. This meant that the urban black church could raise substantial amounts of money and that the capacity of its work force was increased significantly. The urban church, in comparison to its rural counterpart, also enjoyed more sophisticated ministerial leadership. In this regard McAdam found that a far greater proportion of ministers in southern urban churches held advanced de-grees than in rural ones. Given the fact that urban ministers earned higher salaries, they were far more likely to function as full-time pas-tors.[8] Therefore, in terms of organizational strength, the urban church became an institution capable of wielding considerable power. This led Gunnar Myrdal to write in 1944 that "potentially, the Negro church is undoubtedly a power institution. It has the Negro masses organized and, if the church bodies decided to do so, they could line the Negroes behind a program."[9] By the 1950s the black church was capable of mass struggle, and Martin Luther King, Jr., would utilize this power for just this purpose.

Like the black church, black colleges also underwent significant in-stitution-building during the first half of the twentieth century owing to the urbanization of the black population and the consequent improve-ment of black economic conditions. McAdam found that from 1941 to mid-century the enrollment in black colleges doubled from 37,203 to 74,526. Moreover, the income for black colleges rose from roughly $8 million to over $38 million between 1930 and 1947. The number of degrees awarded by black colleges also increased dramatically, and dur-ing the first half of the twentieth century a significant number of these schools achieved full accreditation.[10]

The extensive growth of black colleges was important to the rise of the modern civil rights movement and its leadership because some of these schools became the institutions where the intellectual battle against racial inequality was waged. Within their walls, students and professors debated and wrote about the injustice of racial segregation and domination and generally agreed that they should embrace and promote the drive toward equality. Around the turn of the twentieth century, W. E. B. Du Bois wrote in *The Souls of Black Folk,* "The function of the Negro college, then, is clear: it must maintain the standards of popular education, it must seek the social regeneration of the Negro, and it must help in the solution of problems of race contact and cooperation." [11] The president of Morehouse College, Benjamin Mays, wrote in his autobiography, *Born to Rebel,* that "in my twenty-seven years as President, I never ceased to raise my voice and pen against the injustices of a society that segregated and discriminated against people because God made them black." Mays pointed out that "the leadership of Morehouse College never accepted the status quo in Negro-white relations" and that "throughout its history, Morehouse's leadership has rebelled against racial injustices." [12]

In a comprehensive study of Charles H. Houston, Genna Rae McNeil has demonstrated that during Houston's years at Howard University he developed a first-rate law school there for the explicit purpose of challenging the legal underpinnings of racial segregation. [13] It was this law school that trained the NAACP lawyers who won numerous cases against racial segregation, including the Supreme Court's famous 1954 school desegregation decision. Daniel Thompson in his thorough study of black colleges captured the essence of the argument: "The central mission . . . of Black colleges . . . is still essentially the same as it was in the beginning . . . to prepare students to make necessary and unique contributions to the survival and advancement of black Americans and to improve the overall social condition of the less-advantaged masses." [14] This is not to claim that black colleges have been totally free of conservatism, corrupt administrators, and political censorship by powerful whites who often controlled the purse strings of the schools. However, the argument here is that in spite of such problems, a substantial number of professors and students in these colleges produced trenchant critiques of the racial status quo and waged the intellectual battle against racial domination.

Another responsibility of black colleges was to produce black leaders. Thompson provides an explanation of this: "The sense of leadership responsibility on black campuses has been always stimulated by two interrelated facts: at least 80 percent of the students come from homes and communities where well-prepared, articulate leadership is desperately needed, and because these campuses are relatively small, all students have opportunities, even challenges, to discover and develop their leadership talents." [15] This seems to have been the case at Morehouse where Dr. King received his undergraduate training in the late 1940s. Benjamin Mays wrote, "I found a special, intangible something at

Morehouse in 1921 which sent men out into life with a sense of mission, believing that they could accomplish whatever they set out to do. This priceless quality was still alive when I returned in 1940, and for twenty-seven years I built on what I found, instilling in Morehouse students the idea that despite crippling circumstances the sky was their limit." He went on to point out that "it was a few able, dedicated teachers who made the Morehouse man believe that he was 'somebody.' " The size of Morehouse facilitated this social conditioning because "the student body has never been large. In 1967 the college enrolled 910 students." [16] Given the nature and mission of black colleges it is not surprising that they played a major role in producing men and women who would become major leaders in the civil rights movement. Martin Luther King, Jr., was a product of this college environment, and his personality epitomized the leadership characteristics championed by black colleges.

Institution-building within the family was also significant for the rise of the movement and King's leadership. It is not impossible for great leaders to emerge from conditions of extreme poverty and degradation, but it is unlikely; great leaders throughout human history have usually emerged from the middle and upper classes. They have generally had the privilege of receiving formal education and enjoying the necessary leisure time to develop leadership skills. Therefore, family context is a critical variable that plays an enormous role in providing the resources and environment conducive to the development of leadership skills. Andrew Billingsley has correctly argued that "prominent in the background of Negro men and women of achievement is a strong family life." [17]

The black rural-to-urban migration strengthened the black family. This was true for urban black families in both the North *and* South. It has already been pointed out that in contrast to rural blacks, urban blacks earned more money, lived in stronger communities, and had access to more supportive churches and educational institutions. This general upgrading of the urban black community had positive consequences for the black family. Indeed, Billingsley found that religion, education, money or property, jobs, family ties, and community-centered activities were the chief ingredients of strong family life. He went on to argue that strong black families have a "certain degree of independence and control of the forces affecting the lives of their members" and that they "are often highly influenced by the religious convictions and behavior, the education or educational aspirations of one or more members. They often have an economic footing more secure than the average Negro family in their community. They often have strong emotional ties." [18]

By the 1950s significant numbers of black people had migrated to the cities of the South, hoping to escape the backbreaking poverty and oppression that crippled them and their families in the rural setting. A brief examination of the rural family context of Martin Luther King, Sr.—"Daddy King"—is instructive. Daddy King's childhood was spent in rural Stockbridge, Georgia. His father, James Albert King, was a sharecropper while his mother, Delia King, was a domestic. They had the difficult task of rearing ten children. As a sharecropper Albert King was cheated out of most of his hard-earned annual income by exploitative white landowners. The meager earnings of Delia King contributed to the household but were not enough to raise the family out of poverty. Daddy King recalled that "there was no way to make any money sharecropping."[19] Speaking of the family's overall condition Lawrence Reddick wrote, "life was hard, work and children plentiful, and material rewards slight."[20] As a result, Albert King became an alcoholic and often released his rage by abusing Delia King and the children. This syndrome of black poverty and tense family relations was widespread in the rural South. It engendered an "outward looking" attitude among thousands of rural youths who hungered for city life where they believed opportunities would be greater and social oppression less. During World War I, Martin Luther King, Sr., moved to Atlanta, like thousands of other young blacks who migrated to the city in search of a better life. Within a relatively short period of time he had developed an educational and economic infrastructure for a strong family. And it was in this strong family context that Martin Luther King, Jr., would be nurtured and prepared for his leadership role.

The international scene after World War II also had an impact on the emerging American civil rights movement. During this period, the United States and the Soviet Union were locked in an intense Cold War to determine which would control the balance of world power. By the 1950s a new force had emerged in the world power equation—the Third World. Indeed, the colored peoples of the Third World were smashing colonial regimes and establishing free, independent states with great speed. For example, India with its 400 million people gained its independence from Britain in 1947; in 1949 China with its 650 million people established a Communist state; in 1957 Ghana won its independence; in 1959 Cuba won its revolution and established a Communist state; and during 1960 and the years that immediately followed, numerous African colonies, including Nigeria, Chad, the Congo, Togo, and Algeria, overthrew colonialism and set up self-determining states, while many other African countries were engaged in revolutionary struggles for independence.

Few Americans understood this new reality better than John F. Kennedy who, before becoming president in 1960, served as a United States senator and as chairman of the Senate Foreign Relations subcommittees on the United Nations and on African Affairs. In 1960 Kennedy wrote: "In Asia, the Middle East, and Africa, people long dormant under colonial rule are now for the first time in a ferment of a newly won national identity and independence." He went on to say that the purpose of the revolutions of colored people was to shake off the badge of inferiority white people had imposed on them and that "all this makes for a paramount revolution in the outlook on life itself." However, at this time, the Third World objected to the United States foreign policy of containment and nonintervention, given the fact that this policy was usually employed to back Western European powers attempting to maintain control over their Third World colonies. Concerned that new nations would be drawn to the Soviet Union, causing the United States and the West to lose their grip on the balance of world power, Kennedy called for a new foreign policy. He stated, "it is we, the American people, who should be marching at the head of this world-wide revolution, counselling it, helping it to come to a healthy fruition." [21]

On becoming president in 1961 Kennedy immediately began revising American foreign policy to take the new reality of the Third World into account. His strategy called, first, for winning the hearts and minds of the oppressed in Africa, Asia, the Middle East, and Latin America. In this regard Kennedy argued for the building of strong, native, non-Communist sentiment within these areas through diplomatic relations, intelligent understanding, and economic aid because "man's desire to be free and independent is the most powerful force in the world today." He reasoned that the "strength of our appeal to these key populations—and it is rightfully our appeal, and not that of the Communists—lies in our traditional and deeply felt philosophy of freedom and independence for all peoples everywhere." [22]

Second, Kennedy's approach to increasing American influence in Asia was to make sure that India, a democracy, became more powerful than Communist China. Thus the United States provided India with long-term loans and technical and agricultural assistance so that it would overtake the challenge of Communist China and become the model for the rest of Asia to follow. [23] But Kennedy emphasized once again that the United States could only triumph in Africa, Asia, Latin America, and the Middle East if it were able to convince these populations that America was on the side of equality, freedom, independence, and human dignity across the entire globe.

A serious domestic problem, however—the oppression of black Americans and their rising freedom struggle—hampered Kennedy's grand strategy for influence in the Third World, although he rarely acknowledged its significance in his voluminous writings on the Third

World in the fifties and early sixties. In 1959, for example, he wrote that, "we must seek to understand their [the Africans'] needs and aspirations—and ask them to understand our problems—to understand in particular, I might add, that racial segregation and violence which badly distort our image abroad while weakening us here at home constitute only a small part of the American scene."[24] Nevertheless, Afro-American leaders, Third World leaders, and astute Kennedy advisors would not allow the new president to gloss over American racism and oppression.

Throughout American history Afro-American leaders, including Marcus Garvey, W. E. B. Du Bois, Malcolm X, and Andrew Young, have recognized the link between domestic racism and the oppression of Third World peoples, especially those in Africa.[25] During the rise of the modern civil rights movement, black leaders continued to point out the hypocrisy of, on the one hand, racism at home and, on the other, a foreign policy aimed at winning the allegiance of Third World people. Thus in 1958 A. Philip Randolph told President Eisenhower that racial discrimination "is not a Negro problem but an American problem. . . . In the eyes of the world, and in the hearts of millions of Americans, the problem we have discussed is the barometer of American democracy."[26] Arthur Schlesinger, Jr., pointed out that in the early 1960s Negro leaders were becoming increasingly concerned with United States foreign policy toward Africa. Indeed, as he wrote, "by 1962 American Negro leaders were meeting at Arden House to frame their recommendations on African Policy."[27]

African leaders—who "were reading bulletins from Oxford and Birmingham as if they were local news"—let it be known that they were concerned with American racism. President Leon M'Ba of Gabon thanked Kennedy in 1963 "for the great campaign which he has undertaken . . . against segregation. . . . The United States cannot do otherwise because it is the defender of liberty, equality and fraternity, and because it is the great friend of all the nations of the world." The Algerian leader Ben Bella "ascribed to Kennedy everything he thought good in the United States: the fight against the big trusts, against the segregationists."[28] Similarly, Kennedy advisors who traveled to Africa reminded the president of the concerns of African leaders regarding American race relations. Thus, Harris Wofford wrote the president in 1962 after returning from Africa that "ending discrimination in America would do more to promote good relations with Africa than anything else."[29]

In short, the modern civil rights movement emerged at precisely the time when Third World countries were gaining independence and power. This reality intensified the competition between the United

States and the Soviet Union for world power. A Soviet writer described the dilemma facing the United States: "An objectively inclined person outside the United States could not help but wonder that the United States was resolutely trying to be the 'World Leader.' What could it offer nations when colored Americans who comprised 11 percent of the country's population live in constant discrimination?"[30] This dilemma gave the rising civil rights movement a potent weapon, for mass marches, protest activities, and racial violence would bring the situation out in the open for the whole world to witness. Under these conditions the United States government would be forced to yield or lose its leverage in the Third World. This was the reality that Martin Luther King, Jr., and the civil rights movement exploited in their struggle to free black Americans.

Throughout much of American history blacks were exploited, beaten, and oppressed while most Americans and people around the world went about their daily affairs barely aware of the situation. Indeed, racial segregation and oppression isolated blacks from the American mainstream, making their wretched conditions invisible. The media, however, played an important role in bringing King's leadership and the civil rights movement to national and international attention.

During the 1950s and 1960s, the civil rights movement and advances in mass media, especially television, changed black invisibility dramatically. The media permitted the whole world to witness how the white majority oppressed its black citizens. As early as 1958 over 83 percent of American households owned television sets in contrast to about 45 percent in 1953; over 96 percent owned radios.[31] This rapid expansion —especially that of television—was made possible because new technologies reduced cost, making television sets and radios affordable to most households. The rapid spread of television in the late 1950s coincided with the rise of the civil rights movement, and television provided a window through which millions could watch the black struggle. Another crucial technological advance occurred in 1960 when television news and documentaries shifted from bulky 35mm equipment to the 16mm camera. Erik Barnouw describes the significance of the change. "In 1960 the umbilical cord between camera and recorder became obsolete with the invention of methods for synchronizing them without wire connection. The wire between microphone and recording equipment could likewise be abolished by use of the wireless microphone, which communicated its signals to the recording equipment via miniature transmitters. . . . Now the performer with his microphone, the cameraman with his camera, the sound engineer with his recording equipment, could all be free agents."[32] This advance was extremely important because it made it much easier for the media to cover volatile protest demonstrations.

In July 1962 Telstar I, a communications satellite, was launched into orbit. This revolutionary advance, enabling television pictures to be relayed across the Atlantic and from continent to continent,[33] had profound implications for the civil rights movement. First, it insured that the black struggle could be viewed by audiences across the globe, including those in Third World countries who had access to the technology. By the early 1950s a number of countries had begun to build their own television systems, and the dissemination of satellites greatly enhanced this trend, making it possible for the black struggle in the United States to become a world development. Second, because of satellite communications, American network news adopted a thirty-minute format in 1963 rather than the fifteen-minute format that had been standard. This meant that the civil rights movement was far more likely to be covered and actually televised since the networks now had more room for news.

Global television provided Dr. Martin Luther King, Jr., with an instant worldwide audience that would have been unattainable a decade earlier. His leadership was enhanced and made more effective because advances in the mass media provided him with a screen to both nationalize and internationalize the black struggle.

Black resistance to white domination in America has been one of the dominant features of black existence since the days of slavery. Numerous scholars of the black experience have carefully documented the unbroken link in the freedom struggle of black people since they arrived on American shores in chains. Black protest has always been present in some form.[34]

This persistent struggle for freedom has given rise to a black protest tradition, embracing strategies ranging from armed resistance to nonviolent, massive civil disobedience. The tradition has been transmitted across generations by older relatives, black educational institutions, churches, and protest organizations, and blacks interested in social change have inevitably gravitated to this "protest community" and rejuvenated it.

Both the civil rights movement and King's leadership drew on already existing organizations, experienced leaders, and institutions rooted in the black protest tradition. Prior to the modern movement much of the machinery of the protest tradition was unfocused, overly competitive, and without mass support or an effective strategy. In the late fifties and early sixties, however, this "machinery" was galvanized by a new strategy and spurred on by mass involvement. Martin Luther King, Jr., played a major role as the catalyst of this development and infused the tradition with a new dynamism. The mere existence of this tradition and its associated machinery made it possible for the civil rights movement to become a major force in a relatively short period of time.

Up to this point this essay has identified and analyzed the macrosociological factors—the system of domination, black urbanization, black institution-building, international relations, the development of the media, and the black protest tradition—that facilitated the rise of the modern civil rights movement. I will now demonstrate how a unique set of personal experiences and qualities enabled Martin Luther King, Jr., to become the major leader of the civil rights movement and how his personal qualities meshed with the sociological factors already discussed. The task is to examine how the sociological and personal combined, producing a dynamic charismatic leader and a powerful mass movement.

FAMILY/CHURCH/COLLEGE: THE INTERLOCKING NETWORK

Martin Luther King, Jr., was a product of the urban black family, church, and college. From the very beginning he was thoroughly anchored in this milieu of interlocking institutions and clearly benefited from all its rich resources. In fact, as far as King's childhood and young adulthood are concerned, there were no clear-cut boundaries between family, church, and college. His daily activities intersected each of these institutional spheres, and they shaped his personality in a mutually reinforcing fashion.

King was born into an extended, urban, middle-class black family in Atlanta. It was a household consisting of his maternal grandfather and grandmother along with his father, mother, and two siblings. His father, Daddy King, had inherited the pastorship of the prestigious Ebenezer Baptist Church from his father-in-law, who had died in 1931; this position placed him squarely in Atlanta's black middle class. The family's situation contrasted sharply with the poverty-stricken family in which Daddy King grew up in rural Georgia. For one thing, he derived a substantial and secure income from Ebenezer, and it did not take him long to acquire financial assets within Atlanta's bustling black business community. Indeed, he "became the director of a Negro bank and amassed interests in other enterprises."[35] His home was on Auburn Avenue, which has been described by Lerone Bennett, Jr., as the black Wall Street; located on it were some of the largest Negro-owned businesses and most prestigious black churches in America.[36] Thus, Daddy King, through marriage, hard work, and residential and social proximity to a vibrant, urban black business community, was able to secure middle-class prosperity and status for his family.

Martin Luther King, Jr., and his siblings, in contrast to the over-whelming majority of Afro-Americans of the period, never experienced poverty. Bennett relates that "there was always meat on the King table, and bread and butter" and he reveals the comfortable middle class cir-cumstances of the King family through Daddy King's words: "We've never lived in a rented house, . . . and never ridden too long in a car on which payment was due."[37] Young Martin Luther King, Jr., always wore good clothes. Such family resources were remarkable when con-sidered in the context of the American economy of the 1930s, still reeling from the great depression.

Both parents of Martin Luther King, Jr., were college-educated. His father received his education from Morehouse, a black men's college, while his mother was educated at Spelman and Hampton, two other prestigious black institutions. King's parents not only valued education but had the financial means to insure that their children could receive the best education possible. As a result, Martin Luther King, Jr., was able to acquire a quality education and had the necessary books and leisure time to develop his intellectual powers and oratorical skills.

The King family had the resources that enabled it to protect young Martin from many of the devastating consequences of segregation that scarred the intellects and lowered the aspirations of young black people. His biographers make it clear that the King family was very protective of the children and provided an environment that allowed them to grow up feeling important and the social equals of anybody including "white folk."[38] The family's resources enabled it to provide Martin Luther King, Jr., with an ideal situation in which he could develop his mind and a set of social skills conducive to leadership.

The black church was and is an encompassing institution and this was particularly the case for a preacher's son. The church provided black people with a moral outlook, social status, entertainment, and political organization, and it served as the main reservoir of black cul-ture. The black church was a community in itself. This is why E. Franklin Frazier referred to it as a nation within a nation and why it consumed such a great deal of its parishioners' time. The minister and his family, moreover, never escaped the influence of the church com-munity because they functioned as its first family. The King family began and ended the day with family prayers, and each member was expected to behave according to the values enshrined in the church.

King's maternal grandfather and great-grandfather were Baptist ministers, and, of course, his father—Daddy King—was also a Baptist minister. By the time young Martin was born, Ebenezer had become the Kings' "family" church. The first thing the church did for Martin Luther King, Jr., was to bestow a special status on him. As Maurice Isserman has written, "Black preachers' kids grew up knowing their fathers were exceptional men, honored in their own world."[39] Small wonder that great black leaders including James Farmer, Adam Clayton Powell, Jr., and Malcolm X were the sons of ministers. With regard to King, Stephen Oates has written that "M. L. knew who he was— 'Reverend King's boy,' somebody special."[40] In spite of racial inequality and segregation, Martin Luther King, Jr., grew up in a church environment that honored and respected the minister and the members of the first family. It was the stuff from which strong personalities are often formed.

The black church is an institution where powerful cultural symbols are manipulated and artistically expressed. In the church the preacher is the main manipulator of the symbols that inspire, criticize, and soothe the black masses. Great black preachers are the ones who are able to master oratory in such a way that it provides hope and meaning for people who are constantly crushed by a vicious system of oppression. Daddy King and other ministers who preached at Ebenezer were such orators. The older King explained that "many of the old-time preachers, who could recite scriptures for hours on end, provided me with a great sense of the gestures, the cadences, the deeply emotive quality of their styles of ministry."[41] Services in Ebenezer provided Martin Luther King, Jr., with a natural laboratory in which to observe the symbolic dynamics that connected the minister and the masses. Bennett has captured the results: "Almost from the beginning, however, young Martin made words and symbols central to his orientation to life. Watching his father and other ministers dominate audiences with artfully chosen words, the young boy tingled with excitement; and the urge to speak, to express himself, to turn and twist and lift audiences, seized him and never afterwards left him. To form words into sentences, to fling them out on the waves of air in a crescendo of sound, to watch people weep, shout, respond: this fascinated young Martin." Bennett pointed out that "the idea of using words as weapons of defense and offense was thus early implanted and seems to have grown in King as naturally as a flower."[42]

It was the church, therefore, that played the major role in developing King into a great orator. It is important to point out here that King was developing skills to challenge and inspire the masses. Churches provided the organizational levers through which the energies of the masses could be mobilized for social and political ends. The mass dynamics played out at Ebenezer were duplicated in black churches throughout the nation. To understand them at Ebenezer is to gain an understanding of how they could be set in motion on a national scale.

Finally, the church gave King a sense of destiny, a belief that God works through individuals to accomplish his divine will. Andrew

Young explained how this related to King: "I think that Martin always felt that he had a special purpose in life and that that purpose in life was something that was given to him by God; that he was the son and grandson of Baptist preachers, and he understood, I think, the Scriptural notion of men of destiny. He talked about Moses and of Abraham and he understood, I think, that the cross, or the crucifixion of Jesus of Nazareth, was an event which was not only a cosmic theological event but I think he saw that as a social and political event which could continually reoccur."[43] This clear understanding of the social role of religion was to emerge for King after he went outside the boundaries of his family and Ebenezer—Morehouse College was the setting that placed religion in its proper perspective for him. But it was the black church, with its vast resources and possibilities, that ultimately served as his main social and political arena.

King entered Morehouse College in 1944 at the age of fifteen. His years there were an experience that would shape his social outlook and provide him with the intellectual ammunition to attack social inequality. It was pointed out earlier that some black colleges waged the intellectual battle against racial inequality and that they prepared students to become leaders in the black liberation struggle. Morehouse College excelled in this regard. Major civil rights leaders including James Nabrit, Samuel Williams, John Porter, Julian Bond, Floyd McKissick, Charles Steele, and Kelly Miller Smith attended Morehouse. Steele and Smith, along with Martin Luther King, Jr., were cofounders of SCLC.

By the time King entered Morehouse he was searching for a solution to the race problem. He wrote, "When I went to Atlanta's Morehouse College as a freshman in 1944 my concern for social and economic justice was already substantial."[44] He could not have chosen a better college in this regard, because the race issue was being thoroughly debated there. King recalled, "It was there [Morehouse] that I had my first frank discussion on race. The professors were not caught up in the clutches of state funds and could teach what they wanted with academic freedom. They encouraged us in a positive quest for a solution to racial ills, and for the first time in my life, I realized that nobody there was afraid."[45]

One of the most important lessons King learned at Morehouse was that black religion could be a potent agent for social change. Before going to Morehouse he refused to embrace the black church and ministry because he thought them too emotional and intellectually uninformed. The professors at Morehouse quickly convinced him otherwise and stood as living examples of what the black clergy and church could accomplish and become. At Morehouse black religion and academic scholarship were creatively combined. The college had a strong divinity department and the president of Morehouse—Dr. Benjamin Mays— was an outstanding scholar and theologian.

An important influence on King at Morehouse was Professor George Kelsey, director of the department of religion. Kelsey was a seminary-trained scholar and minister. Through his classroom teaching and informed discussions Kelsey convinced King that "the modern minister should be a Philosopher with social as well as spiritual concerns." [46] King admitted that Kelsey helped change his orientation toward black religion. But it was Benjamin Mays who became King's mentor and profoundly shaped his life and view of black religion. In addition to being a scholar and theologian, Mays was also an activist who thought of himself as a "race man" who had a responsibility to tear down the system of racial inequality. He was very active in the NAACP and other organizations seeking change. But most of all, Mays was important to King because of his views of black religion and his riveting and intellectually informed oratory. In 1933 Mays and Joseph Nicholson published *The Negro's Church,* a landmark study. A major thesis of the book was that black religion was too other-worldly and should be concerned with changing actual social conditions in the here and now. Not only did King adopt this critical view of religion, but he used it throughout his career as a leader of the civil rights movement to prod the black church into active involvement. It is in this sense that Vincent Harding has maintained that King engaged in a continuous lover's quarrel with the black church.

In sum, Morehouse convinced King that black religion could serve as a potent weapon in the fight for racial justice. This conviction was so strong that at the age of seventeen he decided to go into the ministry. In addition to reinforcing the idea that King was "somebody," Morehouse also provided him with a longtime mentor and friend, Benjamin Mays. This influence was enhanced by the fact that Mays served as a bridge between the black college and the church, for while King was a student at Morehouse, Daddy King served on its board of trustees. Mays wrote that "if his father had not been elected to the Board of Trustees of Morehouse College, our friendship would not have reached such meaningful depth," and that "we [Mays and Martin Luther King, Jr.] began a real friendship which was strengthened by visits in his home and by fairly frequent informal chats on the campus and in my office." King knew that to be like Mays he needed to acquire graduate training beyond Morehouse. Morehouse encouraged graduate study; "it is a tradition at Morehouse that an A.B. or B.S. is not a terminal degree; every outstanding student is encouraged to continue his studies." [47]

Clearly, then, King's family, church, and college provided him with an interlocking and resourceful network enabling him to grow intellectually and socially. This stimulating environment is one of the primary reasons why he was able to become a great leader.

KING AND THE EYES OF THE WORLD

King played a key role in nationalizing and internationalizing the black freedom struggle of the 1950s and 1960s. His personal leadership was what journalists call "good copy." As a leader King was exciting, controversial, interesting, dynamic, different, and refreshing. Yet as a personality King was calm, sincere, dignified, eloquent, and elegant. This combination made him extremely attractive to the media. Especially engaging was his strategy when at the center of hostile white forces: to challenge them directly, while at the same time exuding confidence and reason. As Wyatt Walker put it, "Martin Luther King was a hero who would go to jail, who would confront red-neck racists, speak boldly before them without hating them and taking a club to them or trying to shoot back."[48] In the same vein Barnouw, an expert on the media, wrote that King became world famous "less for his fantastic first successes than for the style of his leadership. He was arrested, spat on, imprisoned, fined, and reviled, but he told his followers: We must have compassion and understanding for those who hate us."[49]

But what was even more important than personal leadership style in terms of media coverage was the nature of the civil rights movement itself and the tactics it made famous. This was a mass movement involving thousands of people who challenged the very structure of the society and the democratic values it espoused. It was a development the media could not ignore. The strategy of King and the movement was "mass nonviolent action in the streets to the end that the functioning of the community was disrupted and it was therefore compelled to face the issue."[50] As Barnouw observed, King's "Gandhi-inspired crusade, which always ran the risk of bloodshed, began to draw cameramen and tape recorders."[51] Widespread coverage of this protest movement was enhanced by major technological changes and media expansion in the late 1950s and early 1960s.

Widespread media coverage of King and the movement ended the invisibility of black inequality and of the suffering associated with racial domination. Wyatt Walker correctly pointed out that "the media had a tremendous affect on our movement . . . because it gave a window to America to see what segregation was like. America had never seen it before."[52] The tactic of mass nonviolent direct action that disrupted entire communities and forced white racists violently to attack black citizens under the glare of television forced America to take notice. Public opinion had to come to grips with the wrenching reality that black people were treated like subjects of a vicious totalitarian state in a country claiming to be the leader of the free world.

King was acutely aware of the role the media played in revealing the day-to-day oppression of black people. He was also aware that he possessed a charismatic personality that attracted the media and thus focused the eyes of the world on the obstacles faced by the movement. James Lawson revealed why King as a leader was able to rivet attention on the freedom struggle: "It was the nature of the struggle at that time, that King was the single overwhelming symbol of the agitation, and of the struggle. . . . Any time King went to a community, immediately the focus of the nation was on that community. . . . He had the eyes of the world on where he went. And in the Black community it never had that kind of person. . . . It gave the Black community an advantage the Black community has never had. And has not had since his death."[53] Repeatedly King and the movement used this media visibility to nationalize and internationalize the black struggle, and King made it known to leaders and activists of the movement that they were to capitalize on his charisma and media presence.

It was not long before King began viewing the civil rights movement as part of an entire Third World movement for freedom. In the early 1950s he wrote, "The Negro is not so selfish as to stand isolated in concern for his own dilemma, ignoring the ebb and flow of events around the world. . . . From beyond the borders of his own land, the Negro has been inspired by another powerful force. He had watched the decolonization and liberation of nations in Africa and Asia since World War II. . . . He knew that by 1963 more than thirty-four African nations had risen from colonial bondage."[54] By the mid-1960s he was explicitly arguing that "in one sense the civil rights movement in the United States is a special American phenomenon. . . . But on another important level, what is happening in the United States today is a significant part of a world development." He went on to point out that "all over the world like a fever, freedom is spreading in the widest liberation movement in history" and that "with his black brothers of Africa and his brown and yellow brothers in Asia, South America and the Caribbean, the United States Negro is moving with a sense of great urgency toward the promised land of racial justice."[55]

King, therefore, was aware of the international context of the civil rights movement. Moreover, he was aware of President Kennedy's strategy of gaining power and influence in the Third World. In 1963 King wrote that for the Negro "there is a certain bitter irony in the picture of his country championing freedom in foreign lands and failing to ensure that freedom to twenty million of its own."[56] The presence of African statesmen in the United Nations and the visits of African leaders to the White House amplified the irony. Indeed, "beginning with Nkrumah of Ghana in March 1961, African leaders flowed through the White House in what appeared an unending stream: eleven in 1961, ten in 1962 and in 1963, when the supply was nearing the point of exhaustion, seven."[57] The civil rights movement and its widespread media coverage figured prominently in the Third World, as did the response of the United States government to it.

King spurred the civil rights movement in part by reminding black Americans of their obligation to keep pace with the progress of Third World movements. At the same time he and Third World leaders used Kennedy's strategy toward the newly-emerging nations, expressed in democratic rhetoric, to maneuver the president into appearing as a champion of oppressed masses around the world. However, King clearly understood that Kennedy was, at best, a reluctant champion of black American freedom. Like his predecessors, Kennedy was concerned with blacks so that he could garner their vote, but he was also concerned not to upset Southern whites to the extent that he would lose *their* vote. This is why King wrote that Kennedy's administration "appeared to believe it was doing as much as was politically possible and had, by its positive deeds, earned enough credit to coast on civil rights."[58]

But King and the civil rights movement had an effective technique to force Kennedy, and later Johnson, in the right direction—use of massive street demonstrations and protests while the world observed via radio, the print media, and television. The momentous mass confrontations in Birmingham in 1963 and Selma in 1965 are outstanding examples of this strategy in action. In both instances white oppression, American-style, was played out in blatant forms and was beamed around the world via satellite and other major media. The Birmingham confrontation, with hundreds of others quickly following, was an important breakthrough. In response to these massive demonstrations President Kennedy went on nationwide television and radio in June of 1963 and declared: "We preach freedom around the world, and we mean it. . . . But are we to say to the world—and much more importantly to each other—that this is the land of the free except for Negroes; that we have no second-class citizens, except Negroes; that we have no class or caste system, no ghettos, no master race, except with respect to Negroes. Now the time has come for this nation to fulfill its promise. . . . We face, therefore, a moral crisis, as a country and a people."[59] What this quotation makes clear is that the Birmingham confrontation forced Kennedy to introduce and support national civil rights legislation in order to control the domestic situation and pursue his Third World policy. The process was aided, as it was throughout the turbulent 1960s, by worldwide media so expertly utilized by King and the movement. As King said, the drama took place on a thousand brightly lighted stages.[60] In sum, King's personal leadership style and the mass movement he expertly headed used a technologically sophisticated mass media to take advantage of major domestic and international developments in such a manner as to advance the freedom of blacks in America and Third World people across the globe.

KING AND THE BLACK PROTEST TRADITION

Martin Luther King, Jr., whose courageous actions catapulted him into the leadership of the civil rights movement, was firmly rooted in the black protest tradition and deeply enriched that tradition. Both his father and grandfather, when serving as pastors of Ebenezer, were pioneer leaders of the modern black resistance movement. In the early 1900s King's grandfather—Adam Williams—headed the Atlanta chapter of the NAACP and was active in other protest groups. Oates points out that "when an inflammatory white newspaper attacked Atlanta Negroes as 'dirty and ignorant,' Dr. Williams helped lead a boycott that eventually closed the paper down." Williams was also a leader of a Negro citizen group "that pressured Atlanta into building Booker T. Washington High School, the city's only high school for blacks."[61]

Daddy King, who succeeded Williams as pastor of Ebenezer, followed in the latter's footsteps of activism. Daddy King served on the NAACP's Executive Board and on its Social Action Committee. He was a key leader in the successful movement to raise the salary levels of black school teachers to those of whites. Moreover, in 1935 Daddy King led a march to Atlanta's City Hall demanding the vote for black citizens. According to Daddy King: "More than a thousand people had gathered for the rally at Ebenezer. . . . There were several hundred Negro-Americans marching that afternoon in 1935, down to the Atlanta City Hall, in a demonstration such as no living soul in that city had ever seen."[62] The activism of King's father and grandfather must be placed in the context of the times—it was a radical act for black people to be associated with the NAACP, and it was certainly "revolutionary" for such people to lead protest marches. Yet King's father and grandfather had done so. Moreover, this activity took place under the umbrella of Ebenezer Baptist Church, which thus gave this institution a tradition of activism.

Martin Luther King, Jr., grew up aware of the protest activities of his father and grandfather and that Ebenezer was an activist church. Further, King was introduced to the historical dimension of the black protest tradition through his studies. Lerone Bennett, Jr., who was a classmate of King's at Morehouse, reveals that King's boyhood idols were Gabriel Prosser, Nat Turner, and Frederick Douglass.[63] Given King's personal and intellectual contact with the black protest tradition, it is not surprising that he was in search of a strategy to attack the race problem when he entered Morehouse in 1944.

By the time he finished his undergraduate and graduate studies, he had come to the conclusion that civil disobedience provided both a method and a philosophical basis for approaching the racial problem. While at Morehouse he was introduced to and deeply influenced by the writings of Henry David Thoreau on civil disobedience. At Crozer Seminary in Pennsylvania, still in search of a solution to racial inequality, he studied the works of the great theologians and philosophers. He emerged from these readings much more attuned to how religion could play a positive role in social change, and he gained a great knowledge of the historical and structural nature of human societies. During the same period of time, however, through a lecture in Philadelphia given by Mordecai Johnson, he was introduced to Gandhi and the successful nonviolent movement he had led. King was so impressed that he immediately began an in-depth study of Gandhi, his movement, and nonviolent civil disobedience. King was coming close to embracing a strategy he would later make famous in the United States.

The most profound contribution he made to the black protest movement was his role as a catalyst for mass involvement. Earlier it was pointed out that King grew up in the black middle class and enjoyed all its privileges. Yet his most outstanding feature was his absolute identification with the poor, oppressed, black masses. It has been said that Gandhi's heart was always with the Indian peasants. Likewise, King's preoccupation was with the black masses, first and foremost. His Ph.D. studies at Boston University provided him with a theological and philosophical doctrine that enhanced his identification with all people, particularly the oppressed. That doctrine was "personalism," which maintained that the "clue to the meaning of ultimate reality is found in personality." King wrote that this doctrine "gave me metaphysical and philosophical grounding for the idea of a personal God, and it gave me a metaphysical basis for the dignity and worth of all human personality."[64] Through this philosophy he became convinced that "there is no graded scale of essential worth; there is no divine right of one race which differs from the divine right of another. Every human being has etched in his personality the indelible stamp of the Creator. . . . The worth of an individual does not lie in the measure of his intellect, his racial origin, or his social position. Human worth lies in relatedness to God."[65]

Crucial here is the fact that King, who grew up middle class, went to college, and obtained a Ph.D., firmly believed and acted out the philosophy that all people were equal. This conviction was evident to the masses who flocked to his leadership. Andrew Young captured this important aspect when he said: "I think he made no distinction between people. He was not interested in their wealth or their education, he saw straight through to the heart of a human being. And that was where he tried to relate to people. . . . He was so basically humble and unassuming, and yet he was so obviously talented."[66] King himself provided an informative example of his affinity with the masses. He recalled, "I learned a lesson many years ago from a report of two men who flew to Atlanta to confer with a civil rights leader at the airport. Before they could begin to talk, the porter sweeping the floor drew the local leader aside to talk about a matter that troubled him. After fifteen minutes had passed, one of the visitors said bitterly to his companion, 'I am just too busy for this kind of nonsense. I haven't come a thousand miles to sit and wait while he talks to a porter.' The other replied, 'When the day comes that he stops having time to talk to a porter, on that day I will not have the time to come one mile to see him.' When I heard this story, I knew I was being told something I should never forget."[67] King never made fundamental distinctions between what he called the "Ph.D.'s" and the "no D's."

CONCLUSION

When King arrived in Montgomery, Alabama, in the early 1950s he possessed all the qualities needed to become a leader of the black movement. These included oratorical skills, knowledge of nonviolent mass civil disobedience, a philosophy that wedded him to the masses, an understanding of the black protest tradition, knowledge of the changes occurring in the Third World, and the kind of personal leadership style that would attract the media. Further, he headed a mass-based institution within the black religious community.

By the same token, the times were ready for King. The system of domination imposed on blacks was firmly in place, but at the same time the black community and its institutions—church, family, colleges, and political organizations, for example—were stronger than they had ever been. Additionally, Third World countries were changing the world power struggle, and the media had developed to the extent that it could rapidly convey televised information and images around the globe. Most importantly, the black protest tradition embraced the people and the resources who were ready to intensify the struggle for black liberation. When those forces came together in Montgomery, they had in their midst a leader—Martin Luther King, Jr.

Louis R. Harlan

Thoughts on the Leadership of
Martin Luther King, Jr.

MY EXPERIENCES GROWING up in the South and my graduate training combined to interest me in the civil rights movement. Only half-converted to racial liberalism when I arrived at Johns Hopkins to study under C. Vann Woodward, I wrote a dissertation on racial inequality in southern education in the early twentieth century, later published as *Separate and Unequal* (1958). While I was his student, Woodward served as an historical advisor to the NAACP attorneys in the Brown case and wrote *The Strange Career of Jim Crow* (1955).

Teaching from 1950 to 1959 at a small teachers' college in the old cotton belt of East Texas, I discovered aspects of racial discrimination that were much harsher than I had experienced in an Atlanta suburb. I took my first steps there toward involvement in civil rights by working to register black voters and by joining the NAACP, which had been proscribed by the Texas leg-islature. Moving to Cincinnati, I became a board member of the be-leaguered local ACLU, wrote an article on the desegregation of New Orleans schools during Reconstruction, took part in the March on Washington, and began work on my biography of Booker T. Washington (2 vols., 1972, 1983). I was faculty advisor of the campus chapter of CORE, took part in a rent-strike campaign, and joined a civil rights march through downtown Cincinnati. In 1965 I took part in the Selma–Montgomery march as one of a group of historians organized by Walter Johnson of the University of Chicago.

Moving to the University of Maryland to edit the *Booker T. Washington Papers* with Raymond W. Smock (14 vols., 1972–88), I watched the winding-down of the civil rights movement, and I helped with the local arrangements for the Poor People's March on

Washington. As one of the "faculty" of SCOPE, an SCLC conference for workers in the voting rights campaign, I experienced at first hand the breakdown of the civil rights coalition as the young challenged the old and blacks challenged white liberals. A mere footsoldier in the nonviolent army, I nevertheless saw Martin Luther King often at close range. I marveled at his charismatic power, but also saw it fade before the end of his life. "All of it I saw, and part of it I was."

I t is hard for any contemporary to place a major historical figure such as Martin Luther King, Jr., in perspective. He is so close to us, he looms so large on our horizon, that we have a difficult time gauging his stature and his role in history. That is why nearly all major actors in history go through a cycle: first, they are eulogized as demigods, then some historical iconoclast ridicules their importance and exposes their human failings, and finally a more balanced historical view raises them up again to their true stature. This was the case for Abraham Lincoln and Frederick Douglass and Theodore Roosevelt and Woodrow Wilson, so we can expect Martin Luther King to pass through the same cycle of historical reputation.

Since his canonization as a national hero through the celebration of his birthday, it would be easy now to glorify Martin Luther King beyond all recognition as a superhuman giant whose will and divine inspiration shaped the civil rights movement, whose charisma unfailingly charmed his whole generation, and whose moral authority was absolute. Particularly because of his martyrdom it would be easy to assume that, if only he were alive today, he would accomplish all the unfulfilled hopes and dreams of the civil rights era. It would be easy, but it would be wrong. For at least the past hundred years historians have generally rejected the "Great Man" theory of historical causation. They recognize that leaders play a vital part, both symbolic and real, in social movements of great magnitude such as the civil rights movement, but social forces also play a major part in historical causation and direction.

What, then, were the forces that produced the civil rights movement and determined its cycle of growth, peak, and decline? We do not know all the factors, but we surely know some of them. In the first place, the civil rights movement had been going on a long time and was on the rise when the 1950s began. Civil rights had experienced an earlier upsurge in the abolition movement and the Reconstruction era, followed by a downturn during what we call the Age of Segregation. Early in the twentieth century the cause was revived by the Niagara Movement, led by W. E. B. Du Bois, which handed the torch to the interracial NAACP. It protested, lobbied, and fought through the courts all during the dark days of the 1920s and 1930s for voting rights, for equal education, for fair housing, and for other civil rights goals. Then came World War II, which had a transforming impact on race relations in America, as the historian Richard Dalfiume persuasively argues.[1] The wartime manpower shortage made possible A. Philip Randolph's March on Washington Movement. Though its existence was brief and the Fair Employment Practices Committee which it forced upon President Roosevelt was ineffective, the March on Washington Movement was symbolic of a new black militancy based on hope. Blacks in every community adopted the double-V slogan, victory against fascism abroad and victory against entrenched racism at home. World War II led to the founding in 1942 of CORE by pacifists in search of a positive way to work for human brotherhood and peace. CORE brought to America the concepts and tactics of *satyagraha* that Gandhi had used in South Africa and India and combined these with its own invention of the sit-in.[2]

The Second World War also set the stage for the civil rights movement by redrawing the map of the world and reconstructing its power relationships. The war spelled the end of the European colonial empires and gave birth to independent nations of dark-skinned peoples of Asia, Africa, and the islands, the so-called Third World of nonaligned dark-skinned peoples. At the same time the exhaustion of Europe as a result of the war shifted the balance of power to the two great rival superpowers, the United States and the Soviet Union, whose mutual fear of each other and desire for supremacy led to the Cold War. The Cold War was not only an arms race over nuclear weapons capable of wiping out human life, but a struggle over territory and over the minds of men and women. A large chunk of the uncommitted population of the world was the nonwhite Third World. And what was the most embarrassing feature of American society in its effort to lure the uncommitted Africans and Asians into the American orbit? It was American injustice to blacks—three hundred years of subordination, exploitation, discrimination, and prejudice.[3] The stage of history was set for the civil rights movement. American whites were now willing to make at least some minimal concessions of human rights to blacks, and blacks were spurred on to new levels of militancy by their participation in the war; at the same time, the horror of the Nazi holocaust and persecution of the Jews was fresh in the memory and conscience of the world.

Though the stage was thus set for the civil rights movement without the agency of Martin Luther King, we need only recall the situation in the South at the time King began his ministry of civil rights leadership to recognize how much his example, his personal style of leadership, and his dream altered the direction and accelerated the timetable of the civil rights movement. When the Supreme Court in rare unanimity declared school segregation unconstitutional in the Brown case, it seemed that civil rights was a matter of education.[4] But it should be remembered that in 1954 the country was far less unanimous than the Court. While a few border cities like Washington and Baltimore moved toward compliance, the white South generally took the course of "massive resistance,"[5] and the deep South said "never." As in the slavery crisis a hundred years earlier, the South silenced or punished its dissenters and explored every avenue of the law's delay. In the elected branches of the federal government, President Eisenhower privately disapproved of the Court's decision and publicly refused to endorse it, while his rival Adlai Stevenson openly courted the segregationist South. A southern manifesto of resistance to desegregation secured the names of all but a handful of southern congressmen and senators.

In the middle of this deadlock came the Montgomery bus boycott of 1955–56 and the emergence of Martin Luther King, Jr., as the leader, both symbolic and real, of the civil rights movement, a role he held until his death some twelve years later. It can be argued, as Aldon Morris does in his recent book, that the Baton Rouge bus desegregation campaign was more important because it came earlier and took only three weeks to achieve victory instead of the thirteen months of the Montgomery stride toward freedom.[6] It is also true that CORE, as August Meier and Elliott Rudwick show in their history, brought the Gandhian tactics of nonviolent direct action to America in the sit-ins at a Chicago restaurant a decade earlier than King.[7] Conceding these precedents, I still say that it was the Montgomery action of King that shifted the arena of civil rights confrontation from the courts to the streets and the television screens. It was King who captured the imagination of the country as a whole and of the black communities that furnished many of the foot soldiers of the civil rights army. The Montgomery movement was important not only because it provided a much-needed victory in a time of deepening discouragement on the school front, but also because it thrust to the center of the stage the one figure with charismatic qualities who could inspire his followers and draw the undecided majority into acquiescence and even participation. The Montgomery boycott signaled a shift in tactics and outlook from the legalism of the NAACP, which had reached the limit of its effectiveness at the time of the Brown decision, to the community activism that nonviolent direct action represented. The bus boycott took the fork in the road that led toward the sit-ins, Freedom Rides, and marches of the 1960s.[8]

Let us look for a moment at the steps by which King became the central leadership figure in civil rights and then examine the nature of that leadership. In the first place, how did King come to be the leader of the bus boycott? It was Rosa Parks who precipitated it by refusing to move to the back of the bus, and a test case such as hers had been eagerly sought for months by the Women's Political Council of Montgomery. But black Montgomery was not ready for a woman leader, and the logical male leader, E. D. Nixon, was a Pullman porter subject to frequent trips out of town and thus not available to meet the daily demands of the boycott. So it was partly by default that King, the newest minister in town, became the leader, but he was also the obvious choice because of the excellent preparation provided both by his education and the example of his father, and because of his skill and eloquence as chairman of the protest meeting held in the earliest days of the boycott. During the thirteen months of the boycott King stood every imaginable test of leadership. He inspired his followers to steadfastly refuse to ride the buses, imaginatively organized alternative transport by taxi drivers, undertakers, middle-class car owners, and friendly whites, negotiated skillfully with the bus company and city officials, and stood firm despite arrest and the bombing of his home. Victory came in the form of a Supreme Court decision, in a suit brought by the NAACP, that the state segregation law under which the city operated was unconstitutional. But no one could doubt that the paramount reason for victory was that a black community had firmly and nonviolently refused to accept second-class citizenship. The Montgomery boycott was a sweet victory in the midst of frustration over school desegregation.

During the four years after the bus boycott, King prepared in many ways for the crucial years to come. He founded SCLC and, as its leader, achieved parity with the leaders of the NAACP, the Urban League, and CORE. He moved his base to Atlanta, the hub of the South. He, A. Philip Randolph, and Roy Wilkins led a prayer pilgrimage to Eisenhower's Washington to try to jog the administration toward enforcement of school desegregation. This 1957 effort failed in its immediate objective, but it was a valuable rehearsal for the big event in 1963. A tour of India deepened King's commitment to nonviolence and civil disobedience in response to unjust laws, and brief visits to newly independent Ghana and Nigeria brought home the irony that American blacks were lagging behind their African brothers.

Then came the sit-ins, beginning in Greensboro, North Carolina, and sweeping across the black college towns of the South in the spring of 1960, leading to the formation of SNCC, the enlistment of college students, black and white, southern and northern, and bringing the civil rights movement to full flood. The electrifying arrival of SNCC to the civil rights coalition was simultaneous with the arrival of the generation gap in American society, and the rash, brash young recruits did not acknowledge Martin Luther King as their spiritual leader. He was barely over thirty himself, but his pulpit style, his preacher clothes, his caution, and his occasional appearance in brand-new blue jeans marked him as a middle-aged, middle-class man. Although Ezell Blair and Joseph McNeill were inspired by King's example in the bus boycott to create their own form of nonviolent direct action, the sit-in leaders sought an independent course. When the sit-ins reached Atlanta, King gave them behind-the-scenes support, and Ella Baker of SCLC organized the meeting that founded SNCC at Shaw University.[9]

Rather than relive in narrative those stirring years from 1960 to King's martyrdom in 1968, let us follow David Lewis's lead in dividing them into two periods: King's innovative leadership in pursuit of traditional civil rights goals up to 1965; and his less successful but prescient efforts from 1965 to 1968 to form a new coalition to fight the twin scourges of war and poverty.

Between 1960 and 1965 King was a central figure in a movement that included not only the civil rights organizations already mentioned but also religious groups, Protestant, Catholic, and Jewish, labor unions, most notably the auto workers, civil liberties groups, and occasionally high officials of the Kennedy and Johnson administrations. King was a bit slow in grasping the helm. He did not personally participate in the Freedom Rides of 1961, although SCLC helped to fund them. He arrived on the scene in Albany, Georgia, late and ineffectually, but he learned some hard lessons from that failure which he applied to Birmingham the following year, reaching agreement on an agenda in advance and cooperating with local leadership. With Bull Connor as an unwitting ally, he prepared in Birmingham the climate of national opinion that made possible the March on Washington of 1963 and the Civil Rights Act of 1964 that followed.

Next in the mainstream of events was the voting rights drive at Selma, and when it reached deadlock and a time of divided counsel, King found a way out through the march to Montgomery. There, with the Confederate flags of the state capitol before him and his Dexter Avenue Baptist Church to one side, he halted the marchers and gave a rousing address that matched the "I Have a Dream" speech of two years earlier. I was there, and I'll never forget standing at the end of the speech, holding hands with a nun on one side and a black man on the other, singing "We Shall Overcome." As the crowd dispersed and we headed for the nearest restrooms, an "out of order" sign went up at a nearby gas station as a petty gesture of recalcitrance. Once again, the segregationists played into the hands of the civil rights forces, and the outcome was the Voting Rights Act of 1965.

The best analysis we have to date of King's leadership is August Meier's article, "On the Role of Martin Luther King," written in a magazine of small circulation in 1965, but many times reprinted.[10] Seeking to understand King's charismatic appeal to his following, Meier concluded that his hold on blacks was largely due to his intuitive adoption of the speaking style of the old-fashioned black Baptist preacher, employing moral clichés and an eclectic amalgam of Jesus, Hegel, and Gandhi that passed for intellectual profundity among his relatively uneducated audiences. His hold upon whites was more complex. "For one thing," said Meier, "he unerringly knows how to exploit with maximum effectiveness their growing feeling of guilt." But King went beyond this to express an explicit belief in white people's capacity for salvation. Thus, while he castigated whites for their sins, he also conveyed to whites, in the same way Booker T. Washington had a half-century earlier, that he had their *own* best interests at heart. And he offered them the means of redemption through concession and compromise, a way not afforded by a more overtly radical group such as SNCC.

Actually, King's goals were the same radical ones of social justice and equal rights that animated SNCC and CORE, but he gave the appearance of greater caution, moderation, and openness to negotiation. Meier described him as occupying the "vital center" of the civil rights movement, where he could keep his coalition together, restraining somewhat the rash youths who formed the cutting edge of the movement, while admonishing the laggards to catch up. There were undeniable differences of philosophy and tactics dividing SNCC from King and SCLC, or Snick from Slick, but both factions needed each other and both knew it. And unlike Booker T. Washington in an earlier era, King tolerated differences of approach to the movement's evolving strategy. As Stokely Carmichael of SNCC said in an interview with Clayborne Carson: "People loved King. . . . I've seen people in the South climb over each other just to say, 'I touched him! I touched him!' . . . I'm even talking about the young. The old people had more love and respect. They even saw him like a God. These were the people we were working with and I had to follow in his footsteps when I went in there. The people didn't know 'what was SNCC.' They just said, 'You one of Dr. King's men?' 'Yes, Ma'am, I am.' "[11] By seeming to be more moderate than he really was, King was in a much better position to reason with the Kennedy and Johnson administrations and to negotiate with the segregationists of Birmingham or Montgomery. He could say, in effect, if you do not bargain with me, you must deal next with SNCC, or Malcolm X, or the fire next time.

Martin Luther King was the quintessential black leader, combining the ardor for racial justice of a W. E. B. Du Bois, the political genius and ability to manipulate white opinion of a Booker T. Washington, and the charisma and emblematic leadership of a Frederick Douglass. Some scholars have called King conservative, more in reference to his methods than his goals. August Meier uses the more paradoxical term "conservative militant."[12] What others call conservative I would call wise, and where is it written that a dedicated leader cannot or should not be wise? King was deeply committed, in a religious and moral sense, to nonviolence as a way of life, not just as a tactical means to an immediate end. And while it is true, ironically, that he benefited from the violence of his opponents, he himself never deliberately courted violence that might have led to the death or maiming of his followers. When he rejected rash counsel, as at the Edmund Pettus Bridge in Selma, he prevented needless sacrifice. He did not flinch from his duty when his own end came, but it did not come through any vainglorious foolhardiness on his part.

The cycle of the civil rights movement reached its apogee between 1963 and 1965 with the March on Washington, the Mississippi summer, and the Selma–Montgomery march. Then a succession of shadows fell on its path. When the Johnson administration escalated the war in Vietnam in 1965, it diverted national attention and resources from the civil rights and poverty issues to the death and defoliation of foreign war. Moreover, it weakened to the breaking point ties between civil rights leaders and political leaders. King immediately and repeatedly denounced the war and joined the peace movement. Whatever this may have lacked in short-run expediency, we can now see it was right and just. He had no choice. He had all of his life been committed to nonviolence and peace. Nonviolence was not just a peripheral or a tactical stance. It was central to his thought and feeling. And further, a nation at war would not tolerate the civil disobedience on which the civil rights movement was based.

Another development occurred in 1965 to turn Martin Luther King in new directions. The Watts riot of angry and discontented poor blacks did not take place in the South where the focus of the civil rights movement had been, but far away in Los Angeles, and it set off similar riots in the next three years in other non-southern cities. These riots were among people virtually untouched by the civil rights revolution, or touched only in their rising expectations that were impossible to realize given the conditions of poverty and joblessness in which they lived. The violence of the riots, though it was directed more against property than people, was in itself a repudiation of King's principle of nonviolence. Almost simultaneously came the death and transfiguration of Malcolm X, King's most trenchant critic. King's popularity within the movement sagged perceptibly at the very time when virtually his entire original civil rights agenda had been successfully achieved, and when he was reaching out most creatively toward a new agenda and a new coalition to achieve it. The mutterings against him of the early 1960s now became the full-throated slogans of the Black Power revision of his dream.

In his last years King certainly shifted the focus of his endeavors. In Chicago, in Operation Breadbasket, the main thrust was to force white businessmen to hire the disadvantaged, although fair housing was also an objective. He urged the poor to organize for collective bargaining. Before he died, he was far advanced in the planning of the Poor People's Campaign and its march on Washington, and it was in behalf of decent wages and working conditions for the garbage workers of Memphis that he went to his rendezvous with death. David Lewis in a perceptive essay in 1980 described this as a radical departure from the middle-class agenda of the 1955–65 period to a new socialist agenda, an economic program to translate the new freedom won by the civil rights movement into new opportunity for the previously submerged.[13] I think Lewis is right that this was a change in emphasis, and that to carry it out King sought to develop a new coalition. King lost from his earlier coalition many of the Democratic political leaders, some of the civil rights organizations, and some of the white church-oriented supporters who had subsequently either joined or were held in check by the white backlash. He gained new allies among the antiwar dissenters and, at least potentially, a rainbow coalition of the disadvantaged—Chicanos, native Americans, and poor whites.

King was moving toward a new strategy at the end of his life, but ideologically he was not very different at the end of his life from what he had been at the beginning. A study of his sermons over time will probably reveal a remarkable consistency in preaching the social gospel. For example, King published *Why We Can't Wait* in 1964, well before the ghetto riots and escalation of the war. In a prophetic chapter titled "The Days to Come," he quoted someone as saying, "When you are right, you cannot be too radical," and added the hallowed American words, "If this be treason, make the most of it." The nation, he wrote, "must not only radically readjust its attitude toward the Negro in the compelling present, but must incorporate in its planning some compensatory consideration for the handicaps he has inherited from the past." To illustrate his point, he held up the example of the Indian government's compensatory or preferential treatment of untouchables in housing, jobs, and education. In this same book, published a year before the events of 1965, King proposed a "Bill of Rights for the Disadvantaged," including the forgotten poor whites as well as poor blacks, a foreshadowing of the more detailed "Economic Bill of Rights" in the planning of the Poor People's Campaign. Further, he proposed a law similar to the Wagner National Labor Relations Act of the 1930s that would provide zealous government protection to the disadvantaged in their efforts to organize and bargain collectively for civil rights and equal opportunity enforcement. He also foresaw great potential in the new voting power of blacks and urged black solidarity in order to achieve the maximum effectiveness in dealing with the white majority.[14]

If one finds a new radicalism in King after 1965, it is more a change in strategy than a change in ideas. To speak of radicalism in King, of course, one does not mean the bogey of communism or "communist dupe" that the southern segregationists and J. Edgar Hoover tried to hang about his neck to reduce his effectiveness, but radicalism in the classical sense of going to the roots of American social evils and removing them, root and branch. He began at the beginning, with public accommodations and schooling and voting rights, and later moved toward heavier emphasis on the economic plight of blacks, but liberating the whole person and the whole society were always his ultimate objectives. In the words of the civil rights chant, King wanted freedom, wanted all of it, and wanted it now.

We must finally put King's leadership in a longer perspective. Historically speaking, we cannot now say the last word. A broader and deeper study of the life and meaning of King and his movement awaits the publication of the papers of Martin Luther King, now just under way under the able direction of Clayborne Carson.[15] The historical study of the civil rights movement is still in its early stages. We have the bits and pieces, some eyewitness accounts, and histories of the various organizations in the civil rights coalition, but we still do not have, and it is too early to expect, a satisfactory historical synthesis of the movement.[16] Furthermore, we do not yet know how it all turned out. Some parts of the movement agenda such as voting rights and public accommodations seem to be solid gains, but who would claim that we have achieved equal educational opportunity? And the racial disparity in job opportunities today is a national disgrace. We are torn today between pessimism over the parlous state of civil rights in the America of the Reagan Supreme Court and optimism when we see the spirit of Martin Luther King manifesting itself in South Africa in the work of Allan Boesak and Desmond Tutu. We should remember King as a man worthy of emulation, but we should also remember that the movement of the 1960s was what it was, in contrast to civil rights efforts before and after, because it realized the possibilities of collective action.

Robert Parris Moses

Commentary

BORN AND RAISED IN HAR-lem, Robert Moses received his M.A. in philosophy from Harvard in 1957 and then taught mathematics in New York City before going to Atlanta, on the recommendation of Bayard Rustin, in the summer of 1960 to work as an SCLC volunteer. He remained there briefly, meeting Ella Baker, and then left on a field trip and recruiting campaign for SNCC through Alabama and Mississippi. In Cleveland, Mississippi, he met Amzie Moore, who persuaded him to undertake a voter registration drive in the state the next year. Moses returned to the South in July 1961 after completing the last year of his teaching contract. He settled in the town of McComb in southwestern Mississippi where, as a full-time SNCC staff worker and initially working alone, he established voter registration schools in the surrounding counties and accompanied local blacks to the offices of voter regis-

trars. Along with other SNCC workers who subsequently joined him and local blacks who supported them, Moses was harassed and beaten; he was jailed several times. The threat of violence discouraged most blacks from registering.

Moving in early 1962 to Jackson, Mississippi, where SNCC had opened its state headquarters, he continued his voter registration work and served unofficially as campaign manager for the Rev. R. L. T. Smith, a Jackson minister who ran unsuccessfully for Congress on the Democratic ticket. Later in the year Moses shifted the focus of his work to the area around Greenwood, Mississippi, and in August he became director of voter registration in the state for the Council of Federated Organizations (COFO), an umbrella body, which he had helped found, consisting of SNCC, CORE, SCLC, and NAACP groups operating in Mississippi. He was arrested and jailed in or near Greenwood in 1962 and again in 1963.

Moses was a principal organizer and director of the Freedom Vote or Freedom Ballot, a mock election held throughout Mississippi in November 1963. Sponsored by COFO and open to all blacks over twenty-one years of age, its purpose was to demonstrate that many blacks wished to vote—over 80,000 participated in this election—but were being prevented from doing so. Moses was largely responsible for the 1964 Mississippi Freedom Summer Project, a state-wide voter registration campaign. The Project brought over 1,000 volunteers to the state to establish community centers, open "freedom schools," and register voters, and it focused national attention on the plight of blacks in the state. Also that year he helped organize both the Mississippi Freedom Democratic Party (MFDP) as an alternative to the state's segregationist regular Democratic party and the "Freedom Registration" drive that enrolled over 80,000 people in the new party. Conventions in Mississippi at the county, district, and state level picked a slate of delegates to the Democratic national convention in Atlantic City: the delegation was not seated.

Concerned by the extent of his leadership role and personal following in the movement, about the potential for a powerful leader to dominate a democratic movement through rhetorical skill or intellectual brilliance, through authoritative fiat or personal magnetism, Moses resigned as COFO director in late 1964 and, in early 1965, adopted his middle name (Parris) as his surname, retired from SNCC, and left Mississippi. He was active in the peace movement for a time, and from 1969 to 1976 he taught mathematics at the Samé Secondary School in Tanzania.

I want to begin by saying to the people who are sitting on the symposium panel and the people who are in the audience, I'm not a scholar and I don't have a paper. Our job was to comment on the papers that were presented, and that's what I'm going to try to confine myself to doing.

The one thing that strikes me as I listen and read the papers presented here is that we're in the very initial stages of trying to figure out and write about the movement.

Aldon Morris didn't have a chance to finish his paper, and I'm sorry about that; I wish that he had. There is a part in his paper that I was going to start my comments off with, but he didn't get to read it, so I want to read it to you. He was talking about King and the black protest tradition and he said that the most outstanding feature of King was "his absolute identification with the poor, oppressed, black masses." He talked about his personalism, that the clue to the meaning of ultimate reality is found in personality, that is, in metaphysical and philosophical grounding for the idea of a personal God, a metaphysical basis for the dignity and worth of all human personality. And then this paragraph he didn't get to read: "Every human being has etched in his personality [and these are King's words] the indelible stamp of the Creator. . . . The worth of an individual does not lie in the measure of his intellect, his racial origin, or his social position. Human worth lies in relatedness to God."

I wanted to pick up from that last sentence—that human worth lies in relatedness to God—and ask a question of us: How are we to understand our relatedness to God? And one way in which we understand that is through a metaphor. That is, there is a long-standing metaphor about our relatedness to God, namely that God is an ocean of consciousness and we are individual waves in that ocean of consciousness. We are to think of ourselves as related to God as the wave is related to the ocean. Think about that. It gives you a picture, because we know the ocean and we see the waves, and they rise and fall on the bosom of the ocean, and so in that metaphor we rise and fall on the bosom of God.

Now metaphors are what we use to help us understand reality. Historians use them and scientists use them. I remember that a very important one in my study of the philosophy of science was the Neurath metaphor. Otto Neurath was a social scientist who lived in Vienna. He had a metaphor about the ship of science on the ocean of knowledge. He likened science to a vessel that is floating on the ocean of knowledge, with the scientist as a little man in that ship who is trying to rebuild it all the time, but who can never come to dock, who can't put in at any port. He has to learn how to keep this ship afloat while he's rebuilding it, and he has to do it on the ocean. What he was getting at in that metaphor was that the effort of the scientist to create a precise language of science is forever bounded by the ocean of just ordinary language out of which that precise language has to evolve. The scientist is apt to forget that and is apt to get carried away with his precise language.

I mention that metaphor because when we were having our conferences at Waveland, Mississippi, that metaphor stuck in my mind. At Waveland none of us were allowed to sign our names to any papers because SNCC was fearful of the greater influence that some people might have, and it was trying an experiment in democracy, so each of us was asked to write position papers without signing our name to them. In one of the papers that I wrote I mentioned the metaphor—that SNCC is a boat in the middle of an ocean, and we're inside trying to rebuild it, and we have nowhere to dock. Our problem is, how can we stay afloat while we're rebuilding it and not sink? Well, somebody asked Jim Forman, "What is that? What is this business about a boat?" and Jim got up in the meeting and said that somebody had asked him about the boat and the ocean, and he said, "that's a metaphor." He went on to explain what a metaphor was, and then said, "but I don't like the metaphor. I think we don't want to say that it's an ocean. We need to get some direction in it and say that our boat is on a river, that it's moving someplace." Well, Cleveland Sellers took up that metaphor and came out with a book that he called *The River of No Return*. As you know, some historians have also taken up the metaphor of a river, Vincent Harding, for instance, in trying to explain the whole tradition of black protest.

Aldon Morris presented us with a metaphor this morning, and I want to get back to it. What he said was that "the argument of this essay is that the quality and success of King's leadership stemmed from the interaction of large social and historical factors with the unique combination of qualities that were deeply rooted in his own personality." So here we have the metaphor of convergence—it's a metaphor, it's a picture. He's groping for something to try to give us some sense of what was happening. It was the convergence of these large social factors, which he listed, and personal factors in King's life, which he also listed. My question is—to him and to us—how are we to understand this metaphor? How are we to make sense of it? One way of understanding it is to look back at the question for which this metaphor is the answer, and that question is in the preceding paragraph of Aldon's paper: "How is the emergence and success of such a leader to be explained?"

I want you to consider the metaphor about God again—that God is an ocean of consciousness and we are the waves on that ocean—and think of that metaphor as a metaphor about the movement. Consider that the movement is an ocean of consciousness, protest, rebellion, organizing—fill in other things that the movement is an ocean of—and that the people in the movement are the waves on that ocean. That's how I've always thought about the movement and about my relationship to it, and about SNCC and other people's relationship to it. The movement was this ocean and we were out there; we were the waves on the ocean. Now when you think about the movement in that way you can ask a question different from the one that Aldon asked. Aldon's question is, "How is the emergence and success of such a leader to be explained?" And we can ask, rather, the question, "How is the emergence and the repression, the success and the failure, of such a movement to be explained?"

Let us shift our attention from the wave to the ocean, because the wave is not the ocean. Even if it's a tidal wave, it has no meaning apart from that ocean. The idea is that the history, any history, of the movement, means we have to talk about its failures, its false starts, as well as its successes. We have to offer our young people an understanding of why King was assassinated as well as why he became a Nobel Peace Prize winner. But not only King. We have to offer them an understanding of why Medgar Evers, Herbie Lee, Louis Allen, Goodman, Chaney, Schwerner, Malcolm X, those two Kennedy brothers, why *all* those people were assassinated from 1961 to 1971, and the point is that King's assassination has no meaning apart from the assassinations of all those other people. You cannot understand it as an isolated event. They belong to the ocean that was the movement. That's what has to be studied to get a deeper understanding about who and what Dr. King was.

That really is my major point. That we can ask and should ask of historians that they offer us a history of the movement, and that through that history of the movement we can then understand the relationship of Dr. King to the movement. But without that history of the movement, trying to understand King is as meaningless as trying to understand the wave without the ocean. There is just no understanding to be had. What we're left with is frustration. It's a frustration that Dr. King's sister expressed in the press room, a frustration with young people who don't know how to relate to Dr. King because they see him as a god, so they have no concept that they, too, can be like him. That's what happens when the focus is wrong, is misplaced.

Now, I wanted to take into consideration what some of the conceptual signposts of the movement are, what I've thought over the years were important things in the movement, and I want to put them out there for the historians to think about. There was always within the movement a tension between organizing and leading, or organizing and mobilizing. You can trace the history of the movement in terms of certain great mobilizations. There was Albany, Georgia, there was Birmingham, there was Selma, Alabama. But you can also trace the history of the movement in terms of major organizing efforts. There was the organization of SCLC. There was the organization of SNCC. There was the organization of the Nashville sit-in movement. There was the organization of the March on Washington.

You can trace in the movement the tension in people between their roles as organizers and as leaders, and try to get some sense of what that meant. I think of Ella Baker. She was a great organizer, and she was a leader, too. But one of the characteristics of organizers is that their work emerges, and they themselves subside. If you think of the waves in the ocean, at a certain point they subside back into the ocean, and what you see is what they organized or their work. SNCC is the work of Ella Baker. But it was SNCC that emerged, not Ella. The March on Washington was the work of Bayard Rustin, but it was Martin Luther King, Jr., who emerged, not Bayard. The point is that Bayard did not organize that march so that he could himself emerge as a leader; the march was organized so that someone like King could emerge. And Bayard knew that. He set out to do just that. That's the mark of an organizer. Ella didn't set up SNCC so that she could emerge as the leader of it. Quite the contrary. Ella helped organize SNCC in such a way that she could never possibly be the leader of it. And in doing that she taught us about organizing.

Jim Lawson in Nashville organized the Nashville sit-in movement, and it was that movement that rescued the freedom rides and penetrated into Mississippi. It was the only movement in the whole country at the time that was prepared and absolutely determined to get back on that burning bus. Nobody else, nobody else, not *anybody* in the whole country, was prepared to get back on that bus. Jim Lawson taught and organized those students, but he didn't emerge as their leader. Their leaders went on to become leaders of SNCC. So in the movement there are great examples of organizers and their efforts, and this is not emphasized. It doesn't make good copy, but it made the movement. It was the tissue and the bones, the inner structure of the movement.

So these ideas about organizing versus leading, and the complex roles that people played both as organizers and leaders, need to be examined. Think of a person like Amzie Moore. Amzie Moore was the civil rights leader in Cleveland, Mississippi, but he was an organizer in Mississippi at the state level and never a leader. In the state as a whole he moved like an organizer, never out front, working with people to help them set up certain plans—the voting plan, for example—but in his own town, in his community, he was a leader. Now civil rights leaders got into trouble when they didn't understand that and tried to organize in Amzie's territory. I think that we need to know more about this kind of interplay.

There is the question of nationalism, and I don't have much to say about that. But what needs to be explored is the understanding of the rise of nationalism worldwide in the period following the Second World War, and how it manifested itself in this country in Malcolm, in Robert Williams, and then in the black power movement. Again, using the metaphor of the ocean, the crux of the thing is the phenomenon of nationalism and its manifestation in this country at a time when one wouldn't have expected it to have been manifested.

The other concept I want to bring up is nonviolence. Mrs. King mentioned it when we had the press conference, and I'm sure that that's going to be taken up in other papers. I was watching and aware of nonviolence and how it was being played out within the movement. I've always felt somehow that nonviolence was a way of life and not just a tactic to be used in mobilization—it is a fundamental tool with which a person can try to organize his own life. That somehow never caught hold in the movement, and I think that's something that needs real investigation. The person who comes to mind again is Jim Lawson, because Jim is the only person I know in the movement who actually trained people and then went out and tried to practice nonviolence as a way of life. I'm thinking of those Nashville people, a segment of those Nashville people, who became so prominent in SNCC. We all agreed on nonviolence as a tactic in certain demonstrations at a certain point in history, but nonviolence as a way of life escaped us at that point. It certainly escaped me. I could never talk about it to people we were working with; they carried guns. To the farmers in Mississippi, carrying a gun, protecting your home, was a way of life. We need a real understanding of where nonviolence really fits in and with whom and how.

I say that because there was in this country during the time of the movement an approach to God and to nonviolence about which we were ignorant. That was the approach through yoga, which was being introduced here before and during and after the movement, but we never connected with it. This approach to nonviolence emphasized certain spiritual practices, certain spiritual disciplines. It's an approach that I have tried to study over the past years, and I now understand what we did not have when we were in the movement in the sixties. We did not have access to that kind of knowledge, about how you actually work on yourself with very simple exercises, do very simple things, to transform yourself, to make more manifest that God of whom we are a wave of consciousness. I say that because I think that in the movement which is coming, or evolving again, that if there is going to be nonviolence involved in it, then we have to prepare ourselves for that kind of effort.

Mrs. King mentioned Dr. King's spiritual discipline, and that's something that historians need to tell us about—what it was, what it consisted of—as well as looking into what happened to nonviolence in the movement as it was practiced, and where it played itself out.

So I guess what I wanted to say in commenting on the papers is that I have a question about Aldon's question. And understand that I'm not sure that he actually thinks of the movement that way. Maybe that was just because of being presented with this conference. They asked me to write a paper about the conference and I had two problems. One, I'm not a scholar and I don't write papers. And the other, I don't think about the movement in terms of King, and this was a conference about

King and the movement. I have no qualms about that, but I never thought about the movement in terms of King. It never occurred to me to think about the movement in terms of King. I lived and breathed the *movement*. So I couldn't have written a paper that focused on the movement in terms of King. It may be that Aldon was limited in terms of the scope of the conference. But I just wanted to point out that the other question seems to me more important. Not the emergence and success of an individual, but the emergence and the success of, the failure and repression of the movement as a whole, the study of its false starts as well as its successes, its failures as well as its victories.

Howard Zinn

Commentary

I BECAME INVOLVED WITH the civil rights movement partly through accident (I was getting my doctorate from Columbia University when I was invited to join the faculty of Spelman College in Atlanta in 1956 as head of the history department), and partly through choice (I decided I could not simply teach classes and remain quiescent in the midst of terrible injustice, and when my students began to rebel, I joined them). Even before the sit-ins of 1960, there was a developing resistance to the status quo—for instance, a successful attempt, in which Whitney Young and I worked with students of Spelman and the Atlanta University Center, to desegregate the library system of Atlanta.

In Atlanta, living in the black community, one inevitably encountered the King family. Martin Luther King, Sr., was a prominent local minister, Martin Luther King, Jr.'s sister was a colleague of mine at Spelman, and his brother was a student at Atlanta University. And I came to know King himself, who by now was famous for his leadership of the Montgomery bus boycott, in various situations in Atlanta.

When the sit-ins spread from North Carolina and Tennessee to Atlanta in the spring of 1960, my students were among those demonstrating and getting arrested, among them Marian Wright. I participated in sit-ins and demonstrations, and in 1961 and 1962 traveled to Albany, Georgia, to do a report for the Southern Regional Council on the Albany Movement. When Martin Luther King, Jr., was asked if he agreed with the criticism of the FBI in my report, he answered affirmatively, and this irritated J. Edgar Hoover considerably.

I was asked to become an "advisor" to SNCC, joining Ella Baker, and began to travel to various places in the deep South where SNCC was organizing—Selma, Alabama, Hattiesburg, Greenwood, and Greenville, Mississippi. My articles appeared in *Harper's, The Nation,* and other magazines, and I wrote the first book-length account of SNCC's work in the South, *S.N.C.C.: The New Abolitionists* (1964).

After 1964, when I was teaching at Boston University, and becoming involved in the movement against the war in Vietnam, my great admiration for Dr. King continued to grow as he defied both the white establishment and traditional black leadership to speak out indignantly about what the United States was doing to the people of Vietnam. I was happy to be on the same platform with him at a huge antiwar demonstration in 1967 in New York's Central Park. He had a vision beyond race, beyond class, beyond nation, one that embraced humanity. For this—without forgetting those thousands of people in the movement who sacrificed, as he did, and those who died in the struggle, as he did—he deserves special tribute.

This has been a remarkable day. At first I was wondering what was going to happen, in what direction this conference was going to go, worrying about it, as I always worry when people "do" history. Because you know what happens when people "do" history. They "do" history, and it's done, and there's nothing left to say, and it goes into the library, and then people ignore it. Maybe rightfully. But what we've had here is an interesting development, I think, because as I see this conference it is not an empty exercise in nostalgia—indeed, it is meaningful for the future. This is the way I have always thought of history, and this is the way I have tried to write and present history— in a way that is aimed at the present and the future and that asks, what are we going to do now? It is important for us to take the edge off the notion of charisma and to look more realistically at King—the person beneath that charisma. Aldon Morris, in his very careful analysis of the movement and the interrelationship between King and the movement, was trying, it seems to me, to tell us how we might think of movements and individuals in the future. And Bob Moses made that both explicit and poetic, as he usually does. By the way, when I heard him mention Waveland—I remember Waveland, and I remember how the people in SNCC wrote these papers anonymously, and no one can tell me that when Jim Forman came across that metaphor he didn't know who wrote it. We all deal with metaphors, but some deal with them more than others.

I'd like to continue in that vein, that is, trying to extract from the history of that time, from the movement and King, some things for us to think about. Bob's point about the relationship between King and the movement—his emphasis on the metaphor of the movement as the ocean, his talk about King as a wave and Ella Baker as a wave and Amzie Moore as a wave, and we could add Bob Moses as a wave, and many others—this is very important for us today. Why are we looking at this and why are we studying this if it's not for the fact that today we face problems as serious or more serious than the ones we faced in the 1960s? And today there is no exciting, rousing movement that we can all join. The situation we know demands enormous effort, and we are wondering where that effort is going to come from, and so we need all the guidance we can get. It's very important for us to realize that we cannot wait for charismatic leaders, we cannot look for charismatic leaders. What I am saying goes directly against our modern American culture with all its emphasis on celebrities and *People* magazine, and who's going to be elected president, as if that's the most important thing. That's our American culture, which has become too much of a worldwide culture, and it puts its emphasis on who will save us.

In my work in American history I've been only too aware of how kids in school are taught—as I was taught when I went to school—taught about American history as a succession of saviors. The founding fathers saved us from England, and then Lincoln freed the slaves, and Roosevelt ended the depression, and—well, after that it got vague. But it was only after I got through my formal training in history and began to read for myself that I realized there was a lot going on in this country long before those founding fathers got together in Philadelphia. In fact, the things that these ordinary people did, like rebel from time to time, caused the founding fathers to get together and wonder, how can we contain such rebellions? Lincoln did not free the slaves; instead, there was this enormous movement that went on in the thirty years before the Civil War, and it rose to a crescendo with black abolitionists and white abolitionists and, yes, a movement of people that went beyond those waves of Lincoln and Garrison and Phillips and even Frederick Douglass, who was a great wave. Enormous numbers of people were involved in that movement, which led to sort of the end of slavery. Sort of. And this has been the history of this country that has not been told in the history books. The story of movements that made whatever bits of progress we have had in this country and, on top or in front of which, leaders rose or emerged and became visible.

The leaders, the waves, we most cherish are those who knew what they were, who knew they were waves on the ocean, who understood they were there because of the movement and they could help it along, but who knew that after they were gone the movement would—must

—continue. One of the remarkable things about Dr. King, I thought, was that, exalted as he was in the press and a winner of the Nobel Prize, tempted by this, as everybody is in such situations (such temptations are put before people who become prominent and well known—you know, invitations to the White House and caucuses and little meetings and gatherings of the elite to discuss strategy, and hardly anybody can resist that) King went in and out of that, but at critical moments, when decisions had to be made, he very often, but not always, because he wasn't perfect (he knew that), turned to the people who were in the movement and asked them what he should do.

I remember specifically—and I just heard this again the other night when I was in Atlanta speaking to Lonnie King, who was one of the leaders of the student movement. He was telling me how at a certain point in the fall of 1960, during the boycott of Rich's department store in Atlanta, Lonnie King and Herschelle Sullivan, the two student leaders —Herschelle was a student of mine at Spelman College—I always have to say who was my student because that's how teachers exist, you see, and we would just die if we couldn't say who our students were—and they, Herschelle and Lonnie, decided, "We have to have a sit-in at Rich's department store; Rich's is the big domino that will topple all the others." And so they called Dr. King—because they wanted media attention and King would bring media attention—and they said, "You've got to come and sit in with us on The Bridge at Rich's" (The Bridge was one of four eating places at Rich's), and King hesitated. He was a human being and he had his hesitations. He said, "Look, I'm on probation. I've got four months' hard labor facing me, sentenced in De Kalb County, which is even worse than Fulton County." And Lonnie said, "But you're a leader," and King said, "When are we meeting on The Bridge?" And so he went, and he was arrested, and sure enough he went to jail. There were moments like that.

I speak, we all speak, with such arrogance of people who are not here to defend themselves against the things we say, or to correct what we think we know or remember. Dr. King was, I think, the kind of person who, when he met with the powers that be, even though he came out of the South, found it difficult not to be nice to them. Even though he sort of suspected "maybe they don't have our best interests at heart"—Kennedy, John Doar, Burke Marshall, the others—he had to be nice to the people whom he was meeting face-to-face with, and listen to them and so on. So he came to Fred Shuttlesworth in Birmingham and said, "They suggested we call off the demonstrations in Birmingham for a while," and Shuttlesworth said, "No way." Now King could have listened to Marshall and Doar and Kennedy, or he could listen to a much more insignificant man, Fred Shuttlesworth. But he knew Fred Shuttlesworth was one of those people—one of those other waves in the movement—and that when Eisenhower was getting credit for sending troops to Little Rock in 1957, Shuttlesworth and his wife had sent their kids, the first black kids, into a high school in Birmingham. They had escorted their kids, and Fred Shuttlesworth was attacked by the Klan and beaten with chains, and his wife was stabbed. Federal agents were not around to help them; no troops were around to help them; nobody was around to help. King knew this and much more about Shuttlesworth, and he went back and he said no to Kennedy and Doar and Marshall.

It is very important for people who have been made big waves on the ocean to understand who they are, what they are, and where they come from. I think that King understood this—not always, but often— and he respected the kids in SNCC. It's true that SNCC resented all that hoopla and publicity and the focus on King while those people down there on the earth who *were* the movement were neglected. But I always found that the SNCC people, as critical as they were of King, saw him basically as one of their own and knew that from time to time he would turn to them and listen to them, pay attention to them. And I think that was very important.

What I'm doing is trying to think of what we can learn from that experience, both King's and that of the movement, of both the ocean and the waves. What can we learn that is useful for us today with the problems that we face? And what about our need to create a movement ourselves and not to look for leaders to do that job for us, knowing that the responsibility belongs to all of us because all of us are capable, not of heroic acts, but of small acts, and movements grow as a succession of small acts. I'm not saying a lot about Aldon Morris's paper, but to make up for that I want to tell you that you should read his book *The Origins of the Civil Rights Movement,* which is, I think, one of the most important books on the civil rights movement that has come out in this country. One of the things he does in it is to trace the little things that people do that don't get into the newspapers and don't get into the history books, but that make up the links and connections and roots of a movement, out of which emerge the leaders who become famous. And it suggests to us for the future that any one of us and all of us are capable of becoming links, small links, who are doing little things, connecting with one another and organizing, and in that way we have the possibility of becoming part of some great movement.

There are just a few more things I want to say that I think are important, even though they're specific and controversial and so on. But that's what we need—we don't need placidity and kindness and sweetness and light and all of that. We need things to do. We have to remember certain things from that movement. And one of those things is a skepticism of authority, and this gets back to the skepticism that King very often showed, and that all of us need to show all of the time, that skepticism of authority. Another thing was his sheer honesty. Whatever King's faults were, and he certainly had them, as human beings do, I felt there was one saving thing about him and that was his honesty; he told the truth. And in this era of—why do I say *this* era of lies and disinformation—governments lie and deceive us, really, governments all over the world, in *every* era. The first thing to know about governments is that governments lie and deceive. It's not just something that happened yesterday. And to tell the truth is the absolutely essential ingredient for people to work in any movement.

As I reflect on David Garrow's book on the FBI and King, I'm thinking about the FBI's—I almost said preoccupation but that's a mild word—hysteria, paranoia, madness—about communism. It *is* a madness. Of course there's a reality to communism and there's the Soviet Union and dictatorship—everybody knows that, we don't have to be told that. But there's a madness that is associated with that word, which is attached to everything that anybody does that is an attempt to make progress. The idea is to use the word like a club, to beat people to the ground so they won't speak anymore. It's an intimidating thing, you see. I think of the Democratic party not taking the equal time that was given to them to respond to Reagan after the meeting at Reykjavík. The Democratic party said, "No, we won't take the time." Why? "Because we musn't criticize the president. We'll be accused of being pro-Communist." That really got to me. What timidity. Timidity is not the word. Cowardice. But King, when they said, "King, this guy's a Communist," he didn't rush like some people do to say, "Get rid of this man." Or when they said, "Don't go to the Highlander Folk School because the FBI calls it a Communist place," he went there anyway. That's important today because we know how that word and how that hysteria is used to paralyze people as they try to decide what is right and wrong.

Two last things. One, nonviolence. The establishment would like us to think of nonviolence as just nonviolence—they would like us to think of it as passivity. Dr. King emphasized that nonviolence is not passivity. In fact, the phrase that was used—and SNCC made a point of this phrase—was "nonviolent direct action." That was the phrase. Yes, avoid violence, but don't be passive. Do what you have to do. Liberties are not given; they are taken. That message of the movement is a very powerful one, an important message for today at a time when we need to take direct action to do something about the distribution of wealth, about the economic system that Dr. King, to his credit, became more and more interested in, more and more concerned with. We need a movement around the issue of the shameful waste of wealth in this country when people are in need.

One final thing. I am concentrating on Dr. King, keeping in mind what Bob said about King being a wave on the ocean, about the movement being the ocean, because I think we can learn from every wave as long as we know what it is, who it is, what its limitations are. And there was something in Dr. King that is tremendously important for every movement and that Bob also represented in his own way, and that is the spiritual quality of a movement. Whether it's religion or yoga or emotionalism or music or art or whatever it is, a movement needs that spiritual quality, and Dr. King expressed that. In doing that, and showing us the strength in ourselves, he gave us hope and faith, and we need a lot of that for the future.

Nathan I. Huggins

Commentary

I AM OF THE GENERATION that finished professional training in the early 1960s. For me, the Brown decision of 1954 was the culmination of a long struggle to achieve racial justice. I knew Jim Crow in the South from my service in the Army during World War II. As a northern-reared black youth, racial discrimination in education, housing, and employment had been an overpowering reality of everyday life. No important decision in life outside the family had been free of consideration of race—it made a difference in every way to be black. Even when race might not have made a difference, one could never be sure.

I was just graduating from college when the Brown decision was handed down. I knew—I think all black people knew—that implementation would take time, money, and effort. I expected, however, that the ultimate victory would be brought about as it seemed this initial triumph had come about: with hard and persistent work through the courts, and with blacks insisting on first-class citizenship in every way they could.

Many blacks of my generation, perhaps heirs to Du Bois's "Talented Tenth," saw our best contribution to the struggle in training ourselves professionally so that place could not be legitimately denied us. "You have to be better than any white man to be allowed in the door," was the common lesson we all learned. "Be superior so that if they turn you down, the fault will be on their heads."

I finished graduate school and took my first teaching position in 1962. The Montgomery bus boycott, the sit-ins, and the militant, direct-action, nonviolent strategy and movement were well underway. While I took a modest part in picketing in Cambridge and Boston, and while I had a small role in the local chapter of CORE, it would be a great exaggeration to say that I was a real participant in "the movement."

I was in the "academy," on the sidelines. I experienced "the movement" as most Americans did, on television and in the papers. Many of my students—and some friends a few years younger—suffered considerable conflict because they felt the call to be active and involved in the events that were unfolding, yet there were expectations for them to do well in school or in their professions. It was impossible to do both. I myself did not feel this conflict strongly, or even much at all. I came early to know that I was not (am not) an activist in character or temperament. I am an academic, and the academy, the classroom, and the library are the places where I function well. I would not have done well in the Mississippi summer or on the Freedom Rides. It was better for all concerned for me to watch and comment.

When I agreed to participate in this conference on Martin Luther King, Jr., I did so with the strong conviction of the historian needing to tell the world that great men, no matter how compelling and charismatic, need to be seen in historical context. While I did not want to play the iconoclast, diminishing Dr. King's importance or his role,

I did want to counter what I expected to be a kind of celebration of a martyred hero.

To my surprise, practically all the papers and comments were aimed at dismissing King from the center, challenging his importance as a leader of the movement, and criticizing charismatic leadership in general. I found myself immediately shifting ground. I felt the need to reestablish the historical importance of King and his leadership.

This is all about perspective, and that is what the academic mind is all about. Because we are engaged in multiple perspectives, we are obliged to see things in complex and often contradictory ways. Yes, significant historical change is seldom, if ever, the result of one individual leader, and the individual leader is too often given credit for bringing about the inevitable. Yet, certain individual leaders become essential for our understanding of the history in which they participated.

Minds that take to multiple perspectives, contradiction, complexity, and paradox are not well suited for activism. Still, one cannot always have it one's own way. Dr. King probably would have thought himself, ideally, more the academic than the activist. But history and events made him serve different needs.

I have the unenviable role of being last. I had prepared some comments based on two papers I received, those of Professor Harlan and Professor Garrow. But sitting through the whole day I was excited by many things, and I began to feel that my written comments are no longer pertinent, and I thought I should just jot down some things and talk to you from notes. There's an advantage to that. One, it's going to be a bit fresher, and two, I hope that it will be a little more brief than it would have been had I read this paper. Word processors tend to be verbose.

First, I would like to say a couple of words about an important point made in Professor Harlan's paper about the change in Martin Luther King's leadership role and the way he was perceived once he became directly involved in the problem of poverty and the issue of the Vietnam War. We historians have tended to talk about Afro-American leadership and categorize it in formal ways. We refer, for example, to "accommodationist" leaders, people like Booker T. Washington, who see the world out there and attempt to adapt to it. Then again, we talk about "reformist" leaders. A third category is that of the typical, historical black leader, who was a somewhat emblematic or marginal figure, whose power came not from a constituency of voters, or from a constituency of power, or from a constituency of organizations, but, characteristically, from an influence role. That is, he would be seen—and it was almost always a he (except in the very important case of Mary McLeod Bethune)—seen by whites with power as someone through whom they could have access to black people; he was seen by blacks as a person who had access to white power. It's in that dual role that black leaders normally worked. They were, therefore, often nominated by whites. By implication, they got to be leaders because whites said they were leaders.

. What's striking about Martin Luther King and a whole generation of black leaders, beginning with the end of the Second World War, is that they began to play a different role; they were a great deal more independent. While they continued to have this kind of dual role, they also began to develop more of a power base and a constituency of their own which gave them an independence.

What's so striking about King's move into the problem of poverty and the issue of Vietnam is that it was a truly radical break with the kind of conventional thing black leaders would do in the past, a very radical thing. I don't mean to say that blacks in the past *never* had things to say about poverty. But black leaders, persons who were identified, nominated, understood as leaders, never talked about issues larger than black issues. And they certainly never engaged themselves in foreign policy. What was unique about King's position was that he did raise those issues and that he continued to do so even after it was clear what the consequences would be for his ability to influence the white power structure.

Now, the criticisms of King, interestingly enough, did not come simply from the sources you would imagine, President Johnson and others. They were also from black leaders. Professor Harlan points out that the *Pittsburgh Courier* and other such newspapers said, "How come you're doing this? You're ruining things." Why? Because King was breaking with a kind of tradition, the general understanding of the way black leaders were supposed to behave; this was offensive not only to whites, but to the black leadership as well.

Another negative reaction from the black leadership was to say, "Look, we don't want to engage another issue. Whatever the Vietnam war is, it really isn't our business. Black leaders and black people aren't supposed to be involved in that sort of thing." Perhaps, in a prescient way, some of these black spokesmen recognized that King was adding his voice to another movement, which is to say another ocean, to use Bob Moses's metaphor, which might, as indeed it did, inundate or overwhelm or take over the civil rights movement itself. As the movement against the Vietnam war became *the* movement in the country in the late 1960s, it could be seen as drawing the curtain on the civil rights movement, at least the positive direction, the positive steps of the civil rights movement. So this question of the shift in leadership style is an extremely important one and one which I think we need to pay attention to in terms of the history of black leadership itself.

My next remarks are in some ways more general. They take off from the part of Professor Garrow's paper having to do with spirituality. Partly because I'm last, and partly because I'm leaving tonight and you won't be able to get at me tomorrow, I'm going to take a position that seems unsupported here today. I think it very important to look at an individual as a leader. All that has been said—about the organization, the antecedents of the movement, the antecedents of the organization, the grass roots and all of that—is absolutely true and should not be understated. But we also have to understand that the people who were involved in them were not interchangeable parts. You cannot remove Martin Luther King from that picture and have the story happen more or less the same way.

If you cannot do that, there has to be some explanation in terms of personality and character that is significant historically. Historians have to consider this issue all the time, not just with King but with anybody, at any point in time: how important is the person, the individual personality? We struggle with this, resisting the notion of great men or great women as being shapers of history. We know better. We know that there are movements, that there are convergent forces, and that there are historical processes that shape history at a given moment. But at the same time we also know that individuals are important not only in terms of their own time but in terms of eternity, our historical eternity. We know that as people ourselves, as humans (not as social scientists), we have the responsibility of communicating to others, and we understand that it becomes easier to do that through the medium of personality, through individuals. We, as readers, as students, as people, can identify with individuals much more readily than we can with concepts or metaphors. So the person in history is important. The problem, of course, is how one deals with the historical person in a balanced way so that he or she does not become an icon.

There's another kind of problem here, and Professor Garrow's paper really brings this to our attention. Martin Luther King represents something quite special to us, something that we will never understand. He contains a mystery. Part of the problem is that Martin Luther King believed in God. I say that because I don't believe that most people do anymore, or that most Americans do. People don't say they don't believe in God. Or if you ask "Do you believe in God?" the answer will be, "Yes, yes, I believe in a creator," or something. But it's different to say, "I believe in a Christian God." It's really different. And to understand a person who can say that, one has to accept and understand the meaning of that belief and how it can define the person and shape his or her behavior and perception. We're living in a secular age when we're embarrassed by religion and embarrassed by spirituality. We mention it but we don't know how to include it in our understanding. That's part of the problem. We're embarrassed by it in part because we have trivialized it through a lot of public figures who claim to be "born again," and oftentimes that stands for bigotry. And we say, "Well, that's a charlatan."

But there is a genuine religious experience. People do go through conversion experiences, and these make a difference in their lives. What Professor Garrow has read to us from Martin Luther King's own words are tentative expressions of this conversion experience. I must say as I read those words I kept saying to myself "Martin Luther King is afraid to call this thing what it is." He never really *says* what it is; he *describes* it. Yet, all the characteristics of that statement, that confession, make clear that it was a conversion experience. There are many examples in historical literature of individuals sitting in their closets, in their kitchens, on the bank, under a tree, wherever, and having this conversation with God. And God speaks to them and God tells them something.

We have not been quite able to come to grips with this, and certainly as historians and social scientists it is very, very hard for us to do this.

Part of the reason we have trouble is that we do not honor nonrational behavior. But this nonrational element, as all the very sophisticated social scientists will tell us rationally, is the basis, in the final analysis, of most behavior. It is still the responsibility of the historian and the social scientist to try to discover a way into that nonrational world, to find a way of addressing ourselves to it. It is very hard. It is impossible, let us say. But at least we can make some effort at it. We're willing and we're able to talk about it, but we have conventions that interfere with our understanding. We talk about class and professions and region and gender, and we think we know what such categories mean when we use them. We know what it means when we say that Martin Luther King was middle-class.

So we think we know what we mean when we say the black church is important. Generally speaking, on the heels of that statement, we give descriptions of sociology and other kinds of political roles that the church plays. But we don't talk about black *religion,* which is what the church is about. And we don't understand, when we talk about the black church and the power of the black church, the faith that is involved in it and what that faith can empower people to do. So what is required of us is an involvement in the man—or in the men or women —having this kind of religious experience if we are to get into their historical moment.

Now part of our problem is that there isn't much literature on it. We don't have the blueprint. Most of us are social scientists and scholars who need blueprints to do what we do. We have Weber or Durkheim or some other social science figure or Carl Becker as an historian or somebody who gives us the models, the language, and the questions to raise in looking at a phenomenon. We don't have much in the way of a sophisticated means of analyzing and understanding the religious experience. We might think that we ought to turn to psychology, but psychology is poor for this sort of thing because psychologists deal with religious experience, generally speaking, pathologically. That is to say, if somebody has had it, there's something wrong with them—they're out there and strange.

But there is such a blueprint or model. As I was reading Professor Garrow's paper, it immediately came to my mind: Where does one go as a social scientist, as a scholar, to understand what it is that King is describing and Garrow is telling us about? I suggest William James's *Varieties of Religious Experience.* It's a fascinating book—lectures that he gave in 1901 in Scotland. One chapter is devoted to the divided self. The divided self. I was thinking as I was reading Garrow's paper, Martin Luther King and the divided self. Here is a man who has his self-doubts, who has his ambivalences, who looks at himself and says,

"Why me?" and "Why now?" and "Why all of that?" and "I don't need this." That self is him as much as is the self that is urging him to do something.

There is this fear, or I shouldn't say fear because it's awe. When you look in the face of a fellow human being, who under ordinary circumstances acts civilly at least, and out of this person comes hatred and anger and ugliness and evil, it's awesome to think that you are the instrument of that. You sit across the table negotiating with a white mayor or somebody. It's an awesome experience. You have, in some sense, brought about that evil because you're sitting there making a demand that causes ugliness and meanness to suddenly leap out of the bowels of this person. It's an awesome thing. And how does one go about addressing that? How does one justify being in that room and in a way bringing about that response?

The divided self is something that is described in the language of King. In that session in the kitchen, King's divided self was resolved because he spoke to God and God spoke to him. He felt that. I want to make a confession here. I'm not a born-again person so I don't want you to think that I'm speaking out of some religious conviction. I'm speaking to you because I'm reading here a document which tells me that this is what this man's experience was and I think we ought to honor it. That there is this divided self, this sense of self-doubt, and this resolution that comes about because of not just any old vision, but a Christian vision that comes out of a very real moral tradition and character.

William James's *Varieties of Religious Experience* talks about the conversion experience; it talks about the saintly person and the way in which this new, integrated self begins to become a part of action. The point, of course, that keeps being repeated in these stories, because James's lectures are really first-hand accounts in which people are reporting their own experiences, is that these "saintly" characters are continually revisited by their self-doubt. It isn't a straight line to the truth after that first conversion. But even if they are revisited by their self-doubt, the image of their conversion somehow comes back and makes them see the way.

I'm saying that in the case of Martin Luther King this unified self, this conversion experience, this "call," if you will, is a mission for the man. It allows an intensity of focus and vision to which other people can respond. Now charismatic leadership or charisma is not a one-way thing. It is a two-way or multi-way thing, and you have to have people who are able to respond, who have antennae that are out and ready to receive this vision.

And so this possibility of leadership arises from the vision, and from the unified self that comes out of it. There were other leaders, of course, but King was unique. There could have been a national or international role for any number of other individuals one might think to name. But it didn't happen with them. It might be useful to ask ourselves, "How come King and not somebody else?" There are a lot of claimants to this kind of leadership role. Part of it had to do with the character of the vision, I believe. Part of it had to do with the character of the message. One of the things that was most central to the King message was love. Now the power, the concept of love, is inclusive and not exclusive. And because it is, it allows a universalized response to the charismatic power—that is to say that white people, northern people, European people, strange people, anyone could listen to that message and understand it and could say, "That's me, too."

There were other charismatic figures. One can think of Malcolm X, who was not preaching love. He was preaching a kind of exclusion. He was charismatic, he had an awful lot of power, he had a very single and intense sense of self and vision and purpose and mission. But one cannot imagine Malcolm X drawing universally, getting the same kind of charismatic response, universally. Because in fact what he was saying was that there are boundaries or limits. I'm sure I could have an argument about this with people who think differently, but so much the better. I'm simply making the point that some kinds of charisma have more universal power than others. It's important to make that distinction. And I think in King's case the love and inclusive character of the message and the ability of the viewer to believe him were the ways in which his charisma could be powerful and universal.

This charisma, this leadership, this sense of self, this importance, this role, are things that need to be stressed and to be analyzed. This is not to say that any of us needs to wait for the leader. But we need to understand when we see leaders or when we see historical figures who have certain leadership power or mass appeal, so that we at least are able to recognize what it is, to cite it and to understand the character of it, how it works.

I have two other points to make and then I will be done. One has to do with nonviolence. This needs to be understood in terms of the American context, not as something that was imported. It is my belief that the reason why the strategy of nonviolent resistance became a feasible one among blacks in the South was that it was consistent with a traditional black Christian belief and a kind of stoic Christianity. The statement that King himself made—that undeserved suffering is redemptive—is a truth among traditional black religious people. It is a truth that grows out of an experience of being powerless and where undeserved suffering is the rule of the game. The black religious experience itself, and this stoic Christian experience in particular, creates moral superiority over the oppressor, and that is something that one can go back into nineteenth- and eighteenth-century slave narratives to see again and again and again—slaves, those oppressed people, knowing that they are morally superior to their oppressors. Knowing it! And they knew it out of an inner sense of self.

Now it's out of this morality that one can begin to build the idea of nonviolence and make it work. But it is also, I think, important to understand the limits of this tradition. For example, it is not northern urban, and that's one of the problems with it. The minute that you move into northern urban territory, you're running into real trouble with this kind of message because northern urban blacks believe in a payoff. Now they don't necessarily get the payoff because they believe in it, but they believe in it anyway. That's also part of a very deep American principle, too—pragmatism. You can't be nonviolent in America very easily because that presupposes a moral act for its own sake. At some point along the line somebody in America is going to ask, "What happens? Does it work? Does it win?" And if it doesn't win after a while, then people will leave it. You don't mind, well, you *do* mind getting your head whipped, but you'd like a payoff for your pain. That is very different from having a moral commitment to this insight, believing that the moral commitment is in and of itself of moral value. These are two different things, and the practical, pragmatic approach is an American value, which I think the whole movement had to run against.

Finally, I want to get to the metaphor business. I found in Bob Moses's metaphor of the ocean an enormously powerful and beautiful concept of the movement, and I agreed with it. I also agreed with the metaphor of convergence. I think they're both right. And one can think of a number of other metaphorical possibilities that will present some piece of the truth. But let's not misunderstand. It seems to me that the metaphor of the ocean has its problems. If you don't mind my extending the figure, just as the charismatic individual gets himself killed or his life ends, so in reality movements ebb and flow. It's a mystery to us still, just as it's a mystery about the charismatic figure, to understand why that happens. If it's misguided to wait for the next charismatic leader to come along, it's also misguided to expect the lunar cycle to work so that the ocean will crest, to wait for the ocean to crest. Now I don't think anybody is saying that. But I do think that it's possible to create gods out of movements, too, just as it is out of people. And it's important for us to understand that historical change occurs and movements occur for reasons that we have to try to understand. There's mystery underneath all of this.

TWO

THE BLACK FREEDOM STRUGGLE IN HISTORICAL CONTEXT

John Hope Franklin

Martin Luther King, Jr., and the Afro-American Protest Tradition

I WAS BORN IN THE VIL- lage of Rentiesville, Oklahoma,. and when I was ten moved to Tulsa, where I graduated from Booker T. Washington High School. From Fisk University, where I graduated in 1935, I went to Harvard University, where I earned M.A. and Ph.D. degrees in 1936 and 1941 respectively. As a teacher for more than fifty years I have held positions at Fisk, St. Augustine's College, North Carolina Central University, Howard University, Brooklyn College, the University of Chicago, and Duke University. My books include *From Slavery to Freedom* (1947; sixth edition 1987), *The Militant South* (1956), *Reconstruction: After the Civil War* (1961), and *George Washington Williams: A Biography* (1985). My fellow scholars have honored me by electing me president of the American Studies Association, the Southern Historical Association, the Organization of American His-

torians, the American Historical Association, and the United Chapters of Phi Beta Kappa.

Despite the fact that I never had much personal contact with Martin Luther King, Jr., I admired and respected him enormously. I first met him in the Honolulu airport in the summer of 1959. We had a friendly chat and then he was gone. I have always admired him and have felt personally involved in what he was attempting to do; and I made modest contributions to the cause from time to time.

In August 1963, at the end of my year as Pitt Professor of American History and Institutions at Cambridge University, the British Broadcasting Corporation asked me to serve as the commentator for what was billed as "The British Guide to the March on Washington." With film clips from King's speeches and comments by such personages as Malcolm X, A. Philip Randolph, and James Baldwin, we put together a program that placed the March in historical and contemporary context. Although three thousand miles separated me from the historic March on Washington, I felt that I was an active participant in that event.

Two years later, thanks to the efforts of the late Walter Johnson of the University of Chicago and several other historians, many of us met the Selma marchers on the outskirts of Montgomery and accompanied them to the rally on the grounds of the Alabama state capitol. We succeeded in showing that members of the academic community were not isolated in an ivory tower. Many of the marchers would write about King and the movement, and I would join in those activities, writing a piece called "The Forerunners" for the King commemorative issue of *American Visions*. Some of us, however, prefer to remember when we marched in the ranks behind Martin Luther King, Jr.

Not many years ago, in one of the outstanding centers of philosophical studies in this country—the Negro barber shop—I heard one of the elder sages make this profound observation: "Afro-Americans have very little going for them, but one thing going for them is that they have in recent years shouted to the high heavens in subtle and not-so-subtle ways about the injustices they suffer." Then he proceeded to call the roll of honor of those whose eloquent voices and courageous actions had been crucial in carrying forward the objectives of the black revolution. They were all there, from the Rap Browns and Stokely Carmichaels to the Charles Gomillions and the James Farmers. Then, after a pause, as if to set the next name off from the rest, he said: "And Martin Luther King, Jr." There was no sketch of his life as in the case of the others, no appraisal, not even praise. The name was enough. Then, to indicate what it all added up to, he said, "One of these days these Afros will be not only an annoyance but an embarrassment to the country itself."

The elder sage was more of a philosopher than historian, for if he had examined the past with the care befitting one with his philosophical and mental powers, he would have discovered that Afro-Americans had for centuries been shouting about the injustices heaped on them. And more than once they were an annoyance and even an embarrassment to their country. Martin Luther King, Jr., although a great philosopher *and* activist, a role which I would not accuse my barber shop sage of playing, was also a person with a great knowledge of history as well as a keen sense of it. He certainly knew that Afro-Americans had been shouting about their injustices since the beginning of time, or so it seemed. He knew something of the history and tradition of protest among black Americans. He knew that in their views and attitudes they ranged all the way from the subtle but unequivocal antislavery attitudes in the poetry of George Moses Horton to the fiery, passionate violence in the deeds of Nat Turner.[1] He had his preferences, but first of all he had the knowledge on which to base his preferences.

There were two distinct strains in the Afro-American protest tradition, and the distinction between them is not nearly as clear as it would seem on the surface. One was the quiet, nonviolent protest against slavery, against disfranchisement, against discrimination, against degradation. It was the protest of the helpless, sometimes voiceless, thousands upon thousands who had quite limited means with which to protest. Many slaves had no strong ethical or philosophical position against violence—that would, indeed, be difficult in an institution maintained by violence. Some, with nothing more than their voices, pens, or mild actions, said in their own special way that they found their lot unacceptable. Others knew the futility of violence against powerful, superior forces and concluded that discretion was the better part of valor. Still others, with no immediate opportunity to act otherwise, bided their time, even going so far as to counsel violence.[2]

The other strain was clearly of a violent kind. Blacks, consumed by the rage that their degraded status brought, impatient with what they viewed as mild measures, and willing to die in the effort to end slavery and other forms of injustice, resorted to the sword, the rifle, the vial of poison, and the arsonist's torch.[3] Later, this strain took the form of violence and threats of violence against the indignities of discrimination in housing and employment. Instead of festering like the raisin in the sun, it exploded—in Chicago, Detroit, Watts, Harlem, and Rochester.

Nonviolent action is, of course, the most persistent, the oldest, and the most widespread manifestation of the Afro-American protest tradition. Nonviolent protest is clear, straightforward, unequivocal, and without threats or even guile. Quite often it appeals to the humanity of the perpetrators, and it relies on the paradox, the inner contradiction of the position against which it speaks out. This characterized the position of the 1777 petitioners, allegedly slaves, who sought from the Massachusetts General Court their own freedom. They reminded the members of the legislature that they had, in common with all other men, a natural and inalienable right to the freedom which the "great Parent" of the universe had bestowed equally on all mankind. Regarding the effort of the patriots to secure their independence from Britain, they told the legislature that they, the slaves, had never forfeited their own freedom by any compact or agreement and, when compared with the claim of the patriots, their own case "Pleads Stronger than A thousand arguments in favour of your petitioners." It seemed not unreasonable, therefore, to request that the legislature restore to them the enjoyments that were the natural rights of all men.[4]

It must have been especially embarrassing to the white men fighting for independence in 1780 to have it called to their attention that black men who paid their taxes could not vote. John and Paul Cuffe, black men, refused to pay their taxes. They argued that if it was tyranny for Britain to refuse representation in Parliament to colonists who were taxpayers, it was also tyranny for the colonists to tax free black men while withholding the franchise from them. Amazingly, the colonists did not see it that way and slapped the Cuffe brothers in jail. Set free after a brief period, the brothers received no satisfaction until 1783— two years after Yorktown—when a court decided that they were eligible to vote.[5]

The achievement of independence and the establishment of a new government under the Constitution meant little to black people in the United States. It will be recalled that the slave trade was permitted to continue for at least another twenty years, that for purposes of representation a Negro was counted as three-fifths of a person, and the slave who dared to run away could be pursued by his owner with the strong support of the Constitution, which provided for the return of fugitive slaves.[6] This latter provision was strengthened in 1793 by special legislation called the Fugitive Slave Law.[7] The operation and enforcement of this law was as whimsical as it was incongruous in a New World society boasting of its freedoms. During the administration of George Washington, some North Carolina slaves were manumitted and sent to Pennsylvania to live. One of them was seized as a fugitive slave and jailed under the provisions of the law of 1793, and it seemed likely that he would be returned to North Carolina to someone who would claim him as his slave. Those who petitioned Congress in his behalf called the Fugitive Slave Law a "flagrant proof of how far human beings, merely on account of color and complexion, are, through prevailing prejudice, outlawed and excluded from common justice and common humanity, by the operation of such partial laws in support of habits and customs cruelly oppressive." There followed an eloquent and impassioned plea not only on behalf of the fugitive in question but for that entire class of people who, "distinguished by color, are therefore with a degrading partiality, considered by many, even of those in eminent stations, as unentitled to that public justice and protection which is the great object of a Government."[8]

These were strong words, coming from the lowliest element of the population—words that should have reached the most insensitive of the nation's leaders. But the words did not find their mark. Instead, the new capital busied itself with making certain that the blacks among them would not, under any circumstances, be considered eligible for the enjoyment of equal rights. Thus, it was proposed that blacks be excluded in Washington, D.C., from voting and holding office.[9] It was the author of the Declaration of Independence and the third president of the United States, Thomas Jefferson, who signed these bills into law. I have no record of blacks protesting against these new indignities. Perhaps black Americans were too numb, too dumbfounded by the entire experience of Revolution, the blatant discrimination in the Revolutionary army and in constitution-making for a special, privileged few, to think that protests would achieve anything.

If many blacks were discouraged by the new wave of oppression manifested by the vigorous enforcement of the Fugitive Slave Law, others were moved to new forms of desperation. For the moment, at least, mild nonviolent protests were deprecated. Instead, some blacks, who concluded that "they had as much right to fight for our liberty as any men," decided to fight. In Richmond, in 1800, Gabriel, the slave of Thomas Henry Prosser, decided that he had suffered enough of bondage and determined to fight, even die, for his freedom. He began to organize a revolution to overthrow slavery in Virginia and possibly elsewhere. He enlisted several thousand Negroes in the cause and began to amass a formidable cache of arms and ammunition. Except for his betrayal by one of his so-called supporters, it would have been a bloody, if unsuccessful, affair. As it turned out, Gabriel and more than thirty of his coconspirators were executed in September and October 1800.[10]

It became clear to the black realists that violence was not the road to certain freedom, especially when there were traitors who could not always be identified and when superior firepower was on the other side. The realization did not eliminate acts of desperation, however. The cook, disgusted with the liberties her owner took with her, could and did, on occasion, mete out to him a deadly potion of arsenic or strychnine that relieved her of further annoyance from him. Field hands, weary of the unreasonable demands of the owner for whom they worked "from day clean to first dark," just might end their obligations by "dispatching him" during one of his customary visits to the fields to supervise them. Then, there were Denmark Vesey, whose Charleston plot was discovered in 1822 before it got off the ground, and Nat Turner, bold visionary, despondent, bitter, and foreboding, who came close to starting something big in 1831. By the time that Turner and his cohorts had killed sixty whites, the relatives and associates of the victims and law enforcement officials knew that this was a desperate situation that required desperate measures. They killed more than a hundred slaves in the encounter and executed a score or more, including Turner, as they meted out justice to those whose crime was that they sought freedom.

Martin Luther King, Jr., thought that the acts of Denmark Vesey and Nat Turner were ill-advised at best and utterly futile at worst. "The courageous efforts of our own insurrectionist brothers, such as Denmark Vesey and Nat Turner, should be eternal reminders to us," he declared, "that violent rebellion is doomed from the start. . . . Beyond the pragmatic invalidity of violence is its inability to appeal to conscience. Power and morality must go together, implementing, fulfilling and ennobling each other. In the quest for Power I cannot bypass the concern for morality. I refuse to be driven to a Machiavellian cynicism with respect to power. Power at its best is the right use of strength. The words of Alfred the Great are still true: 'Power is never good unless he who has it is good.' "[11]

King was so convinced that nonviolent protest was the only valid tactic for Negroes that he spent much more time promoting the concept of nonviolence than in speaking out against violence. On one occasion, he said, "If every Negro in the United States turns to violence, I will choose to be that one lone voice preaching that this is the wrong way. Maybe this sounded like arrogance. But it was not intended that way. It was simply my way of saying that I would rather be a man of conviction than a man of conformity. Occasionally in life one develops a conviction so precious and meaningful that he will stand on it 'til the end. This is what I have found in nonviolence."[12]

If King knew of George Moses Horton, I have no doubt that he admired him. He would admire him for his poetic talents, the content of his writings, and his remarkable courage as a slave in speaking out against the institution. This gifted North Carolina slave who wrote poetry for men at the University of North Carolina to dispatch to their lady friends never hesitated to raise his pen against slavery. Even if his protests represented no one except himself, he expressed sentiments that inarticulate, enslaved black men and women also shared. In his best known poem, "On Liberty and Slavery," one senses an outcry of personal anguish for being trapped in a degraded status:

> *Alas! and am I born for this,*
> *To wear this slavish chain?*
> *Deprived of all created bliss,*
> *Through hardship, toil and pain.*
>
> *. . .*
>
> *Come Liberty, thou cheerful sound,*
> *Toll through my ravished ears!*
> *Come, let my grief in joys be drowned,*
> *And drive away my fears.*

> *Say unto foul oppression, Cease:*
> *Ye tyrants rage no more,*
> *And let the joyful trump of peace,*
> *Now bid the vassal soar.*
>
> . . .
>
> *Bid slavery hide her haggard face,*
> *And barbarism fly:*
> *I scorn to see the sad disgrace*
> *In which enslaved I lie.*[13]

No poet of the American Revolution or of the movement for equal justice spoke more eloquently or more courageously in favor of freedom than George Moses Horton, North Carolina slave.

With much more bombast and fire than Horton, David Walker protested slavery at an unusually high level of volatility. This North Carolina, free Negro expatriate, living in Boston, was as opposed to slavery as he would have been had he been ground down under its oppressive heel. One supposes that, even as he peddled second-hand clothes for a living, he brooded over what he could do about slavery. Then, in 1829, he brought out his *Appeal in Four Articles,* regarded by many as the most dangerous pamphlet, the most blatantly antislavery tract written by a black person in the years before the Civil War. Walker said:

> I have known small collections of coloured people to have convened together, for no other purpose than to worship God Almighty . . . to the best of their knowledge; when tyrants . . . would also convene and wait almost in breathless silence for the poor coloured people to commence singing and praying. . . . as soon as they had commenced, the wretches would burst in upon them and drag them out and commence beating them as they would rattle-snakes. . . . Yet the American ministers send out missionaries to convert the heathen, while they keep us and our children sunk at their feet in the most abject ignorance and wretchedness that ever a people was afflicted with since the world began. Will the Lord suffer this people to proceed much longer? Will he not stop them in their career?

Walker never spared the owners of human flesh as he invoked the wrath of the Almighty against them. In speaking of the inhumanity of the slaveholders, he rose to a new crescendo:

> It appears as though they are bent only on daring God Almighty to do his best—they chain and handcuff us and our children and drive us around the country like

brutes, and go into the house of the God of justice to return him thanks for having aided them in their infernal cruelties inflicted upon us. Will the Lord suffer this people to go on much longer, taking his holy name in vain? Will he not stop them, PREACHERS and all? O Americans! Americans!! I call God—I call angels—I call men, to witness, that your DESTRUCTION *is at hand,* and will be speedily consummated unless you REPENT.[14]

It may appear on the surface that Walker was advocating violence, but he was not. It may even appear that he had advocated a position unacceptable to Martin Luther King, Jr., but he had not. He was, on the one hand, challenging the oppressors to accept their own teachings; on the other, he was invoking the wrath of God against the oppressors if they would not desist. If the oppressors reacted violently, that was because they continued to commit evil acts which they would defend by violence, if necessary. The position taken by Walker was not unlike that taken by King in the letter to his fellow clergymen from a Birmingham jail:

In your statement you asserted that our actions, even though peaceful, must be condemned because they precipitate violence. But can this assertion be logically made? Isn't this like condemning the robbed man because his possession of money precipitated the evil act of robbery? Isn't this like condemning Socrates because his unswerving commitment to truth and his philosophical delvings precipitated the misguided popular mind to make him drink the hemlock? Isn't it like condemning Jesus because His unique God-consciousness and never-ceasing devotion to His will precipitated the evil act of crucifixion? We must come to see . . . that it is immoral to urge an individual to withdraw his efforts to gain his basic constitutional rights because the quest precipitates violence. Society must protect the robbed and punish the robber.[15]

Henry Highland Garnet went even closer to the brink than David Walker in extending a threat that some would describe as a threat of violence. A minister in the Presbyterian church and a former newspaper editor, Garnet became embittered when whites destroyed Noyes Academy in New Hampshire rather than permit him and a few other young black men to attend school there.[16] Eventually he became completely radicalized, opposing not only slavery but also general economic and political exploitation, especially what he called "the unholy system of landlordism and the labor monopolists." In 1843, at the National Negro Convention—itself a major protest organization that had been in existence since 1831—Garnet captivated his audience with his fiery denunciation of slavery, calling on slaves to strike and threatening the advocacy of armed rebellion.

> Tell them in language which they cannot misunderstand, of the exceeding sinfulness of slavery, and of a future judgment, and of the righteous retributions of an indignant God. Inform them that all you desire is FREEDOM, and that nothing else will suffice. Do this, and forever after cease to toil for the heartless tyrants, who give no other reward but stripes and abuse. If they then commence the work of death, they, and not you will be responsible for the consequences. You had better all die—die immediately, than live as slaves and entail your wretchedness upon your posterity.[17]

But in predicting violence Garnet did not advocate it. He did not even counsel slaves to strike back, but there is a veiled hint that slaves should not turn the other cheek. Even if Garnet did not advocate retaliation, he stands closer to the tradition of violence than either Walker or King.

The premier spokesman for slaves and free Negroes before the Civil War was, of course, Frederick Douglass, who was an authority on both groups since he had been a slave and was later a free person. No one was more eloquent in his protests against the hated institution of slavery, and no one could be more powerful in his arguments that slavery was a curse to black and white alike. He told of its horrors and argued that blacks as members of the human race deserved better than to be dragged in the mire of human degradation that was slavery. He chided white Americans about Independence Day. In 1852 he told his listeners at Rochester, "This Fourth of July is *yours,* not *mine. You* may rejoice, *I* must mourn. To drag a man in fetters into the grand illuminated temple of liberty, and call upon him to join you in joyous anthems, were inhuman mockery and sacrilegious irony. . . . Go where you may . . . search out every abuse and when you have found the last, lay your facts by the side of every-day practices of this nation, and you will say with me that, for revolting barbarity and shameless hypocrisy, America reigns without a rival."[18]

With all of his eloquent bombast, Douglass seemed to equivocate on the use of violence. He would have nothing to do with John Brown's scheme to free the slaves by arming them and, if necessary, killing their owners,[19] but on one occasion he expressed apprehension that slavery could be destroyed only by bloodshed. In the audience was Sojourner Truth, a stern but nonviolent enemy of slavery, who believed in the divine deliverance of her people from thralldom. Sojourner arose, and interrupting Douglass with that deep, rich voice of hers she shouted, "Frederick, is God dead?" "No," he replied, "and because God is not dead slavery can end only in blood."[20] Sojourner was not persuaded, and in fact neither was Douglass. But by the time of the Civil War, both of them had become advocates of the sword. As a devoted admirer of Douglass, Martin Luther King, Jr., surely stood with Douglass in his renouncing an attack on slavery such as John Brown proposed. His attempts to dissuade various factions from advocating violence during the civil rights movement is reminiscent of the rejection of Brown's plan for freeing the slaves. While Douglass never lifted his own hand in the fight for freedom and the Union during the Civil War, he nevertheless recruited soldiers for the cause.[21] One suspects that this would have been a bit more than King could take from one whom he admired so much.

The reluctance of many Americans to concede that emancipation was an objective of the Civil War portended the nature of the problems that freedmen would face at the close of the war. Citizenship and equality for the former slaves were not seriously discussed in 1865. In every former Confederate state, where the vast majority of blacks lived, remnants of the slave system were in evidence everywhere.[22] New laws made vagrants of blacks who had no visible means of support, thus creating the machinery for delivering them once more into the hands of their former masters. Laws excluded blacks from voting or testifying in court against whites, imposed curfews on them, forbade their possession of firearms, and even prohibited them from making "insulting" gestures toward whites, whatever that meant![23] Northerners knew what was happening in the South, but their war weariness and their anxiety to get on with the business of building huge business establishments dampened what ardor they had for equal justice for blacks.

Blacks themselves were as alert as anyone to the efforts to deny them citizenship and, indeed, to drive them back toward involuntary servitude. Once again, in the tradition of nonviolence that their forebears had established, they met in conventions to call attention to their plight and to protest the injustices imposed on them. Martin Luther King, Jr., would not have argued with their tactics or their objectives. Richmond blacks asserted that "invidious political or legal distinctions, on account of color [are] inconsistent with our own self-respect." At the convention in Nashville, blacks complained that the federal government had left them without protection after knowing what services they had rendered "to the cause of the preservation of the Union and the maintenance of the laws." They were even more distressed that the Tennessee delegation, all white, of course, and with some former Confederates among them, were being seated in Congress when their state legislature had spent most of its time passing laws so unjust to the former slaves. Delegates to the convention in Raleigh, North Carolina, declared that they wanted fair wages, adequate education for their children, and the repeal of "all the oppressive laws which make unjust discriminations on account of race or color." Then, they went to the heart of the matter: "We want the privilege of voting. It seems to us that men who are willing on the field of danger to carry the muskets of the Republic, in the days of Peace ought to be permitted to carry its ballots; and certainly, we cannot understand the justice of denying the elective franchise to men who have been fighting for the country, while it is freely given to men who have just returned from four years fighting against it." [24]

Similar sentiments and declarations came from groups meeting in Norfolk and Alexandria, Virginia; Jackson, Mississippi; Charleston, South Carolina; Mobile, Alabama; and Savannah, Georgia. It was obvious to the most casual observer that in the years following the Civil War Afro-Americans clearly saw the things they wanted and those to which they were entitled. And they were anxious to tell everyone that they were well aware of their rights. Everywhere they demanded the vote, the abolition of the hated black codes, and measures to relieve suffering and privation. No latter-day civil rights spokespersons would be more articulate or precise or unequivocal in stating the objectives and aspirations of their people.

But there was violence, too, and plenty of it. It was as though whites were quite certain that once the slaves were free they would wreak havoc by plunder, arson, and murder. Thomas Jefferson had said as much a half century earlier. In explaining to his young friend Thomas Coles why they could not give up slavery, he said that it was like having a wolf by the ears; they could not let slavery go because, like the wolf, the slaves would commit indescribable violence against their former masters.[25] But the violence in 1865 and 1866 was the violence not of blacks but of whites against blacks. In Memphis they slaughtered almost 50 Negro women; in New Orleans 35 blacks were killed and 127 wounded.[26] Only blacks, it seemed, upheld the tradition of orderly, peaceful, nonviolent protest. At the meeting of the National Equal Rights League in 1865, for example, the members asked that the following amendment be adopted and added to the Constitution of the United States: "That there shall be no legislation within the limits of the United States or Territories, against any civilized portion of the inhabitants, native-born or naturalized, on account of race or color, and that all such legislation now existing within said limits is anti-republican in character, and therefore void." [27] It is not clear how such an amendment would quell the uprisings against the freedmen, but it is clear that the black protests were at least civilized and worthy of a responsible citizenry.

As others in the United States, particularly certain white reform and neo-abolitionist groups, joined in the effort to define the place of blacks in American life, blacks themselves began to set forth anew their vision of a nation where there would be no color or race distinctions. Happily, with fewer constraints than in the antebellum years, they could use their own fledgling institutions—schools, churches, benefit societies, and fraternal organizations—to beat the drums for progress. They used the platform, the pulpit, the press, and the proverbial grapevine to get their message across. It was essentially a message of hope, of love, of conciliation, and of aspiration. Their institutions were producing leaders who spoke clearly and eloquently for the causes they espoused. When the planters of southern Louisiana indicated an unwillingness to pay black workers regular wages and enter into agreements regarding work, pay, housing, supplies, and the like, the black workers of Avoyelles, Louisiana, made it clear that if they had nothing else, they had sufficient self-esteem to state categorically what they wanted. In part, they said, "We consider ourselves, although poor and houseless, as much a part of the nation and society as they, and that we have at heart the tranquility of the country and that we will zealously work for Reconstruction, the establishment of common schools, opposition to slavery, universal suffrage, protection to all in the enjoyment of equal rights before the law, [and] the perpetual maintenance of the Union." [28]

It was this spirit that caused blacks to defy local whites and take their children to school, even as whites fired on the schools or burned them to the ground. They voted, even with the threat of economic reprisals or worse hanging over their heads. Not only did the Ku Klux Klan and the Knights of the White Camellia flourish as the premier anti-Negro terrorist organizations of the period, but their numerous satellite groups such as the White Line, the Constitutional Union Guards, the White Brotherhood, and the Pale Faces were thriving in various localities. No black voter could know if his exercise of the franchise would bring him death before sundown, the loss of his job, or a mere flogging, but he voted. When whites railed about black political domination, which everyone knew was a myth, black voters did what they could to make their meager influence felt until murders, lynchings, mutilation, arson, and other barbarities drove them away from the electoral process and to a more civilized if less effective communion with each other. [29]

The Civil Rights Act of 1875 was the first legislation in whose enactment black Americans had some official role. Introduced in 1870 by

Senator Charles Sumner of Massachusetts, it languished in Congress for half a decade and was not actually passed until 1875, just before the Democrats, elected in the fall of 1874, took control of the House of Representatives. Among those who kept the proposed bill alive, as Sumner lay dying, were the black members of the House. This was the kind of advocacy Afro-Americans hoped would obviate the necessity for the usual protests. Robert Brown Elliott of South Carolina told his colleagues in the House that he supported the Civil Rights Bill "because it is right. The bill . . . appeals to your justice but it demands a response to your gratitude" for all that Negroes had done in the nation's wars as well as in its economic development. John Roy Lynch, representative from Mississippi and a former speaker of his state legislature's lower house, said that "when every man, woman, and child can feel and know that his, her, or their rights are fully protected by the strong arm of a generous and grateful Republic, then all can truthfully say that this beautiful land of ours . . . is, in truth, the 'land of the free and the home of the brave.' " [30] An incipient black congressional caucus was showing its mettle within a decade after the close of the Civil War.

The Civil Rights Act was as ineffective after its passage as its opponents had predicted when it was under consideration. When the Supreme Court declared it unconstitutional in 1883, neither its supporters nor its critics were surprised.[31] Terrorists were not affected, for they had continued their work of dismantling the Reconstruction machinery and had even accelerated their attacks on blacks and their friends. The situation had reached the point where some desperate individuals began to express their disgust and distress without any hope of actually involving the government of the United States. Ida B. Wells-Barnett was such a person. As early as 1887 she refused to be seated in a Jim Crow car and unsuccessfully took her case to the Tennessee Supreme Court. Dismissed from her position as a teacher in the Memphis school system, which she criticized, she began a one-woman crusade through her newspaper, *Free Speech,* against lynching, rape, and other forms of violence against black men and women. A mob destroyed her press offices while she was on a speaking tour in the North.[32]

After she moved to Chicago, she continued her crusade, an example of which was her pamphlet *The Reason Why the Colored American Is Not in the World's Columbian Exposition.* It was strange, she said, that in a world's fair celebrating the four hundredth anniversary of the discovery of America, blacks, who had contributed a "large share to American prosperity and civilization," were deliberately excluded. It was both ingratitude and insensitivity, she concluded, as she recounted the "Afro-American's Contribution to Columbian Literature." [33] It must have been embarrassing to the fair's officials to see this courageous black woman standing at the entrance of the fair and passing out copies of her pamphlet to visitors. Two years later, in 1895, she published *A Red Record*. In this work she argued that the system of anarchy and outlawry had grown in the previous decade to be so common "that scenes of unusual brutality failed to have any visible effect upon the humane sentiments of the people of our land."[34] Her alarm over the growth of mob violence prompted her to appeal to world opinion in the hope that it would help eradicate those forms of barbarism. Things got worse before they got better, but Wells-Barnett pointed the way toward peaceful, courageous, persistent, nonviolent protest.

Even when there was heated debate over means as well as ends regarding the place of Afro-Americans in the life of the country, there was a lack of interest in the ultimate solution. If Booker T. Washington thought that the emphasis should be on winning the approbation of whites through hard work and W. E. B. Du Bois believed that one should demand that to which he was entitled under the Constitution, both would claim to have logic and common sense on their side. Despite the popularity of Washington with the press and the general public, his perceived lack of interest in the struggle for political and legal equality alienated him from aggressive, ambitious, and idealistic young black Americans. That is why, both in terms of the enactment of laws and in their judicial interpretation, the United States in subsequent years moved closer to Du Bois than to Washington.[35]

Even before the end of the Washington–Du Bois controversy, it was clear how young Americans stood. The sorry, sordid picture of Negro life in America in the early twentieth century moved a group of young men in 1905 to organize to attain full citizenship through determined and aggressive action. The day of temporizing was over, they reasoned, and they must fight to the bitter end to gain their rightful place in American life. Led by Du Bois, the group met in Niagara Falls, Canada, in June 1905, and drew up a plan for action. They demanded the franchise, freedom of speech and criticism, the abolition of all distinctions based on race, respect for the working man, and recognition of the basic principles of human brotherhood. In the following year they met at Harpers Ferry, and, faced with the widespread disfranchisement of blacks and an increase in violence, Du Bois later admitted that the manifesto that he wrote for the occasion was "a tumult of emotion." In part, it said:

> Never before in the modern age has a great and civilized
> folk threatened to adopt so cowardly a creed in the
> treatment of its fellow-citizens, born and bred on its
> soil. Stripped of verbose subterfuge and in its naked

nastiness, the new American creed says: fear to let black men even try to rise lest they become the equals of whites. And this in the land that professes to follow Jesus Christ. The blasphemy of such a course is only matched by its cowardice.[36]

By the beginning of the twentieth century the Afro-American tradition of protest was well established. It was at least as old as the nation itself, having its roots in trying to do something about the predilection of the founding fathers to make distinctions based on race that would hardly have been worthy of men still in their European caves. The tradition was, on the whole, nonviolent, but it was too much to expect every violated female slave and every brutalized male slave to turn the other cheek. It is a wonder that most of them did, but long before he spoke on the subject, Martin Luther King's spiritual ancestors adhered to his view that violence in the face of the overwhelming power of one's adversaries was not only imprudent but futile. Resorting to violence, King said, would be "imitating the worst, the most brutal, and the most uncivilized value of American life."[37] The tragedy was that all too often blacks turned their hostility and frustration toward the larger society inward, not in terms of peace, but in terms of violence, bringing heartbreak and suffering down on their own families and neighbors.

It is difficult to live in a society as violent as American society has been, through history, tradition, and culture, without becoming infected with the virus of violence. This is especially true when one has so much about which to protest and so few means of making that protest. To the extent that protests have been peaceful and nonviolent, they have nurtured and reaffirmed King's views and actions. To the quite limited extent that they have been violent, the violence that they have evoked has been an object lesson for any sensible person to follow. There is no way of knowing, moreover, how important the threat or fear of violence has been as a factor in the decisions of persons in power to make concessions, but one cannot build a society or a community on such idle speculation.

As Martin Luther King, Jr., himself said on one occasion:

> Humanity is waiting for something other than blind imitation of the past. If we want truly to advance a step further, if we want to turn over a new leaf and really set a new man afoot, we must begin to turn mankind away from the long and desolate night of violence. May it not be that the new man the world needs is the nonviolent man? Longfellow said, "in this world a man must be either an anvil or a hammer." We must be hammers

shaping a new society rather than anvils molded by the old. This not only will make us new men, but will give us a new kind of power . . . power infused with love and justice, that will change dark yesterdays into bright tomorrows, and lift us from the fatigue of despair to the buoyancy of hope. A dark, desperate, confused and sin-sick world waits for this new kind of man and this new kind of power.[38]

THREE

Martin Luther King, Jr., and the Ideology of Nonviolent Social Change

Cornel West

The Religious Foundations of the Thought of Martin Luther King, Jr.

I WAS BORN THE SECOND son of Clifton and Irene West on June 2, 1953, in Tulsa, Oklahoma. I lived in Topeka, Kansas, from 1954 to 1958 and grew up in Sacramento, California (1958–70). The fundamental influences on my character and outlook are my loving family (especially my brother Clifton) and Shiloh Baptist Church pastored by Rev. Willie P. Cooke. From an early age I felt called by God to bear witness to the profound crisis in western civilization and to exemplify prophetic engagement with the plight of the wretched of the earth. As a youth, I was drawn to the courage and sincerity of Malcolm X (as articulated in his classic autobiography and speeches), the internationalism of the Black Panther Party, and the defiant theology of James Cone. Needless to say, the grand example of Martin Luther King, Jr., has always been not so much a model to imitate but rather *the* touchstone for personal inspiration, moral wisdom, and existential insight. I heard him speak in person only once—when I was ten years old—and remember not his words but his humble spirit and sense of urgency.

I graduated *magna cum laude* from Harvard College (1970–73) with a major in Near Eastern Languages and Literature, specializing in Hebrew and Aramaic. Yet my courses with Samuel Beer, Talcott Parsons, Roderick Firth, Martin Kilson, H. Stuart Hughes, John Rawls, Charles Price, Terry Irwin, G. Ernest Wright, Israel Scheffler, Hilary Putnam, Paul Hanson, and Preston Williams meant the most to me. I received my M.A. and Ph.D. degrees in philosophy from Princeton—the first Afro-American to do so—in 1975 and 1980, respectively. My dissertation was entitled "Ethics, Historicism, and the Marxist Tradition." My formal graduate education was shaped most by Sheldon Wolin, Thomas Scanlon, Thomas Nagel, Raymond Geuss, Walter Kaufmann, Richard Rorty, Ronald Dworkin, David Hoy, Richard Grandy, Carl Hempel, Arthur Lewis, Gerald Cohen, Paul Benacerraf, and Gregory Vlastos. I stayed at Princeton only two years and returned to Harvard to write fiction and my thesis. I was a teaching assistant for Stanley Cavell and Martha Nussbaum and spent time studying literature with Joel Porte and cultural politics with Daniel Aaron. I also took courses on Hegel from J. N. Findlay at Boston University and from Hans-Georg Gadamer, then visiting at Boston College. As in my undergraduate years, I worked in breakfast programs in Jamaica Plains and the prison program at Norfolk State Prison.

I started teaching philosophy in 1977 at Union Theological Seminary in New York City. Along with great colleagues like James Cone, James Forbes, Jr., Dorothea Sölle, Samuel Roberts, Ann Ulanov, Beverly Harrison, Tom Driver, Milton Gatch, David Lotz, Donald Shriver, and my closest friend, James Melvin Washington, I deepened my prophetic Christian faith and sharpened my intellectual skills. In 1980 I joined the editorial collectives of *Social Text* (with my friends Stanley Aronowitz, Anders Stephanson, Sonia Sayres, Fredric Jameson, and others), *Boundary 2* (with Paul Bové, Jonathan Arac, William Spanos, Michael Hayes, Joe Buttigieg, Daniel O'Hara, and Donald Pease), and the Black Philosophers' Society (with Al Pretty-

man, Howard McGary, Lucius Outlaw, and others).

I left Union for Yale Divinity School in 1984, returned to Union in 1987, and went to Princeton University in 1988 (primarily to work with my colleague, the great Toni Morrison) where I am professor of religion and director of the Afro-American Studies Program. I have held visiting positions at Barnard, Columbia, Haverford, Williams, Princeton Theological Seminary, Harvard Divinity School, and the University of Paris VIII. I also taught in the Timbuktu School at the Rev. Herbert Daughtry's House of the Lord Pentecostal Church in Brooklyn for five years and at the Center for Workers' Education in Manhattan. I have been a member of the National Executive Committee of the Democratic Socialists of America since 1983, and I cherished my friendship with its late leader, Michael Harrington. I have written three books—*Prophesy Deliverance! An Afro-American Revolutionary Christianity* (1982), *Prophetic Fragments* (1988), and *The American Evasion of Philosophy: A Genealogy of Pragmatism* (1989)—and co-edited three books—*Theology in the Americas: Detroit II* (1982), *Post-Analytic Philosophy* (1985), and *Out There: Marginalization and Contemporary Cultures* (1990). My wonderful son, Clifton Louis West, is a joy of my life.

I am convinced that a new insurgency is stirring among progressive white people, women, gays, lesbians, the elderly, and especially people of color, and I plan to play a major role in its flowering. In short, I have only begun to fight in the perennial struggle for freedom and dignity—a struggle that must build on the rich legacy of Martin Luther King, Jr.

I would like to begin with three epigraphs that give us some sense of the religious foundations of Martin Luther King's thought. I begin with Amos 5:21–24, a recurrent reference throughout King's writings and sermons:

> I hate, I despise your feast days, and I will not smell in your solemn assemblies.
> Though ye offer me burnt offerings and your meat offerings, I will not accept them: Neither will I regard the peace offerings of your fat beasts.
> Take thou away from me the noise of thy songs; for I will not hear the melody of thy viols.
> But let justice run down as water, and righteousness as a mighty stream.

The second epigraph is from Luke 4:18, a passage that fundamentally informs King's sense of Christian ministry:

> The spirit of the Lord is upon me because he hath anointed me to preach the gospel to the poor; he hath sent me to heal the brokenhearted, to preach deliverance to the captives, and recovering of sight to the blind, to set at liberty those who are oppressed.

The last epigraph is from the Negro spiritual that was briefly quoted earlier at this conference:

> *I've seen the lightning flash,*
> *I've heard the thunder roll,*
> *I've felt sin breakers dashing,*
> *trying to conquer my soul.*
> *But I heard the voice of Jesus,*
> *saying still to fight on.*
> *He promised never to leave me,*
> *never to leave me alone.*

Martin Luther King, Jr., was the most significant and successful "organic intellectual," to use Antonio Gramsci's phrase, in American history. The term intellectual (which I have not heard yet at this conference) needs to be emphasized. King *was* an intellectual, a religious intellectual. Now to some secular minds that might sound oxymoronic or self-contradictory, but King revelled in ideas, he took the life of the mind seriously. As an organic intellectual, he tried to relate those ideas to common, ordinary people and to remain ensconced and enmeshed in their world. Never before in our past has a figure outside elected public office linked the life of the mind to social change with such moral persuasiveness and political effectiveness. A full account of why and how King emerged as such a figure would need to consider the distinctive historical conditions of post–World War II America—with its world power status, its unprecedented economic boom, and its apartheid-like structures of racial domination in the South—that set the stage for the moral vision, personal courage, and political determination of King and those who struggled alongside him.

Yesterday we considered the relationship between the individual and society, between human agency and structural constraints, with each informing the other in a complex interplay. I agree with Professor Huggins's point that while the individual is unintelligible without understanding the larger social forces, the individual is also irreducible. And if the individual makes a difference, then the *kind* of individual one is makes a difference.

In the limited space of this essay, I shall focus on the four principal intellectual and existential sources (by existential I mean the forms that shape one's being, one's sense of self)—preeminently religious in character and prophetic in content—that informed King's thought. The first, and most important, of these sources was the prophetic black church tradition that initially and fundamentally shaped his world view. The second was a prophetic liberal Christianity that he encountered in his higher education and scholarly training. The third was a prophetic Gandhian method of nonviolent social change that he first heard about in a sermon by Mordecai Johnson, then president of Howard University, and that he utilized in his intense intellectual struggle with the powerful critiques of Christianity and the Christian love ethic put forward by Karl Marx and Friedrich Nietzsche. The last source was that of prophetic American civil religion, which fuses secular and sacred history and combines Christian themes of deliverance and salvation with political ideals of democracy, freedom, and equality. I shall argue that these four religious sources constitute the major pillars of King's thought, and I shall start at King's beginning, that is, in the bosom of the black Baptist church.

It is very important to note at the outset that this black church tradition is not monolithic or homogeneous, but complex, diverse, and heterogeneous. The black church—a shorthand rubric that refers to black Christian communities of various denominations that came into being when African-American slaves decided, often at the risk of life and limb, to "make Jesus their choice" and to share with one another their common Christian sense of purpose and Christian understanding of their circumstances—is unique in American culture and, indeed, unique in the New World. This is one of the fundamental differences between black people in the United States and those elsewhere in the Americas, where blacks were not able to control their own ecclesiastical institutions or have their own preachers and pastors speaking to them in a language they could understand. Being a black Baptist in America was quite different from being a black Anglican in Jamaica or a black Catholic in Brazil. The black church in the United States is the major institution created, sustained, and controlled by black people themselves; it is the most visible and salient cultural product of black people in America. The profound insights and superficial blindnesses, immeasurable depths and immobilizing pettinesses, incalculable richness and parochial impoverishment of that complex, hybrid people called African-Americans surface most clearly in the black church—all of the faults and foibles, all of the grand struggles and achievements.

Let us be very clear and let us never forget that the great American prophetic figure of our time, Martin Luther King, Jr., was a child of the black church, an individual product of the major institutional product of black people in this country. And when I talk about King being an individual product of the black church, I'm talking about the kind of *person* he was. I'm talking about someone who exemplifies, embodies, and exudes the very ideals and values that he talks about. He doesn't just talk about love; no, he has a love affair with black America. He doesn't just talk about care, but he actually exemplifies his care. He doesn't just talk about sacrifice; he lives a sacrificial life. That's a value —integrity—that comes out of the black church. (Of course, such values do not come only from the black church—black people have no monopoly on virtue—but the black church takes such values very seriously.) When I talk about King as a product of the black church, I'm referring to how he was shaped in this institutional setting. It was within the black church context that he acquired such values as integrity, love, care, sacrifice, sincerity, and humility, and came to take them so seriously.

The black church was created under economic conditions of preindustrial slavery and socioeconomic circumstances of "natal alienation." (This is Orlando Patterson's term in *Slavery and Social Death* to describe a social condition in which people have no legal ties of birth in either ascending or descending generations, no right to predecessors or progeny. Hence they are confined to a perpetual and inheritable state of domination and are defined as dishonored persons with no public worth, social standing, or legal status. They are only of economic value, mere commodities to be bought, sold, or used.) In this regard, the black church has signified and continues to signify the collective effort of an exploited and oppressed people, of a degraded and despised people, of a dominated and downtrodden people of African descent to come to terms with the absurd in America and the absurd as America. African-Americans did not have to read Albert Camus or Eugène Ionesco to discover what the absurd was. They lived it every day, and many continue to live it *every* day.

The black church was a communal response to an existential and political situation in which ultimately no reasons suffice to make sense or give meaning to the personal circumstances and collective condition of African-Americans. With the "death of the African gods" (to use Albert Raboteau's phrase in his very important book *Slave Religion*), black people creatively appropriated a Christian worldview—mainly from such dissenters in the American religious tradition as Baptists and Methodists—and thereby transformed a prevailing absurd situation into a persistent and present tragic one, a kind of "Good Friday" state of existence in which one is seemingly forever on the cross, perennially crucified, continuously abused, and incessantly devalued, yet sustained and empowered by a hope against hope for a potentially and possibly triumphant state of affairs.

The ground of this hope was neither rationally demonstrable nor empirically verifiable. Rather, it was existentially encountered in an intense personal relationship with Jesus Christ, whose moral life, agonizing death, and miraculous resurrection, literally and symbolically understood, enacted an ultimate victory over evil—over collective slavery and over personal sin (another term we haven't used, but that King took very seriously)—a victory that had occurred but was not yet consummated, an evil that had been conquered but was not yet abolished. The Christocentric language of the black church—of Jesus as the bright morning star against the backdrop of the pitch darkness of the night, as water in dry places, a companion in loneliness, a doctor to the sick, a rock in a wearied land—exemplifies the intimate and dependent personal relationship between God and individuals as well as between God and a seemingly world-forsaken people.

This is one of the reasons that what David Garrow was talking about is so very important. The "kitchen experience" is not so much a conversion (I disagree with Nathan Huggins here), it simply made available to King the depths, the riches of the Gospel he had already accepted as a young man in Atlanta. It had to become real to him. He was standing on the edge of life's abyss. The old church folk used to say faith is stepping out on nothing and landing on something. King was experiencing this for himself. That's not necessarily conversion; it's a deepening of that perennial process of becoming a Christian.

My point is not simply that this is the broad, black Christian worldview that King heard and adopted at his father's church, Ebenezer Baptist Church in Atlanta, but also that this worldview put the pressing and urgent problem of evil, the utterly and undeniably tragic character of life and history, at its very center. (Let me emphasize that we're talking here about tragedy; we're not talking about the pathetic. The tragic generates moral heroism, what William James called the strenuous mood; it fosters struggle, engagement, commitment, decision. The pathetic devalues and delimits agency; it is mere deferential and submissive behavior.) The major focus of the prophetic black Christian world view is neither an escapist pie-in-the-sky (often a caricature of black religion, even among some black intellectuals) nor a political paradise on earth (the heresy of certain liberal appropriations of Christianity). Rather, the stress is on marshalling and garnering resources from fellowship, community, and personal strength (through meditation and through prayer —there is an irreducible core of God-individual relations even within the corporate body of the church; King understood this very well, and Robert Moses made this point: one tries to acquire an internal moral discipline as an individual, but is always linked to some community) to cope with overwhelmingly limited options dictated by institutional and personal evil. In short, this black Christian perspective affirms a sustaining eschatology, always forward-looking, always prospective, as well as a moral critique of pervasive white racism, but its emphasis is on survival and struggle in the face of the alternatives of absurdity and insanity, of feeling that the world is so chaotic and confusing that there is no way of getting one's bearings as one encounters the deep crises and traumas of life.

This is one of the reasons I like the title of David Garrow's book *Bearing the Cross*. I think in many ways that phrase gets to the center of it. Howard Thurman, another crucial figure in King's intellectual formation, argued in *Jesus and the Disinherited* that the logic of Christian social action is martyrdom. I can see such a claim forever dangling in the closet of King's mind. If you're going to talk seriously about the Christian Gospel in America you have got to come to terms with death, with dread, with despair. I think King understood that; his life is a statement of it. And it's the depths of that seriousness, I think, that makes King different from us, because in our middle-class coziness we don't want to confront the depths of seriousness the way he did. (Let's be honest with ourselves. This is not to say we cannot be like King. But it's erroneous to claim that King was just like us. He was *not* completely like us. Some of us don't have the courage to take a stand like he did. We have the potential to do it, but whether we actualize it is a different question.)

The principal African resources in black Christianity were threefold. First, a kinetic orality permeated black sermons and songs, black prayers and hymns. A sense of community was constituted and reinforced by an invigorated rhetoric, rhythmic freedom, and antiphonal forms of interaction—the call and response forms. Fluid, protean, and flexible oral stylizations of language gave black church life a distinctively African-American stamp, a stamp that flowed from black cultural agency in a society that tried to deny and downplay any form of black agency and black creativity. This is very important, and this is where there is a link between King and Marcus Garvey. Garvey's name has not been mentioned here, but if we are talking about black leadership we have to talk about Garvey. On this particular point King understood that you have to affirm black capacity and potentiality, acknowledging your African heritage without idealizing and romanticizing it, acknowledging the degree to which it formed who and what black people are. When Garvey said, "Up you mighty race, you can do what you will," King would have agreed, but he would have moved in a different direction. King affirmed black capacity and potentiality in a society that, in many ways, in his day, was organizationally geared to denying it and, of course, in many ways, in our own day, still continues to deny it.

The second African resource was a passionate physicality that accented black control and power over the only social space permitted them in American society—that is, their bodies. I think Michel Foucault's recent work is very useful in understanding this. Given overwhelming oppression and exploitation, the only thing one has is one's body, and the question is, What does one do with that body in terms of trying to impose order on the world? Self-assertion of somebodiness, one's own somebodiness, enacted by bodily participation in stylized forms of spiritual response in a black church liturgy signified a sense of "homefulness" for an exilic people. This raises a significant point relating to the issue of integration. On the one hand, King believed in the egalitarian integration of black and white persons, but on the integration of the black church he took a different view. Not because he believed that a separatist Gospel ought to be preached. No, not at all! But he knew that the church is one of the few places where black people could feel at home and, as long as their exile continued, there had to be some spaces in the society where they could be themselves—not uncritically, but culturally. They had to have some sense of being agents, some sense of being subjects in history, and the black church provided a space for that.

The third African resource was a combative spirituality that promoted the central roles of preacher, deacon, and choir—the preacher preaching, the deacon praying, and the choir singing. Each had to meet a weekly challenge of feeding a flock that was so hungry, encouraging the discouraged, and giving hope to the downhearted. Much hangs on that sermon, that prayer, and that song. It's not simply the sermon, prayer, and song, in and of themselves. People's lives hang on those performances. This is one of the reasons why the black church is so histrionic and performative. It understands that people's lives are depending, relying on what is put forward in that church service, that liturgy. This stress on the performative and the pragmatic, on pageantry and the histrionic, put a premium on prospective moral practice or forward-looking ethical struggle for black Christian parishioners. This sense of struggle paradoxically cultivated a historical patience and subversive joy, a sober survival ethic and an openness to seizing credible liberation opportunities. Professor Huggins talked about this patience in terms of stoicism. I'm not sure that's the right term; it's a different tradition. There are stoic dimensions of it, yes.

> *Nobody knows the trouble I've seen;*
> *Nobody knows but Jesus.*
> *Nobody knows the trouble I've seen;*
> *Glory, hallelujah!*

It doesn't follow. There's a dialectical reversal here. There's a paradox, a tension-ridden paradox. Glory for what? Based on what?

The theology of the black church was, for the most part, traditionally Augustinian with an African-American difference. It accented the traditional Protestant Christian doctrines (and here, of course, I'm not saying that Augustine was a Protestant, but rather referring to the fact that Martin Luther and John Calvin and others appropriated Augustinian sources in initiating the Protestant Reformation in western Christendom) of divine majesty, sovereignty, and mystery, of sin and grace, of forgiveness and love, filtered through the black experience of oppression. This filtering process linked God's plan of salvation to black liberation—making them inseparable though not identical—and bestowed upon black people a divine source for self-identity, that is, children of God, that stood in stark contrast to the cultural perceptions and social roles imposed upon them by a racist American society.

This African-American difference not only highlighted the dignity of a people (both as a community and as unique individuals) who were denied such dignity in their surroundings, but also accented the strong universalist and egalitarian Christian notion of all persons having equal value and significance in the eyes of God—the *imago dei,* being made in the image of God. In this way, the black church put forward perspectives that encouraged both individuality and communal fellowship, both personal morality and antiracist political engagement, both a grace-centered piety and a stress on Christian good works. To put it crudely, the black church attempted to provide a theological route between the Scylla of a quietistic, priestly, American Christianity that legitimated racism, and the Charybdis of a secular, self-righteous, Promethean view that elevated human powers at the expense of divine grace and divine aid. The black church tried to hold together both the dignity and depravity of persons in such a way that God, like Yahweh with the children of Israel, identifies with the disinherited and downtrodden, yet even the disinherited and downtrodden are sinners in need of conversion and sanctification. Human beings can change and be changed, both individuals and societies, yet no individual or society can fully conform to the requirements of the Christian Gospel, hence the need for endless improvement and amelioration and relentless critique. (I would find it difficult for King to be in any human society and not bring prophetic judgment to bear on it.)

This complex dialectical interplay of human finitude and human betterment in black church theological perspectives makes African-American Christianity more evangelical than fundamentalist. This is so because fundamentalist Christianity is preoccupied with the claims of science and historical criticism of biblical texts; it views the Bible not only in literalist terms but, more importantly, in the form of propositions within a *closed* revelation, that is, only certain biblically derived propositions constitute divine revelation. Black evangelical Christianity, on the other hand, is primarily concerned with human fallenness, and this infuses our readings of the Bible. Biblical texts indeed remain the authoritative guide to Christian life, yet the focus is on moral conduct and spiritual development in light of *continued* revelation, that is, openness to divine purpose—especially through the Holy Spirit—grounded in the Bible but appropriated by individuals and communities in the present. I think it is no accident that the one denomination founded by African-Americans, namely Pentecostalism, with Rev. William Seymour on Azusa St. in Los Angeles in the early 1900s, is a form of Christianity that affirms and emphasizes the Holy Spirit. In short, fundamentalist Christianity is rationalistic in orientation and legalistic in effect, leaning toward bibliolatry—the worship of the Bible; black evangelical Christianity is dramatic in orientation and moralistic in effect, affirming a biblically informed perspective, but resisting all forms of idolatry.

My claim is that black church viewpoints not only fundamentally shaped King's thought, but influenced the themes and elements he responded to and accentuated in his encounters with liberal Christianity (at Morehouse College, Crozer Theological Seminary, the University of Pennsylvania, Boston University, and Harvard University). Even his appropriations of the Gandhian conceptions of love and social change and of American civil religion are grounded in his black church formation. In this way, the black church's influence on King's views is the most primordial and decisive source of his thought. In his own writings and sermons, he simply presupposed this influence and always assumed that his being a black Baptist minister spoke for itself regarding this black church influence. (I think the pioneering work of James Cone and David Garrow demonstrates this.) For example, King's choice of Georg Wilhelm Hegel as his favorite philosopher was not because he was convinced of the necessary developments of the *Weltgeist* put forward in *The Phenomenology of Spirit,* but rather, as he said, because Hegel held that "growth comes through struggle"—a view King was quite disposed to, given his formation in the black church. Furthermore, King's preferred method of looking for partial truths in opposing positions, in rejecting extremes and affirming a creative synthesis of opposing views in a tension-ridden harmony is, on the surface, Hegelian. But it is, on a deeper level, rooted in the dialectical mediation of the dualistic character of the self (spirit/nature) and world (history/eternity)—a mediation both King (in an African-American context) and Hegel (in a German Lutheran context) inherited from Christian thought. The point is not that King did not learn much from Hegel and liberal Christianity, but rather that Hegel and liberal Christianity supplemented the influence of the black church.

This supplementary character of intellectual sources subsequent to King's black church formation can be seen quite clearly in his encounter with liberal Christianity in his formal higher education and training. For example, at Morehouse College King's concentration in sociology reinforced his theological and moral condemnation of the hypocrisy of white southern Christians and their alleged adherence to the Christian Gospel. Walter Chivers, his sociology professor, conducted detailed empirical investigations of lynchings in the South—those happenings that occurred every two and a half days between 1880 and 1922, producing that strange fruit that southern trees bear that Billie Holliday sings so poignantly about. Chivers had already developed his self-styled ethical critique of American capitalism, a critique that influenced King in significant ways. More pointedly, King's black church perspectives were further refined under George D. Kelsey, head of the department of religion and author of one of the most powerful texts in Christian ethics, criticizing American racism and Christianity, *Racism and the Christian Understanding of Man,* and Dr. Benjamin Mays, Morehouse College president. By avoiding fundamentalist traps, shedding parochial images of mere cathartic preaching, and linking sophisticated intellectual pursuit to serious Christian commitment, King became convinced at Morehouse that his vocation lay in becoming a minister in the black Baptist tradition and came to understand the Christian minister as an intellectual engaged in the service of the kingdom.

King's response to the Euro-American Christian academic world was to select those viewpoints that gave philosophical and theological articulation to the deeply held themes and beliefs he had acquired in the black church. I would like to mention four of these central religious themes. The first was the dignity and sanctity of human persons. I would emphasize sanctity here because dignity comes out of a very different tradition, a stoic tradition of natural law, whereas sanctity is based on the religious concept of one's relation to God, one's being made in the image of God, which gives one a special status. The second theme was the moral obligation and social responsibility of Christians to resist institutional evils such as racist segregation. King did not have to read Walter Rauschenbusch to take seriously the social gospel. He had already learned it at Ebenezer, and while Rauschenbusch would still teach him much, he would simply be building upon King's sense of being a Christian, morally engaged in political activity for change. The third theme was the significance of personal immortality, and the last, the power of Christian love to make a difference in personal and social life.

At Crozer, King took nearly one-third of his courses under George Davis. Like the black church, Davis saw God as a deity intimately and intricately involved in human history, a "working, toiling God" who labors through human beings to realize the ultimate end and aim of history. This objective was the recognition and appreciation of the value of human personality and the unity of humanity—the brotherhood and sisterhood of human beings. Influenced by the social gospel of Rauschenbusch, Davis linked his personalism to political and social engagement.

Yet it was the work of L. Harold DeWolf at Boston University who provided the liberal Christian resources most congenial and amenable to King's refined black church perspectives. In his six courses with DeWolf and in writing his doctoral dissertation (under the guidance of DeWolf) on the conception of God in Paul Tillich and Henry Nelson Wieman, King found an acceptable and respectable academic theology that best expressed the major themes and beliefs of his black church background. DeWolf's personalism provided King with a professional theological language that put forward the four basic themes King had inherited from the black church tradition. During his years in graduate school, King tentatively adopted limited liberal Christian ideas about the natural goodness of people and the progressive direction of human history. Yet later, in the heat of battle, he fell back more and more on the classical Christian ideas of sin, grace, and hope within the context of the black struggle for freedom. While he found his graduate school texts in many ways intellectually stimulating, they were ultimately not as sustaining as he would have liked them to be.

In short, Davis and DeWolf supplemented King's black church viewpoints, supplements that resulted in slight revisions, emendations, and new academic forms for his evangelical foundation. King indeed called himself an evangelical liberal, an apt description after adopting Kelsey's dramatic, nonliteralist reading of the biblical texts, Mays's Christian modernist view of a highly educated and politically engaged black minister, Davis's stress on human history as the crucial terrain for divine activity, and DeWolf's full-blown personalism that undergirded a social gospel.

The major challenges to King's black church formation came from the critiques of religion put forward by Karl Marx and Friedrich Nietzsche. King took very seriously Marx's argument, based on Ludwig Feuerbach's formulation, that religion was the opiate of the people, the instrument of those who rule, that it disinvests people of their own powers and invests God with all power, thereby rendering people powerless, submissive, and deferential toward the status quo. King also took seriously Marx's focus on the vast economic disparity between the rich and poor—exemplified for King by the class inequality in America where the top 1 percent of the population owned 28 percent of the wealth and the bottom 45 percent owned 2 percent of the wealth. But we are talking about two aspects of Marx here. One is the Marx who presented a trenchant critique of religion, to which King had to respond. Then there's the Marx who talked about economic and class inequality, and this is a Marx that King would appropriate. King's black church formation led him to conclude that many forms of religion did render people submissive, but also that prophetic Christianity could empower them to fight against oppression and struggle for freedom and justice. King remained convinced all his life that there was a need for a vast redistribution of wealth and a de-emphasis on material possessions in a profit-oriented capitalist society. Later in life, he acknowledged the necessity of some form of American democratic and libertarian socialism—an indigenous form of egalitarian distribution—to preserve the constitutional rule of law and protect individual liberties, but also to secure and promote a "person-centered rather than property-centered and profit-centered" society. In regard to his response to Marx, King wrote:

> I read Marx as I read all of the influential historical
> thinkers—from a dialectical point of view, combining a

> partial yes and a partial no. Insofar as Marx posited a metaphysical materialism, an ethical relativism, and a strangulating totalitarianism, I responded with an unambiguous "no"; but insofar as he pointed to weaknesses of traditional capitalism, contributed to the growth of a definite self-consciousness in the masses, and challenged the social conscience of the Christian churches, I responded with a definite "yes."

In short, King succumbed to neither a knee-jerk negative reaction to Marx without reading and grappling with him nor an uncritical acceptance of Marx's atheism that overlooked the contribution of prophetic religious people to struggles for freedom.

Nietzsche's view of Christian love as a form of resentment and revenge of the powerless and impotent toward the powerful and strong led King briefly to "despair of the power of love in solving social problems." Following both the black church tradition and liberal Christianity, King had concluded that the Christian love ethic applied only in individuals' relationships, not for group, nation, or class conflicts. And if Nietzsche was correct, even individual relationships of love were but power struggles masquerading as harmonious interactions. This created a real intellectual crisis for King. Could the love ethic of Jesus Christ transcend relations between individuals and actually become a potent, progressive force in the social sphere? The black church did not provide resources to answer that question, nor did liberal Christianity. When he heard Mordecai Johnson talk about Gandhi, King's intellectual excitement, I can imagine, must have been indescribable because the Gandhian method of love-motivated (*agapic*) nonviolent resistance provided King with both a response to Marx and an answer to Nietzsche. It gave him the means to apply the love ethic of Jesus Christ in the social sphere, as a moral and practical method—a way of life and a way of struggle—by which oppressed people could fight for freedom without inflicting violence on their oppressor or humiliating their opponent, thus preserving the possibility of transforming the moral disposition of their adversary.

For King, this method of nonviolent resistance required more internal moral discipline than Marxist revolutionary activity would, because one had to accept suffering without retaliation, to receive blows without striking back. For him this was not cowardice but courage, not fear but fortitude. Nonviolent resistance also went beyond Nietzschean resentment and revenge, in that resistance was directed at the forces of evil rather than against persons who commit the evil. The enemy, for King, was injustice and oppression, not those who perpetrate the injustice and oppression.

Needless to say, this Gandhian viewpoint goes against most of our common instincts and moral intuitions. In this sense, the application of the love ethic of Jesus Christ in the social sphere requires not only tremendous moral discipline and fortitude, but also—and here we reach the crucial element in King's thinking—a profound trust in the redemptive power of love and in the salvific plan of God. King believed in the fundamental trustworthiness of human existence, that creation was essentially good and only existentially evil. (That's a belief that many of us find not so much problematical, but difficult to live. I speak as a Christian, so I believe it, but I know the problems of trying to live it. And secular folk don't even believe it!)

This trust presupposes that the unearned suffering of *agapic* nonviolent resisters can educate, transform, and even convert one's opponents. The aim is not simply to rely on the moral sense or conscience of the adversary but, if need be, to force the adversary to develop such a moral sense and conscience. And if one concludes that no such development is possible—that the adversary not only has no moral sense or conscience but, in addition, no longer even has the *capacity* to develop one—then we are forced to admit that we are doomed to an unending cycle of violence and oppression, that human history is the slaughterhouse that Hegel said it was, with the old victims of violence soon to become the new perpetrators of violence. That's the nightmare that hangs in King's closet. Is that what human history is? All the evidence is on that side. Such a nightmare—an inevitable conclusion for Marx and Nietzsche in King's view—calls into question the very power of the love ethic of Jesus Christ. For King, to accept such a nightmare means only self-destruction awaits us. To accept such a view, for individuals, for groups, for nations, is to acquire and preserve "power without compassion, might without morality, and strength without sight." But King says, "No. There's an 'over-againstness' of this Christian Gospel, and so my life will in fact become an example of refusing to succumb to that kind of despair." But he took that despair seriously. It was not academic for him. Indeed, the despair forever seeps in on one, and at times one does seem to succumb to it.

The last major resource for King's thought was American civil religion—that complex web of religious ideas of deliverance and salvation and political ideals of freedom, democracy, and equality that constitute the evolving collective self-definition of this country. This first new nation, as Seymour Lipset put it—born liberal, born modern, and born bourgeois—gave birth to a grand social experiment unprecedented in human history. Its Declaration of Independence constituted, for King, a great moral event and document—it didn't have sacred status like the Bible, but it was canonical and classical. His appropriation and interpretation of American civil religion led him creatively to extend the tradition of American jeremiads—a tradition of public exhortation that joins social criticisms of America to moral renewal and calls America back to its founding ideals of democracy, freedom, and equality. King was convinced that despite the racism of the Founding Fathers, the ideals of America would be sufficient if they were only taken seriously and lived in practice. In this sense he was a patriot, quite different from the kind of patriot who is trotted out year after year now. This is so very important if we are to engage in the struggle for which King is being celebrated. He was a patriot in this sense, but his understanding of what the Declaration was all about had tremendously progressive and prophetic implications. Thus, his condemnation and lament of America's hypocrisy and oppression of poor whites, indigenous peoples, Latinos, and black people was put forward in the name of reaffirming America's mission to embody democracy, freedom, and equality.

King did not support or affirm the bland American dream of comfortable living and material prosperity. Rather, he put forward his own dream, grounded and refined in the black church experience, supplemented by liberal Christianity, implemented by Gandhian methods of nonviolent resistance, and rooted in the American ideals. King did not say "My dream is America's," but rather "My dream is rooted in this tradition, but I'm going beyond it. My dream relates to these despised people who have been locked out." In fact, part of the greatness of King was to extend his dream to the international arena. Here, on this one issue, there was a link between King and Malcolm X and even the Black Panther party: the fact that black people, poor people, were part of an international struggle against colonialism, imperialism, and racism. When King read the Declaration of Independence he saw a colony rebelling against British imperialism, and he accented that progressive potential.

King's thought remains a challenge to us principally in that he emphasized the anticolonial, anti-imperialist, and antiracist consequences of taking seriously the American credo of democracy, freedom, and equality. He never forgot that America was born out of revolutionary revolt and subversive rebellion against British colonialism and imperialism, and that while much of white America viewed the country as the promised land, as the city on the hill, shining for the world to see, black slaves saw it as Egypt, the land of bondage. King never forgot that in the early twentieth century, as Europe's poor, huddled masses were yearning to come to America, Marcus Garvey was leading the largest mass movement of black folk to get out. The contradiction was very clear. He was not a Garveyite, but he understood Garvey's appeal. Through his prophetic Christian perspective, King saw just how far America had swerved away from its own revolutionary past. In its support of counterrevolution in Vietnam, Guatemala, Colombia, Jamaica, and South Africa—and today we can add Chile, Nicaragua, and South Korea—the United States betrayed its own ideals. King acutely observed in 1968: "The greatest irony and tragedy of all is that our nation, which initiated so much of the revolutionary spirit of the modern world, is now cast in the mold of being an arch-antirevolutionary. We are engaged in a war that seeks to turn the clock of history back and perpetuate white colonialism."

King's universal and egalitarian religious and moral commitments, as well as his historical consciousness, led him to internationalize the American ideals of democracy, freedom, and equality and to measure not only domestic policies but also United States foreign policy by these ideals. And he found both sets of policies wanting. He knew some progress had been made, yet so much more was needed; even present gains could be reversed, as we have witnessed in the past few years. Regarding domestic inequities, King proclaimed: "If the problem [of injustice to the poor and blacks] is not solved, America will be on the road to its self-destruction." And on the eve of his murder, he was just as emphatic about the need for action on the international scene: "If something isn't done, and in a hurry, to bring the colored peoples of the world out of their long years of poverty, their long years of hurt and neglect, the whole world is doomed."

The unique status and legacy of Martin Luther King, Jr., is that as a black Baptist minister, he embodies the best of American Christendom; as an organic intellectual, he exemplifies the best of the life of the mind involved in public affairs; as a proponent of nonviolent resistance, he holds out the only slim hope for social sanity in a violence-ridden world; as an American prophet, he commands the respect even of those who opposed him; and as an egalitarian internationalist, he inspires all oppressed peoples around the world who struggle for democracy, freedom, and equality. What manner of man was he—this child and product of the black church, open enough to learn from other traditions but rooted enough in his own tradition to grow, who now belongs to the nation and to the world—a nation and world, as was said of Amos, still "not able to bear all his words" even as they try to honor him.

Richard H. King

Martin Luther King, Jr.,

and the Meaning of Freedom:

A Political Interpretation

FOR A STUDENT OF TWENTIETH-century southern history, culture, and literature, it has been impossible to ignore the tremendous impact of the civil rights movement on the region as well as the nation. And it seemed inconceivable as a southerner and one-time participant in the movement—in Chapel Hill and Tuscaloosa—that I would not write about it at some point in my life. In 1983 I moved to England after teaching for fifteen years at the University of the District of Columbia, an institution that was itself born in the latter days of the movement in 1968. Only then was I able to achieve a perspective on the civil rights movement and begin to be able to write about it.

At that point what I discovered I wanted to do—and what needed doing—was not another history of the movement as a whole or a study of a campaign or community central to its development. Rather I decided to focus on the meaning of certain seminal political ideas and to treat the movement in the broadest terms as the key to the revival of "the political" in postwar America. It seemed to me that "freedom" rather than "rights" or "equality" or "justice" was the key to the political thinking of the movement. The task, then, was to try to understand the meaning or meanings of freedom as the term was used in the rhetoric of civil rights leaders and participants.

From this it followed that I would have to deal with perhaps the central figure in the movement: Martin Luther King, Jr., black southerner, minister, holder of a doctorate in philosophical theology, student of modern social and political thought. King's life and thought seemed to exemplify more clearly than most that crucial intersection of action and experience, theory and practice—freedom as a theological claim and freedom as the richly complex means and end of action in the world. My contribution to this volume is a first approximation of an understanding of Dr. King's understandings of freedom as a political idea—and as a personal experience.

The motions of grace; the hardness
of the heart; external circumstances.
—**Pascal,** *Pensées,* **No. 507**

W hy was the rhetoric of freedom so central to the civil rights movement? What made it so resonant with the dreams and struggles of the southern movement? One way to deal with such questions is to study the meanings of freedom in the writings and the public rhetoric of Martin Luther King, Jr. For if King was hardly a typical participant or leader, he was nevertheless a representative figure in and of the southern phase of the movement.

This essay will first explore the way King reconciled a sense of choice and the act of being chosen, of freedom and fate, in his own life. His public life can be described as having been organized around four fundamental choices, each a variation on the relationship between choosing and being chosen, activity and passivity. These constitute what I call King's "choice to be chosen" as a public, even heroic, figure. It should be added that I am not referring here to clearly identifiable moments of choice as such, but rather to basic decisions that emerge over time as having already been made and that give shape and coherence to King's life. This essay will then examine the various political expressions of his understanding of freedom. And, finally, I will discuss certain problems arising from King's concepts of freedom.

THE CHOICE TO BE CHOSEN

An essential indeterminancy lies at the core of the modern concern with identity, since neither the social structures nor the fundamental assumptions exist to give us a sure grasp on our identity. Nor is it clear whether the self for which we search is there waiting to be discovered or whether self-identity refers to the self constructed from the circumstances and choices confronting us. Indeed, it may be of little value to talk of identity at all—whether found or constructed—until the life in question is over and can be narrated.

The difficulties with identity are heightened considerably for black people living in a "white" world. For they may be burdened by—or gifted with—what Du Bois called "double consciousness," a reverberating, ricocheting sense of self produced by the mirroring but distorting presence of the white "other," a presence that perpetually calls coherence or worth into question. This precarious location of the self between paranoia and dissolution, a siting that Ralph Ellison's trope of invisibility captures, is threatened as well as protected when the black person in question is a world-historical figure.

Indeed, the relationship between the self-conception of a political hero and his historical setting has been a central theme in modern historical and political speculation. For Machiavelli the basic conflict was between individual *virtu* and *fortuna,* between the power of the political leader and the recalcitrant obstacles thrown up by history. Thus lawgivers create and impose institutions; princes preserve and extend those institutions; and prophets call the citizens of a republic back to first principles, all in an effort to create a realm of permanence against the depredations of time and fortune.[1]

At the opposite pole from Machiavelli's master of political circumstances stands Hegel's more ambiguous world-historical individual: "Such individuals had no consciousness of the general idea they were unfolding, while prosecuting those aims of theirs," yet "they had an insight into the requirements of the time—what was ripe for development." What counts in our evaluation of such figures is not their motives but their achievements. Nor are such historical heroes necessarily happy: "They attained no calm enjoyment; their life was labor and trouble; their whole nature was naught else but their master-passion. When their object is attained they fall off like empty hulls from the kernel. They die early like Alexander; they are murdered like Caesar; transported to Helena like Napoleon." Though such individuals think they are free to achieve their desires, they are actually the instruments of a rational process called history.[2]

Closer to home, Emerson's essay "Fate" repeats some of these essential concerns, with a democratic accent added. Similar to Machiavelli in emphasizing individual power, Emerson still insists on retaining the Hegelian conjunction of necessity and freedom. After first delineating what he understands by the term fate—"the laws of the world," "necessity," whatever "limits" us in our biological and racial endowments —Emerson argues that fate includes within itself individual power or freedom: "Freedom is necessary." The nature of things includes its own self-surpassing, brought about by individual intellect, will, and moral sentiment, "So far as a man thinks, he is free," while fate consists of "causes which are unpenetrated." That Emerson wants it both ways marks him, perhaps, as typically American.[3]

Thus where Machiavelli envisages a conscious actor imposing form on meaningless history, and Hegel portrays an unconscious actor controlled by reason in history, Emerson imagines that we are conscious actors in a meaningful order of things: "No statement of the universe can have any soundness which does not admit its ascending effort."[4] What unites all three, however, is the sense that the political efforts of the hero must be in some sort of harmony with the times. Even Machiavelli says, "He is happy whose mode of procedure accords with the needs of the times, and similarly he is unfortunate whose mode of procedure is opposed to the times."[5] Ultimately, however, time wins out in any individual or collective life and undermines the actions of the hero.

Detour though this may seem, it is directly pertinent to our understanding of Martin Luther King's sense of destiny. In fact, King had studied Hegel, including *The Philosophy of History*, at Boston University's Divinity School and was even then developing a nonreligious description of his Christian sense of calling.[6] A particularly cogent example of King's self-consciousness about "choosing to be chosen" exists in his announcement to his Montgomery congregation that he was moving to Atlanta: "I can't stop now. History has thrust something upon me which I cannot turn away. I should free you now."[7] Striking here is the conjunction of freedom and necessity. In obeying "history," King will free the congregation of his presence. But more significantly, he implies that he will liberate them in a deeper sense from their old attitudes and unjust institutions. It is also important to note King's understandable reluctance to call attention to his own ambition. His statement to the congregation might be read as an ingenious combination of high ambition, even hubris, with humility. In general this moment in Montgomery was the Emersonian moment in King's public life when freedom and necessity seemed to coincide, when causes were penetrated by intellect, will, and moral intention.

This sense of a life marked by the coincidence of freedom and destiny, choice and calling, stayed with King. Not long before his death he offered a more abstract, less personal version of the same theme when he affirmed that the "essence of man is found in freedom," but that "Freedom is always within destiny. It is the fulfillment of our destined nature. We are always both free and destined." King also emphasized that he was speaking of freedom of the "whole man" and not just "freedom of the will." Freedom in this abstract, metaphysical sense was thus not just an inner capacity but a condition of being in and making decisions about the world: "the capacity to deliberate, decide, and respond."[8]

Of particular interest is that the language King used to describe his sense of freedom and destiny was secular as often as it was explicitly Christian. This is not to say that he abandoned his religious faith as he took up his public role. The repeated connections he made between himself and Moses, as in the "I've been to the mountaintop" image, or between himself and St. Paul, as in the "Letter from Birmingham Jail," testify to King's deeply felt Christian commitment and the use he made of its allusive resources. What pushed him to a nonreligious description of his public role was perhaps the need to justify having chosen a public role against the "powers and principalities," where humility and soft-spokenness, the Christian virtues generally, were not efficacious. How to explain his calling as a Christian to an increasingly secular world?

Though this "choice to be chosen" was fundamental in King's life, it was probably not the first crucial choice in his life. What was absolutely essential for a public figure such as King was his willingness to risk his life, to face death as a real possibility. A deep personal crisis in January 1956 led him to this position. Much later at Birmingham he asserted that "No man is free if he fears death."[9] Here, too, we find that King seemed to feel most free when he accepted the ultimate limitation upon his freedom. This risk of life is central to any understanding of what it meant for King (and for many participants in the movement) to be political.

In general there is a fine line between willingness to risk one's life and deliberately courting fatality. In this connection we might consider King's two youthful attempts at suicide less as attempts at self-destruction than as experiments in self-punishment, an impulse perhaps later transformed into his willingness as a leader to undergo unearned suffering. But when King became an adult he no longer actively pursued a confrontation with death but waited, in a sense, for it to come to him. After President Kennedy was assassinated, King told his wife that "This is going to happen to me also."[10] Premonitions of death were always present, to the point that some of his aides felt him to be excessively morbid. Thus the choice to risk his life encompassed the same mixture of activity and passivity we find in so much else in his life.

Questions of life and death lead inevitably to a third crucial choice of King's public life—his decision to embrace nonviolent direct action as a way of life and a mode of action. In this area he came closest to explicitly recognizing the complex mixture of activity and passivity in his own life and in the collective lives of black southerners. In countering Reinhold Niebuhr's claim that passive resistance was just that—passive—King sought to transcend the violence yet mobilize the psychic energy of black southerners, to replace their fear with civil courage, and to transcend their sense of "unfreeness" by emphasizing that to be nonviolent was a choice. Thus nonviolent direct action issued from free men and women; it was not just the predictable response of oppressed people lashing out at their oppressors.

Whatever the other problems with nonviolence, it was, then, a brilliant, creative response to a historical double-bind. Whichever way blacks acted, white people were sure to say, "No, that's wrong" or "Isn't that just like black people?" King broke this double-bind by shifting the focus of the question away from *whether* black people were going to act to *how* they were going to act. To choose nonviolence was a way of refusing to be a prisoner of the culture.

Finally, if the rejection of violence arose from King's "choosing actively and affirmatively what not to do," his fourth crucial choice— to become a Baptist preacher in the South—reflected an affirmation of what "one is never not." [11] Those familiar with King's life know that for a time he resisted becoming a minister at all and later was intent on avoiding the emotionality of Baptist fundamentalism to the point that at Crozer Seminary he studiously avoided seeming "black." Behind his decision to earn a Ph.D. at Boston University Divinity School was his desire eventually to teach and write. Like Gandhi, King was a budding colonial intellectual and left his homeland to get educated. While in the North he had to sort out class and status as well as race and regional affinities. Yet, as did Gandhi, King returned home to lead a movement drawn from all classes. As Gary Wills has suggested, "By trying to run away from his destiny, he equipped himself for it." Indeed, the appeal of the Memphis campaign may have been closely linked with the chance it gave King to come back to home territory, to replenish his depleted resources, to reestablish his psychic roots. [12]

What did it mean to live a life organized around such choices, to be aware of one's role and have it continually confirmed by others? My sense is less of a man who imposed himself upon events than of a man who imposed himself upon *himself* in preparation for what history would confront him with. As with Lincoln, there is a certain aura of sadness and constraint around his public persona. Moreover, lacking Lincoln's public sense of humor, King created himself as a figure of gravity to the extent that one is brought up short by remembering how young he was; it is almost impossible to look through the prepared public face and see the private man. Though it is easy to discount the judgments of memory, most accounts testify to King's self-control, to the willed quality of his demeanor, from early on. He was like a finely tuned string stretched to maximum tension. This may explain a certain lack of flexibility in his public image.

Yet such *gravitas* inevitably masks inner conflicts, desires, and guilts. No strong-willed and high-spirited son of a father possessing those same qualities could have grown up without having to learn considerable self-control, and those two suicide attempts bespeak considerable aggression turned inward upon the self. The creation of Martin Luther King, Jr., the public figure, only exacerbated the gap between the inner and outer selves. One friend heard him say "I am conscious of two Martin Luther Kings. I'm a wonder to myself." [13] At times the costs of self-discipline, ambition, and publicity became apparent, and the relentless self-critic, egged on by an overweening superego, emerged. As William Miller wrote of King, "When he did obey what seemed to be an occasional irresistible compulsion, he said that he felt seriously called to be a martyr, a suffering servant, a disciple—but he found it extremely difficult to admit that he was worried about what he regarded as the destiny God had given him." [14] Another friend, Stanley Levison, remembered that Martin "could be described as an intensely guilt-ridden man. . . . It was a continual series of hammer blows to his conscience and this kept him a very restive man all his life." [15] Aside perhaps from Lincoln, it is difficult to think of any other American leader of whom such words could be spoken. I take this to be a sign of strength, not weakness, indicative of a man whose inner resources had not been depleted by his public role.

Occasionally we can see behind the mask. One scene in Landau's film "Montgomery to Memphis" shows King joking ruefully at how afraid he and his colleagues had been when they found themselves conducting a mass meeting in Mississippi with Sheriff Raney standing ominously behind them. The scene is moving and poignant because it forces us to see how young King was and how frightened he often must have been. King's mellifluous public voice concealed a sharp tongue that was revealed when he exploded at Whitney Young for criticizing his (King's) public opposition to the war: "Whitney, what you're saying may get you a foundation grant, but it won't get you into the kingdom of heaven." [16] And there were those moments in his speeches—the extemporaneous last part of "I Have a Dream" or the concluding moments of his last speech in Memphis—when he pushed through the measured public self to something more fundamental. In those moments the role and the circumstances and the self were one.

In general King's life displays an ascent from the oppressive and benighted South to liberty and literacy, and then a reimmersion in the southern black experience, a pattern that literary historian Robert Stepto has identified as paradigmatic in the canonical texts of black American writing. [17] Moreover, all this was done under the glare of modern publicity and the vastly accelerated pace of twentieth-century public life in

America. It is instructive to recall that Gandhi's public career lasted over a half-century while King's was compressed into just over twelve years. It was a career made up of alternating periods of public involvement and private withdrawal, but the withdrawals were increasingly too brief and too inadequate to recharge emotional and intellectual batteries.[18] Once in step with the *Zeitgeist*—his public career began just after the 1954 Supreme Court decision and in the same year as the Bandung Conference—by 1968 he found himself working alone, out on a tight-rope without a safety net.

Yet King had entered into his destiny willingly; he did choose to be chosen. Indeed he was perhaps personally most free in those last years when the tides of history were flowing in a different direction, for then he chose against the *Zeitgeist*.[19] Thus he had the courage to remain the person he had become, to make choice and destiny indistinguishable. By speaking out strongly against the war in Vietnam and searching for new ways of addressing the social and economic plight of poor Americans, he cut himself off from the channels of power controlled by the white and black establishments. As he wrote in 1967, perhaps as a kind of self-admonition: "Ultimately a genuine leader is not a searcher for consensus, but a molder of consensus."[20]

THE POLITICAL MEANINGS OF FREEDOM

Though Martin Luther King, Jr., tended to equate freedom and destiny when speaking in theological terms (or when referring to an individual life), his concept of political freedom was more complex. This is fortunate since the freedom-as-destiny idea has an unhappy legacy as a specifically political idea. If we understand it to mean that the goal of the actions of an individual or group is to establish freedom, then it is fairly comprehensible and defensible. But if the equation of freedom and destiny means that freedom is whatever happens to that individual or group, then the equation of the two terms is highly dangerous and can be used to justify the unjustifiable. Generally King linked freedom and destiny in the former sense when applying it to the political realm.

It must be emphasized, however, that King's ethical and political positions derived from his theological stance.[21] His philosophy of nonviolent direct action was based not on utilitarian or Kantian grounds, that is, he did not claim that his position was what maximized happiness, nor was it derived from adherence to some categorical imperative, although he did seem to think that it could also meet these criteria. Rather, justification for nonviolent direct action was grounded in a transcendent personal power at work in the world through specific historical events.

King's "evangelical liberalism" *cum* personalist theology led him to detect traces of God's presence in history and in human nature, fallen though the world might be. Whereas for neo-orthodox thinkers the distance between God and humanity was so vast that Christ offered the only hope of bridging that chasm, liberal theology tended to see a much closer connection, with Christ providing an ethically blameless life as a model for human emulation. Because human beings were created in God's image and a moral or natural law existed against which human arrangements could be measured, there were hints in the world of human action of how to relate the Christian message to political, social, and economic realities.

By extension, then, for King (as for his fellow southerner, Lillian Smith) segregation was not simply an unjust social and psychological reality, but also a symbol of separation and alienation from self, others, and God. It was, finally, a denial of freedom.[22] And to subvert this alienating power of segregation, King argued that Christian love, *agape,* was absolutely central. *Agape,* as he defined it, is: "understanding and creative, redemptive goodwill for all men. . . . We love men not because we like them, nor because their ways appeal to us, nor even because they possess some type of divine spark; we love every man because God loves him."[23] Such a claim about *agape* does not deny that each person possesses a divine spark, only that the ultimate injunction to love your enemy does not derive from that "fact" or from any merit a person may possess. The seminal political virtue for King derives from the nature of God's relationship to his creation. By extension, the goal of political action informed by *agape* is the "beloved community," the necessary context for the exercise of human freedom, which is both a utopian ideal and a real future possibility. Finally, there is, wrote King, "some creative force that works for universal wholeness . . . though the arc of the moral universe is long, it bends toward justice."[24]

Shifting from the abstract language of theology and ethics to the more concrete language of biblical faith, we can say that King believed in a personal God at work in human affairs. He was particularly drawn to the "Exodus event," a historical example of God's intervention in history that prefigured the way God had helped deliver black Americans from slavery and then sided with their struggle against segregation and oppression. With this in mind we can also understand how King's references to himself as a Moses-figure leading his people out of bondage to Pharaoh struck obvious chords in the consciousness of black Americans. "We, too, are in bondage," he wrote in 1963, and he went on to claim that the freedom songs of the movement served the same purpose as spirituals had one hundred years earlier. Thus the first meaning of freedom in King's political thought referred to the corporate experience of deliverance from oppression by God's action in history as sacred and secular.[25]

King also linked the biblical event and the experience of black Americans with the fate of the nation: "The sacred heritage of our nation and the eternal will of God," he wrote, are consonant with "our echoing demands."[26] By implication black Americans had succeeded the Puritans as the chosen people in God's redemption of secular history through the national community. It was as though only the Americans literally acquainted with slavery and systematic oppression could be carriers of liberation for the entire nation. As King wrote in *Where Do We Go from Here?* black Americans had the mission of "enlarging the whole society and giving it a new sense of values."[27] In this respect his sermons and writings assume the functions of a jeremiad. In invoking the Constitution and the Declaration of Independence, they call America back to its first principles or point to their future realization, a more logical position for a black leader since the black American propensity for historical nostalgia is distinctly limited. Generally, political action aimed at furthering black freedom has national, even eschatological, significance since it unites secular and sacred, the black experience and God's purposes for the nation. From King, American civil religion received its first explicitly black interpretation.

Though freedom as collective liberation was important for King, it did not quite convey the transformation of the self experienced by those actively engaged in protest and direct action. From this perspective, direct action might be seen as a form of preparation in the wilderness before the promised land was reached. This second form of freedom, what I call freedom as character, has to do with liberation from an old self and acquisition of a new one. Political action becomes a kind of therapeutic exercise.

King described this self-transformation in several ways. In his early writing he spoke of the "lack of self-respect among black people," and, using the metaphor of maturation, said that the "Negro, once a helpless child, has now grown up politically, culturally, and economically."[28] After Birmingham he talked of a positive sense of being "somebody" and that the black man "had to win and to vindicate his dignity in order to merit and enjoy his self-esteem."[29] Later, under the impetus of black power and black consciousness, he issued a "psychological call to manhood" and spoke of his "deep feeling of racial pride" and an "audacious appreciation of his [the Negro's] heritage." Echoing Du Bois, he went on to add that the "Negro's greatest dilemma is that in order to be healthy he must accept his own ambivalence."[30]

But King also assumed that freedom was "never voluntarily given by the oppressor." To maintain otherwise was a contradiction in terms, since "growth comes through struggle."[31] This Hegelian lesson implied that, though the struggle need not be a violent one, freedom as character or self-transformation could only come through a literal or figurative risk of life. Significantly, King couched the confrontation between police and protestors in the seeing/being-seen figure so central to the oppressor/oppressed dialectic. As he described the scene in Birmingham, there were "hundreds, sometimes thousands, of Negroes who for the first time dared look back at a white man, eye to eye."[32] And King vividly captured the reversal from passive to active, unequal to equal, submissive to assertive, impotent to potent, when he wrote: "Bull Connor's men, their deadly hoses poised for action, stood facing the marchers. The marchers, many of them on their knees, stared back, unafraid and unmoving. Slowly the Negroes stood up and began to advance. Connor's men, as though hypnotized, fell back, their hoses sagging uselessly in their hands."[33]

It is also important to stress the shared nature of such public action against segregation: the creation of a new self was not the result of individual but of collective action. Moreover, King's intention was to keep open the possibility of seeing the white enemy as a subject not an object, an end not a means, a "Thou" rather than an "It." More immediately, solidarity was created among the protestors, and a sense of oneness was created in the "war for the transformation of a whole people."[34] Thus, not just courage but also solidarity were defining qualities of the new free self in which the old dishonored aspect had been replaced with dignity and self-respect.

Interestingly, the vocabulary King used to describe such transformations of the self was largely psychological or medical rather than religious. Analogous to his concern with the therapeutic effects of action was a diagnosis of American society in terms of health and sickness as much as right and wrong. In *Where Do We Go from Here?* he described the "congenital deformity of racism" that characterizes white society and added that "the preparation for the cure rests with the accurate diagnosis of the disease."[35] King also applied the pathology model to the history of black America. Its central quality was "pain," and it was "scarred by a history of slavery and family disorganization" that rendered the black family "psychopathic." The images were mixed, however, when he described the contemporary task as "a battle against pathology within and a battle against oppression without."[36]

In keeping with this pathology model, King conceived of nonviolent direct action as a way to expose the "dangerous cancer of hatred and racism in our society." The white liberal must be made to see "the need for powerful antidotes to combat the disease of racism." Another of his favorite tropes for such exposure derived from the Socratic effects of bringing "tensions in the open."[37] Perhaps the missing figure implied by the pathology and Socratic gadfly metaphors was the contemporary one of the psychoanalyst, a figure who combines the Hippocratic and Socratic functions, albeit uneasily and somewhat confusedly. Seen in this way, King's nonviolent direct action exposed the sickness of the white segment of the national psyche and revealed a complementary disorder in the black part, but also identified healthy areas and strengths waiting to be encouraged.

Yet both types of freedom—collective liberation and self-transformation—were ostensibly peripheral to the explicit public goals of the movement: the destruction of racial segregation and black disfranchisement. Though it later became fashionable to dismiss such goals as superficial (or "bourgeois" or "white western") they were obviously important to black southerners and were goals that some white Americans, even in the South, could support. Furthermore, it may seem to be straining to identify the securing of rights, expressed constitutionally as "equal protection of the law," with any normal definition of freedom. But modern liberalism in Anglo-American political culture and thought has tended to define freedom in this way, as equal standing before the law. More exactly, according to the liberal notion of freedom, the individual should be free to pursue his or her private interests within a framework of civil rights. The individual citizen is primarily a rights-bearer, while the point of engaging in political action is to protect one's private sphere of concerns by securing protection of rights—in short, to cordon off civil society from state power.

King worked with a concept of natural law as the source of "constitutional or God-given rights." In particular, he frequently invoked the founding authority of the Declaration which, along with the Constitution, he identified as "the great wells of democracy."[38] By extension, he implicitly held to the doctrine of "incorporation," identified with Justice Hugo Black, according to which the Fourteenth Amendment made the Bill of Rights apply to state as well as to federal actions. The relationship of King (and the civil rights movement generally) to these constitutional questions was also crucial in that King translated the legalistic rhetoric of the federal jurisdiction vs. states' rights debate back into a moral discourse about just and unjust laws. Thus King located himself firmly in the tradition of radical liberalism by echoing the abolitionist argument for natural rights and higher law doctrines in opposition to slavery. The general significance of the "Letter from Birmingham Jail," a document aimed primarily at an educated, white, middle-class audience, lay in its function as a liberal *apologia* for civil disobedience and an indictment of white moderates, particularly in the South, for temporizing.[39]

Crucial here is a claim King first voiced in Montgomery in 1955 and last articulated in Memphis in 1968—"the great glory of American democracy is the right to protest for right."[40] This claim bore a close resemblance to a phrase in Hannah Arendt's *Origins of Totalitarianism*, in which she spoke of the "right to have rights." Although she eschewed any reference to natural rights as such, Arendt went on to speak of this as the right "to live in a framework where one is judged by one's actions and opinions" and "to belong to some kind of organized community."[41] Thus we can read King to be saying that black people insist on inclusion in the polity as a matter of right rather than as a favor to be granted them as though they were aliens seeking naturalization. To protest publicly was in itself to assume that the protestors were members of the political community, that a place in the public arena was theirs by right. To assert this was a kind of performative assertion, creating what it asserted.

The analysis of the difference between just and unjust laws in the "Letter from Birmingham Jail" is crucial to comprehending King's concept of freedom as equal standing. He began by citing Aquinas to the effect that "An unjust law is a code that is out of harmony with the moral law" and "not rooted in eternal law and natural law." King realized that few people thought in such natural law terms, so he shifted to psychological standards by claiming that an unjust law "degrades human personality."[42] Still, this begged the question of what it was about an unjust law that degraded. King's answer was that segregation implied a false sense of superiority over those who were discriminated against and treated as "things." He then moved back to theological language by quoting Paul Tillich to the effect that if sin is separation and segregation is separation, then segregation is sin. Though the logic was faulty, King felt justified in urging disobedience to laws preserving segregation as a kind of moral and ontological separation.

Even then King was not quite satisfied. He shifted from substantive to procedural criteria by asserting that a just law had to apply to a majority as well as to a minority, that is, it must provide equal protection. Moreover, he added an explicitly political dimension when he implied that no law, even if it met the previous criterion, was just if it was imposed upon a minority that had no part in its formulation or enactment. Indeed, if we take this participatory criterion as an overriding or, at least, a necessary condition for calling a law just, then King seems to imply the basic right of a citizen to have an active voice in the making of laws. Higher law and natural rights advocates have not generally included such political participation among basic rights.

Finally, opposition to unjust laws implies a form of civil disobedience, the ultimate meaning of the right to protest for right(s). Within the purview of freedom as equal status, civil disobedience is the attempt to rectify aberrations in a fundamentally just structure of laws and institutions. It is not revolutionary; rather, in the willingness to suffer the consequences, the practitioner of civil disobedience demonstrates the highest devotion to the spirit (as opposed to the letter) of the laws. Indeed, appeal to higher law or natural rights doctrines can be understood as a way of reassuring the audience of citizens that one is not aiming at anarchy or revolution.[43] Thus, King's concern with freedom as equal status before the law for individual black citizens was less appealing than freedom as collective liberation or as self-transformation, but it was absolutely essential that it be taken up and asserted.

The dividing line between freedom as equal status and freedom as political participation, the fourth meaning of freedom, is a subtle but important one. Freedom as participation is everywhere implied in King's writings and speeches (and actions) but rarely spelled out explicitly. We might grasp its elusive presence by suggesting that in every public protest *for* rights, justice, or jobs there was also an implied assertion that *by* protesting collectively the protesters were asserting their status as citizen-participants who planned to revitalize the speech and action of the political community. Citizens in this concept of participatory freedom are more than rights-bearers; they are active participants, and their political action is the source of power and a sign of self-empowerment. To use King's locution against Arendt—citizen-participants *protest* for rights while rights-bearers *have* rights.[44]

The closest King came to articulating this particular concept of freedom was in a quotation from Cicero: "Freedom is the participation in power."[45] What is important here is that politics is more about appearing, speaking, and acting on matters bearing on the *res publica* than it is about power, interests, or rights per se. Political participation is an end in itself rather than just an instrument to the achievement of power, interests, or rights. One acts politically not only to gain freedom, but also to demonstrate one's freedom. Political action is already a species of freedom.

A distinction made by Arendt is also relevant to our understanding of civil disobedience as a manifestation of participatory freedom. In "Civil Disobedience" she sharply distinguishes conscientious objection from civil disobedience and places the civil rights movement in the latter category. More than a theoretical quibble, this distinction bears directly on the question of the role of conscience in politics and particularly on King's elevation of Thoreau and Gandhi to canonical status in the history of civil disobedience. Arendt points out that in appealing to conscience both Socrates and Thoreau were engaged in a negative action against something. The appeal to conscience is by its very nature a solitary act and thus obviously not capable of generalization; one acts essentially from self-interest, albeit of the highest sort; one cannot live with oneself if one continues to obey the law. By contrast, for those engaged in civil disobedience, "concerted action springs from an agreement with each other, and it is this agreement that lends credence and conviction to their opinion, no matter how they may have arrived at it."[46] (It might also be added that Thoreau was certainly no advocate of nonviolence, nor did Socrates present a very strong case for civil disobedience, since the whole thrust of the *Crito* was to refuse to escape from Athens.) Although Arendt has been criticized—unfairly, I think —for seeming to exclude moral concerns from political action, especially civil disobedience,[47] her point was that appeal to conscience is individual and hence apolitical, while a decision to break the law as a group is arrived at collectively, whatever the provenance of that decision might be.

Here Arendt puts us on to something important about King's nonviolent direct action and civil disobedience. First, the motives for participation in direct action ranged from King's principled philosophy of nonviolence to a tactical, pragmatic decision to be nonviolent. What counted, if we follow Arendt, was the decision to act collectively in public. Moreover, though white participants in the movement may have broken the law for reasons of conscience—segregation laws seemed a clear violation of right(s)—it is not quite correct to say that black people were acting from reasons of conscience in challenging and disobeying segregation laws. For blacks it was not a question of deciding that segregation and disfranchisement were unjust. That was obvious. Rather, it was a matter of acting upon some primordial sense of self-respect and, as King showed, giving reasons for acting upon that impulse in the effort to convince nonparticipants and opponents.

There might be objections here that in acting from self-respect, courage, and solidarity, black participants were ultimately acting in their own self-interest. (Even Arendt might be read to suggest this.) If we want to stretch self-interest that far, then such an objection is true. But it does violence to the idea of self-interest to include in this concept risking one's life to register to vote or to buy a sandwich. More importantly, King's attempt to widen the horizons of participants in the movement, to link the cause of black southerners with the implementation of the republic's founding principles, was an attempt to identify the self-interest and self-respect of black Americans with the public interest of the nation in general. All disputes about the possibility or desirability of loving one's enemies aside, this was the truth in King's claim that "the Negro" was acting not only "to free himself" but also "to free his oppressor from his sins."[48]

Less consciously, but just as importantly, nonviolent direct action and civil disobedience can be interpreted not just as a protest against unjust laws but also as a massive effort to illuminate or enlarge the public realm of free action in the South and in the nation. King caught something of this capacity of public action to illuminate the dark corners of domination when he wrote in reference to Birmingham: "It [the power structure] was imprisoned in a luminous glare revealing the naked truth to the whole world." [49] In illuminating the way things were in Birmingham, in showing it "like it was," participants were also illuminated and revealed to be citizens. They emerged from private obscurity into the public gaze of those authorities whom they "dared look back at" and into the gaze of the nation. Obtaining political power, by extension, was not only a way of protecting one's rights and interests; it was also a way to "keep on keeping on" being citizens.

There is, finally, another sense in which collective public action exemplified an aspect of political freedom. What was manifestly the case in the heyday of the movement was the display of what Arendt calls "public happiness," what Pat Watters, a white journalist, meant by the "undeniable joy in the mighty doings of the movement." [50] The sermons and speeches of King and other leaders, the responses of the audiences or congregations to those public addresses, the exuberance of the freedom songs, and the high spirits of the marchers all testify to the sheer happiness of speaking and acting in public. In the process the only quasi-public space historically available to black people—the church—was transformed into a genuine public space as were, paradoxically, the jails where protestors were incarcerated and the courthouses, formerly closed to the public appearance of blacks. Spirituals, blues, and black popular music were reshaped into freedom songs. Here, ironically, black southern culture proved much richer in resources for nurturing public action than anything the white churches or white political organizations, even those friendly to the movement, had to offer. King and the civil rights movement taught the South and the nation to be political and to be free in the fundamental meaning of those terms.

CRITIQUE AND IMPLICATIONS

There is not enough space here to explore all the implications of King's political life and thought as they bear on the problem of freedom. Nor is there a way to assess the degree to which the various concepts of freedom I have discussed are theoretically or historically compatible. Still, I would like to suggest several crucial points at which questions can be raised and then discuss some of them.

A standard criticism of the civil rights movement and King himself, then and now, is that they ignored, even short-circuited, efforts to transform the structures of capitalist America, and thus were more concerned with surface than with fundamental matters. King granted the point in a limited way in his last years by increasingly emphasizing the importance of economic and social change. The order of emergence of his concerns is crucial, however, since he implicitly maintained that the "spirit of the times" and the requirements of the southern black community demonstrated the need for a psychological and political awakening before economic and social issues could be confronted directly.

Put in terms of restrictions rather than requirements, black and white American radicalism was then (and still is) notoriously weak on economic theorizing. Indeed, the period of King's emergence coincided with the proclamation of the "end of ideology"; and whatever general validity that assertion may or may not have had, it did point to the pervasive belief that neither socialism nor free-market capitalism carried much conviction in economic matters. More pointedly, failure to think socialist thoughts in the early 1960s can be traced not only to the lingering after-effects of McCarthyism, but also to what seemed to be the irrelevance of conventional socialism.

What about King's own sense of the conjunction of freedom and destiny in his own life, of his sense of chosenness? Unless we believe that there is some perduring, constituting meaning to history or that God intervenes in history, we must take King's understanding of his historical vocation as the way he had of explaining himself to himself and to others, of giving coherence to the story of his public life. Such individual stories are probably necessary for all of us, but if we cannot accept the metaphysical or religious assumptions informing a life story such as King's, it is difficult to know what to do except translate it into other terms.

King's sense of chosenness did, however, express itself in a way that had specific political impact—as the strong, even charismatic leader in the mobilization of the southern black population. A standing criticism, expressed by activists such as Ella Baker when she was with SCLC and also stated by SNCC, was that King's charismatic style of "Moses-type" leadership, drawing as it did upon the preacher-congregation relationship, hindered as much as it encouraged the emergence of self-reliance and political independence among participants.[51] The alternative model of politicalization offered by SNCC stressed the way communities should arrive at their own needs and then generate leaders in touch with their communities. If a leader was imposed and the community mobilized without being organized, the old patterns of dependency would be perpetuated.

This line of criticism leads to an examination of the group liberation concept, based on the Exodus analogy. Of the sense of chosenness as a people and of the role of Afro-Americans in the "redemption" of America, the same can be said as about King's sense of chosenness—such self-conceptions are ways of explaining and justifying actions and of expanding perspectives and self-images. Their danger lies, ironically, in accepting the myth of American exceptionalism and its world-historical or divinely-appointed service to freedom. The dubious nature of such claims and the dangers entailed in them are all too clear. Indeed, it is easy to link collective liberation with a parallel myth of black chosenness and virtue. The founding principles of the republic to which King often appealed are worthy of consideration, not because they are inscribed in the nature of things or are uniquely granted by God or history, but because they seem worth preserving as informing principles of a decent political order.

There is another problem with the idea of group liberation as expressed through the Exodus story when combined with the language of anticolonial, national liberation movements. Though both posit a goal of liberation from oppressors, the Exodus analogy imagines a physical departure from bondage and the conquest of a new land or a return home, while the colonial analogy imagines the literal expulsion of an oppressor and the reassertion of control over the homeland. Both models of liberation run up against the demographic, geographical, and cultural realities of America. As a result, the group liberation and self-determination concepts have tended to refer to new forms of individual and group consciousness rather than to political liberation as such. Black self-determination has had to be internalized, as it were.[52]

These historical circumstances, when linked with his own vision, led King to emphasize the close connection between direct action and the transformation of the self. But what are the political and moral implications of a therapeutics of political action? Here we must link the therapeutics of action with participatory freedom. In the republican-civic humanist conception of politics, freedom was closely related to the assumption that citizen participants were committed to act for the public good rather than purely from self-interest. This was a rough definition of political virtue, a quality informing participation as well as strengthened by participation.

Did King have a concept of political virtue? The answer would be a qualified yes. King and his followers were willing to risk their lives for a cause transcending immediate self-interest. Furthermore, his idea of *agape,* the commitment to recognize the oppressor as a human being and to forgive him or her, was an analogue of public virtue, despite its essentially religious provenance. As a principle, *agape* informed public action and the protestor's attitude during that action. It was not an injunction to establish a personal relationship with one's adversary.

It was easy, as the momentum of public protest and mass mobilization increased, to forget the centrality of *agape* and to see participation as a way of transforming the self rather than as the expression of an already transformed self. The issue here is whether political participation is a means to the end of self-transformation or, rather, does it presuppose a transformed self or, at least, transform the self incidentally in the process? Insofar as the latter is the case, King's philosophy of nonviolent direct action—along with Gandhi's—was the most creative re-visioning of political action in this century, for it acknowledged the importance of psychological liberation—as Arendt really does not—without raising it to supreme importance and thereby losing sight of more general objectives.

But if political participation becomes primarily a way to change the self, we are entering the dangerous ground Max Weber warned of when he wrote, "He who seeks the salvation of the soul, of his own and others, should not seek it along the avenue of politics."[53] It is dangerous because, if self-transformation is the goal of political action, then self-interest and self-respect are combined without the mediating or moderating force of an impersonal, other-regarding virtue such as *agape*. The result may then be something like the Fanonist fantasy of the therapeutics of violence. Once this occurs, the risk of life and striving for self-respect tend to degenerate into a desire for self-proving and self-defeating macho confrontations with the "enemy," while solidarity tends to congeal into a stifling ideological conformity that makes thought and debate all but impossible. King never succumbed to the despair of such a position, but his emphasis upon the therapeutic effects of political participation was easily corruptible.

Another problematic aspect of King's emphasis upon freedom as a change in the self lies in the various and sometimes contradictory tropes and analogies he used to describe such a transformation. At times he spoke of the shift from child to adult; at others, from boyhood to manhood; and at still others, he used the nobody/somebody trope. The question must be asked, in what sense and for whom had black people seemed to be "children" at one point and "adults" later? If black males achieved "manhood," then what did black women achieve? Though the nobody/somebody trope was less fraught with problematic connotations, King might have evaded some of them by talking of self-transformation in terms of a shift from private to public self-descriptions. Language more explicitly political might have allowed him to articulate the desired transformation in the sense of self without implying that black men were in some sense "boys," or that black people were "children" (as white racists had always asserted) or that black men, but not black women, underwent a fundamental transformation in becoming a free self.

I am not sure, however, how to sort out King's deployment of psychological or medical language to describe American society, black or white. It might, for instance, be claimed that it is very questionable whether a sick society can help itself. While this might justify King's self-appointed role as gadfly (or therapist), it does tend to deny that the racist is responsible for his or her racism, just as we do not hold a TB patient responsible for his or her disease. It is not clear what we gain by jettisoning moral discourse, however.[54] Furthermore, using the language of pathology begs the question of whether racism is always, or even often, a pathological phenomenon rather than a "normal" response to environmental influences on the part of whites. That is, unless the quality of being free from racist feelings is built into the notion of psychic or social health—and if it is, there has probably never been a healthy person or society—it is not immediately obvious that all racists are psychologically disturbed. It is precisely the power of racism that it does not depend on mentally ill people to perpetuate it. This is not to excuse it, but rather to suggest that it may arise from a lack of "moral imagination" or be adopted out of self-interest.[55]

More strikingly and controversially, King never quite reconciled his belief that certain aspects of black society were pathological with his celebration in later writings of Afro-American steadfastness and achievement. The depth of the problems in urban ghettoes struck him particularly after his experience in Chicago. Yet unless corrective measures were to be imposed from "the top down," some measure of popular participation would be demanded. Are people involved in pathological institutions or situations themselves pathological? Are they politically capable? All these questions are raised by the language of pathology, but neither King nor anyone else has found a way to answer them satisfactorily.

The larger conceptual point raised by this examination of King's rhetoric of freedom is that any way of talking about individuals or society involves figurative language, vocabularies of description, that shape as much as they reflect "reality." If this is inevitable, then one of the central tasks of political and social thought is to consider the implications of the descriptions employed and to guard against the confusion of figurative speech with reality, all the while remembering that reality never comes to us except under a particular description.[56]

If we move toward freedom defined as equal legal and political status, then several questions suggest themselves. One criticism of nonviolent direct action claims that it depends as much on coercion as on persuasion.[57] The subtext of King's message, so this criticism goes, would be that direct action functioned as a safety valve or as an alternative "creative force" for black anger and frustration—that is, if you don't let us march, the place will go up in flames.[58] Indeed, by 1967

King had come to admit that "ethical appeals" and "persuasion" had to be "undergirded by some form of constructive coercive power."[59] This was, it seems to me, less a change in philosophy than a shift in the way King described what he was about. Coercion of a kind had always been part of direct action insofar as boycotts, picketing, and mass marches threatened to disrupt the artificial civil and economic tranquility of the community in question. In this respect King had come back around to effective agreement with Reinhold Niebuhr. But King had not thereby abandoned the principle of nonviolence. Just as there are distinctions between persuasion and coercion, there are also important distinctions to be made between violent and nonviolent forms of coercion. Thus David Garrow's claim that King moved from nonviolent persuasion to nonviolent provocation is correct in general, but it is less than momentous. The shift, if it consciously occurred, was an example of shrewd but not cynical thinking. That having been said, the most serious aspect of Garrow's thesis is perhaps the greater danger to which the shift exposed protestors rather than any betrayal of moral principle per se.[60]

Some have also noted that King rarely, if ever, disobeyed federal laws or federal court injunctions, and for that reason his advocacy of civil disobedience fell short of being very radical. In other words, he knew that ultimately the federal government and northern public opinion were on his side and that segregation and disfranchisement had no constitutional legs to stand on. King never advocated, so this line of reasoning goes, anything like disobedience to something comparable to the Fugitive Slave Law, and thus he never brought the full force of federal power down on himself and the movement.[61] By extension, protest for rights in this view was not an appeal for limitations upon governmental power in the name of individual rights within civil society, but an appeal to federal power against state power.

There is something to be said for this line of reasoning, but not a lot. Most notably, this accusation of moderation neglects the constant danger that participants risked from state and local authorities, not to mention the threat from private (white) citizens in the South. Nor was it at all obvious at the time that the Kennedy-Johnson administrations or the Congress would intervene on behalf of civil rights workers and protestors—and certainly the FBI would not. One of the horrors of the situation was that civil rights workers depended upon the initial refusal of federal protection before they could attract national and world attention and thus obtain that protection. A kind of symbiosis existed between the movement and the federal government, but it was a tortured rather than an harmonious one. Thus it distorts matters considerably to see the struggle for civil and political rights as already settled before it began. Such a view assumes a benevolence about history and about the operation of power in America that is quite misplaced.

Most readers will undoubtedly find the notion of freedom as participation the most obscure and the most questionably linked to King's thinking. Indeed, he did not consider political freedom as the highest good for a Christian. To criticize him for not developing the idea of political freedom in any explicit way is to commit the fallacy of irrelevance, as though King should have read his Aristotle, Machiavelli, and Arendt more closely (or at all) and in the midst of considerable physical and psychological pressure inclined himself to savor the joys of political action as such. At the beginning I tried to indicate that he was rarely at one with his public role, which must have seemed more of a burden than a joy. What is striking, however, is the degree to which King's writings and public appearances do manifest some of the liberating effect of acting and speaking in public.

Of the notion of participation itself as a species of freedom, there will be even more skeptics, since it goes against the grain of our belief that politics is instrumental and primarily about power, a view shared by realists and radicals alike. All that can be said here is that though freedom as political participation is perhaps the one "exalted moment" of public life, just as romantic love is perhaps the one exalted moment of our private lives, it cannot in the nature of things maintain itself in its original form, but will become routinized. Still, its appearance in history should be cherished as a reminder of the best we can be and do as public beings, as citizens.

CODA: FORGIVING AND FORGETTING

In her book *The Human Condition* Arendt wrote movingly not only of the great power of love but also of its antipolitical effects. For, she claimed, love eradicates the necessary distance between human beings and thus destroys the space of action and judgment she calls the "world." Yet she suggests that a political expression of this power which she calls "respect" or "friendship" does exist. It is "a regard for the person from the distance which the space of the world puts between us, and this regard is independent of qualities which we may admire or of achievements which we may highly esteem."[62] The crucial link between Arendt's idea of respect and King's concept of *agape* is that both are impersonal attitudes, detached from any particular merit or quality the other may—or may not—possess. And because King called for it as an attitude toward enemies and not just toward allies and comrades, *agape* becomes an attitude that not only preserves the space between friends but also closes some of the distance between enemies. It enjoins an impersonal regard for their persons and projects. And *agape* imagines, at least implicitly, a future when all citizens can inhabit the public world together.

Furthermore, such an attitude presupposes "forgiveness," a quality

Arendt contends is the politically necessary means of breaking the cycle of vengeance so endemic to politics. Forgiveness in turn depends upon a kind of forgetting as well, what Nietzsche referred to as "learning to forget," the prerequisite for creative action in history.[63] It is not that the oppressed should literally forget what has been done to them. That would neither be possible nor desirable. Rather, as King said, "we forget in the sense that the evil deed is no longer a mental block impeding a new relationship."[64] In forgetting one incorporates and transcends the past.

Forgiving and forgetting would not be ways for black Americans to excuse what had been done to them. They would, rather, free black Americans from the embittering force of remembered suffering and injustice. Thus King's ultimate significance, one which remains to be absorbed fully, lay in his effort to incorporate the complex dialectic of forgiving and forgetting into politics. Thereby he suggested a way of beginning things anew, of taking action to rectify and yet go beyond the history of vengeance, and of transforming the compulsion to repeat into the capacity to act.

Mary Frances Berry

Commentary

I HAVE BEEN AN ADMINIS-
trator, a teacher, a scholar, a lawyer, and a movement activist.
Before I was all that, I was a black
person growing up in the South,
who graduated from high school
the year of the *Brown* decision. Like
all other black kids in Nashville,
Tennessee, I attended segregated
schools; like all black people, we
lived where white people told us to
live; and like all Southerners, I was
as suspicious and as afraid of
"them" as they were of "us." I was
in the Birmingham bus station in
1956. When I walked over to the
white waiting room to purchase a
newspaper, I was violently told to
leave. I didn't know it, but it was
the same day that Autherine Lucy
entered the University of Alabama.
I guess they thought I was going to
try to integrate Alabama all by myself.

When I "went north" to graduate school, the University of
Michigan was just awakening to
the movement—and they had
quite some waking up to do. I remember well the day that Martin
Luther King was assassinated. My
black classmates and I began to cry,
uncertain of his fate. When some
white students began honking car
horns and shouting—happily—
"King is dead," we knew he was
gone.

King had been there throughout my early adulthood. I wanted
to join him, but I followed the advice of a college teacher: When this
movement wins, we will need educated people, and you will be
ready. But I had believed King
would still be alive. With his death,
we inherited the gift he left: that
each of us could change the world
through nonviolence, with love
and struggle.

T hank you very much to all the people who are responsible for inviting me here today to talk on this panel. When I discovered what I would be talking about—when I learned the subject of the papers that I would be commenting on—I wondered why I was in this particular session since I'm neither a philosopher nor a theologian. Indeed, if I were at a scholarly meeting, with people who were sitting around talking about dry scholarly topics, I would begin with a complaint that I did not have an opportunity to read Professor West's paper because I received no copy of it. But since this is not such a meeting, I will say that the time that he took to prepare it was well worth it, and I enjoyed listening to it.

Let me just say that when I thought about the topic of nonviolent social change and nonviolent direct action and the ideology of nonviolence and what the meaning of freedom in it was and what the religious foundations of Martin Luther King's thought had to be—as I listened to people talking about what he was and what motivated him—it seemed obvious to me that he was, of course, as all people are, a product of what they've learned, of what their experiences have been, of their education; they're part of what they eat, of what they do with their lives. It reminded me also of a question that a reporter, who had the unenviable task of following me around all day and all evening last week, asked me at the end of the day:

> Which one is the real you? Are you the almost-preacher
> I just heard talking to that black audience at the church,
> or are you the person who was out there talking to the
> little kids in the street, and you responded to them when
> one of them said, as a mother called out the window,
> "Her not callin we cuz us don't belong to she," you
> seemed to know what she was saying. Or are you the
> scholar who was sitting there in that meeting of learned
> people talking about all kinds of issues related to the
> Constitution. Are you the teacher that I saw in the class?
> Are you—Which one of these things are you?

You can ask the same question about Martin Luther King, Jr., writ large. He was all of the things that Professor West talked about. And he was more than all of those things. There were elements in everything that he was that were attractive to different groups of people. Of course he was attractive to the black masses in part because it resonated in their ears when he spoke from the black prophetic religious tradition. After all, it was their tradition, and he was part of them. And of course he was attractive to a white America generally since he spoke in tones that reflected the broad sacred and secular traditions of American society.

And, of course, what he had to say could resonate anywhere in the world because he was not enunciating just Christian ideas and principles. In every one of the major religions there is the idea of risk-taking in a good cause, the idea of peace, and the idea of good triumphing over evil. So these things have a value that extend beyond our own society and, indeed, throughout the world.

You can ask, as some people do, why other leaders in our past did not gain the same acclaim and recognition. Why will this era be known, whether we like it or not, as some people may not, as the age of Martin Luther King, Jr., and of black people and of all people who are interested in progressive change in this country? A short answer is that violence has a respectable history and respectable origins in American society. After all, the American Revolution was a violent undertaking and, indeed, violence is as American as cherry pie, as someone said. But King made nonviolence as a tradition as respectable or more respectable than the tradition of violence. He became the embodiment of nonviolent social change.

Do you ask, why him? Well, if he had not existed he would have had to have been invented. And I don't mean in the sense of saying that it is a question of leaders changing history, or history changing and then there are leaders. I mean, yes, he was chosen, but I heard Professor King talk about a SNCC tradition of leaders coming up from the needs of the masses, and the masses picking them. And then there's another tradition of the elite. As I understand the history of what happened to King, he was chosen by the masses and leaders of the people in Montgomery who knew their needs and saw him as a person who could meet their needs. Now we all have experiences with leaders being chosen. There are all kinds of leaders who are chosen at particular times in our history and in our present-day life. The real question is not whether one is chosen; it is, are you *worthy* of being chosen? And some people are and some people are not. There are people who are chosen who turn out to be a terrible mistake, and you know it as soon as you make the choice. But whatever else you say, he was worthy of being chosen, and it was a terrible burden for him to bear. We have not heard enough about that, in my opinion, in these sessions or elsewhere.

The terrible burden of being chosen and being expected to be worthy, of always having to go to the well one more time, of having to produce a highwire act over and over again, of having to do what Arthur Flemming always tells me about, making silk purses out of sows' ears. There's a terrible burden involved in that; King was worthy of the choice.

Now Professor King talked about categories of freedom, and I was very interested in the discussion. I think that these categories could fit, from the standpoint of a philosopher who talks about them, whether we are talking about collective liberation so that people could become totally new, changed by the process, or whether they should be rights-bearers, whether they were participants who not only had rights but protested for rights. I guess freedom—whatever categories one uses—for the people who were involved in the whole civil rights movement and for those of us who struggle today, is defined very simply. It is the right of people to have control over their own destiny and to have a say about what happens to them. And that is what the masses of people who were in that movement and who followed his leadership would have understood as the meaning of freedom.

When I think about King embodying nonviolent social change I think of him as a historical figure. I think of his meaning in our time. And in that sense it doesn't really matter so much where he got all that he was; what matters is what he did with it and what we learn from it and what we do with it in our time. And what we learn is the whole idea of a leader and a movement being a molder of consciousness.

I didn't fully understand what Martin Luther King, Jr., talked about until the last two or three years—the whole concept of *agape,* the whole concept of love, the kind of love based in its rightness. I understood it on the night before Thanksgiving two years ago when I was sitting in the embassy of South Africa with the ambassador, Walter Fauntroy, and Randall Robinson. I noticed that all during the discussion we were having with the ambassador that as long as it was superficial and light he could talk to us without averted eyes and smile and laugh and chat. But when the moment came that we looked him directly in the eye and made a demand and said, "We want freedom for people in South Africa. We are here as people to say to you that if you don't understand that, we are about the business of doing what is necessary to make you understand that," he averted his eyes; he couldn't look at us, he could *not* look at us.

It was not a question, as Professor King talked about, of black people not being able to look other people in the eye, as during the civil rights movement, of having to learn to look them in the eye. We knew, we were transformed enough, we could look anybody in the eye, including him, but the ambassador could not look *us* in the eye because he was not accustomed to looking at black people as people who were human beings with dignity, on the same footing, who could be challenging, aggressive, and refuse an order, as people with whom he could talk, negotiate, discuss, and exchange ideas.

And that was important. I understood because we loved him, not as himself but as what he represented, and we understood that he was not yet ready for the stage of nonviolent social change which is to humiliate a person into understanding what is necessary to negotiate. And we understood that nonviolent social change involves action, and that action would be necessary to get him to the point where he would understand that he must look at us, and that he must understand that we were people and that we could share a discussion. His responses, of course, created a movement. Because had he responded to us in the sense that Martin Luther King, Jr., was talking about, we could have had discussions. But since he wasn't ready—there has yet to come a point when he will be ready—and it tells you what all of the Afrikaners have to come to, the point when they understand what it means to feel humiliated because of who they are and what they do. There's a basis of love —to talk to people about what is necessary to be done. I understood it finally then. And I understood also that what it requires, this kind of nonviolent social change, is shared values. If people have no values in which they believe, there's no way for you to connect with them. But since the Afrikaners say they have those values—we will see in the fullness of time.

Now the other thing that I understand about all this is that King did not mean simply that one would use nonviolence to get political participation and political action. One of the other important things that we learned from the movement and from him is that you use nonviolent social change to leverage political action. It is a connection that we make all the time now, that protest is an essential ingredient of political activity. You have politics, you get involved in that, but outside it is the leverage that you use once you're there. And it's not a question of transforming yourself by engaging in politics and hoping that's going to transform you. I would maintain that you have to be transformed already in order to understand how to engage in any kind of activity, and then the transformation may go on.

There was another point that Professor King made questioning whether Martin King's way and the way the nonviolent social change movement undercut more massive social and economic change that could have taken place in this country, and whether it therefore might have been counterproductive. He was saying some people suggested that, although he himself did not maintain that view. I would say that that probably is beside the point because the entire civil rights movement can be looked at in two ways. The first is to focus on the various steps of nonviolent social change—the raising of consciousness, the humiliation, the pricking of the conscience of one's adversary, and the negotiations as a way to achieve progress. But you can also look at the movement as a whole—the whole movement was consciousness-raising. You can use nonviolent social change to go beyond politics to deal with the problems of economics and other problems in our society, but you cannot take the next step until you take the first step. People have to do the first thing before they know the first thing won't do everything and that they need to do something else, if you see what I mean. So I don't see the movement in that sense as raising the question about whether you could have done everything and changed the whole society had it not existed.

To give another quick analogy to help you get that concept, some people say in the "Free South Africa" movement that instead of talking about sanctions or apartheid we should have immediately started talking about what kind of socioeconomic help was necessary for the people in South Africa. But if we had started there we never would have gotten to first base. You first had to know what apartheid was, and then know what you would do next, and then get to what you would do next. So there's more work to be done, but the important thing is that King demonstrated that you can use nonviolent social change in order to achieve justice.

The other thing that I don't particularly like about some of the discussion about King, especially among scholars, is the questioning why he was not more clear about all the concepts that he espoused in his life. Why didn't he write treatises more than he did about all these principles and explain all the ins and outs of all of them? We fault him for ambiguity on X point and Y point or a lack of consistency here, there, and everywhere. I think it is remarkable that he gave us as much as he did about what he did. I mean it is difficult enough to be in the center of public life as he was all of his life, carrying that burden. Why should we also expect him to be always handing out to us what exactly everything meant? Also, scholars wouldn't have any work to do if he had been that clear about it.

Finally, Martin Luther King, Jr., was the worthy carrier, the extender of a tradition that he expanded beyond most people's imagination. What he did, whatever he did, he did nothing during his lifetime to erode or tarnish the contributions he had made. You know there are people who do things that make contributions, and then they do something that tarnishes it all. And you say, "Oh my gosh. Now why did he have to do that?" He was human and he made errors, but King was worthy; he was worthy throughout his life, and he did nothing in the end to erode or tarnish those contributions. What he left for us is the demonstration that nonviolent social change works; it works in our time. And we would not be here in this room if it had not been generally accepted that he was the embodiment of that tradition. We would not be here in the halls of Congress; there would not be a statue of him in the Capitol; nobody would be talking about a day dedicated to him or anything else. So the question as to what is the importance of nonviolent social change and what is the importance of Martin Luther King, Jr., is answered by our very presence here.

Vincent Harding

Commentary

VINCENT HARDING, WHO teaches at the Iliff School of Theology in Denver, was born in New York City. After serving two years in the United States Army, he went to Chicago in 1955; there he attended the University of Chicago (receiving his M.A. in 1956) and worked, between 1955 and 1961, as a lay pastor in churches on the city's South Side. In 1961 he and his wife, Rosemarie Feeney, moved to Atlanta to participate in the black freedom struggle in the South. As the Mennonite Service Committee Representatives to the Southern Freedom Movement between 1961 and 1965, Harding and his wife served as civil rights teachers, activists, and negotiators in South Carolina, North Carolina, Virginia, Georgia, Tennessee, Alabama, and Mississippi. Returning to Chicago, Harding received his Ph.D. from the University of Chicago in 1965. His dissertation, on Lyman Beecher, was directed by Sidney Mead and Martin Marty. Harding subsequently became chair of the department of history and sociology at Spelman College (1965–69) and director of the Martin Luther King, Jr., Library-Documentation Project and the Martin Luther King, Jr., Memorial Center in Atlanta (1968–70). Harding has published voluminously— articles and essays, fiction and poetry—and helped create the major CBS television series, "Black Heritage." His most recent books are *The Other American Revolution* and *There Is a River,* histories of the black struggle for freedom, justice, and transformation in the United States, and *Hope and History,* a book for teachers who wish to include the freedom struggle in their curriculum.

I 'm very glad for the kind of experience we've had here, talking about the life and spirit of King, and even more importantly, talking about what that life and spirit mean for our life and our spirit now and in the future. I think the spirit here has been very, very good. I've been glad to see some friends who I haven't seen for a long time; glad to catch up; very, very happy to see Coretta Scott King and to sit with her and review notes about our children.

I want to say something about a question I raised last evening that I'm still struggling with—how to deal with the official King. Several people came up to me and spoke to me in very helpful ways, and one of them was Martin's sister, who some of you don't realize is here, but Christine King Farris is very much here. She said, "Vincent you're worried about this matter of the military band and everything like that. Don't you know that that's the way America does so much of its celebrating?" And I said, "Yes, isn't that right, Christine. But maybe that's one of the things that Martin wants us to struggle with creatively. Are there some new ways to celebrate? Indeed, are there some better ways to celebrate a peacemaker than by having military bands? What about the Howard University Gospel Choir?" Martin was a man of such imagination and creativity I suspect that he's urging us now to keep thinking, keep moving, keep going forward, refusing to be satisfied with any of the things that we find now because, as Chris said, "Martin didn't believe in going out of America; he wanted to be in America." And I agree, but he wanted to be in America so that he could transform America, and not just to lie back with what was there.

I would like to end our morning session with a further reflection on what we've been doing and on what our sister and brothers have been saying. As so often happens in these situations when we're dealing with King, we spend so much time talking about his earlier movement years that we never get to the later ones. I'd like to start off at the end, because I think where King ended is in a sense an invitation to us to go on. Ten days before Martin King was assassinated, his dear friend and marching colleague Rabbi Abraham Heschel introduced King to a group of Jewish leaders. March 1968. King was walking the tightrope that the other brother King refers to. And the rabbi said, "Martin Luther King represents a voice, a vision, and a way. And I invite all of you to take seriously this voice, this vision, and this way." Indeed the rabbi finished with these words: "I am convinced that the whole future of America depends upon how seriously we take this voice, this vision, and this way." The whole future of America depends on it. I believe that. And I want us to spend just a moment thinking about what that voice, vision, and way had become by 1968.

In the last year of his life Martin could be heard saying things like this: "The dispossessed of this nation, the poor, both white and Negro, live in a cruelly unjust society. Therefore they must organize revolution against that injustice. Not against the lives of their fellow citizens but against the structures of injustice through which the society is refusing to lift the load of poverty." That was King in his last year. The tightrope that he was walking, in my view, was a tightrope between the two things that people say cannot go together—revolution and nonviolence. King was trying to put them together. For by revolution he did not mean people picking up guns and shooting someone down so that the more successful violent people could take over from there. By revolution he meant a fundamental transformation of the values, the institutions, the life, and the direction of society.

The last document to which Martin's name is attached, published after he was assassinated, written sometime in March, maybe February 1968, is a document that ended up appearing in *Playboy* at the beginning of 1969. Why it took so long to appear is probably a very interesting story in itself; I'll let David Garrow tell me that one. But here is what he was saying in the late winter of 1968, his last days: "Millions of Americans are coming to see that we are fighting an immoral war that costs 30 billion dollars a year, that we are perpetuating racism, that we are tolerating almost 40 million poor during an overflowing of material abundance. Yet they remain helpless to end the war, to feed the hungry, to make brotherhood [and sisterhood] a reality. This has to shake our faith in ourselves." King, sensitive man, understood so often how we were feeling about ourselves. He said,

> If we look honestly at the realities of our national life it
> is clear that we are not marching forward, we are grop-
> ing and stumbling. We are divided and confused. Our
> moral values and our spiritual confidence sink even as
> our material wealth ascends. In these trying circum-
> stances the black revolution is much more than a strug-
> gle for the rights of Negroes. It is, rather, forcing
> America to face all its interrelated flaws: racism, pov-
> erty, militarism, and materialism. It is exposing evils
> that are rooted deeply in the whole structure of our
> society. It reveals systemic rather than superficial flaws,
> and it suggests that radical reconstruction of society it-
> self is the real issue to be faced.

Now, what does it mean to follow the voice, the vision, and the way of a man who eighteen years ago was calling for, working for a "radical reconstruction" of American society on behalf of the poor, the weak, the needy here and overseas? Cornel, in his presentation which so richly enlivened us, did what we so often do. He came to the end and had almost no time to deal with this revolutionary King. This King who believed in the revolutions of the poor around the world. This King who was deeply troubled by a nation that tried to suppress the revolutions of the poor. We've got to deal with him. That's where King was at the end of his life. That was the vision that Rabbi Heschel was talking about and the question is, what do we think that means for us now?

Therefore I will be both scholar and rabblerouser by asking some questions of us all, both scholars and nonscholars. What would this kind of vision, this kind of way, this kind of direction be? What would King, for example, be saying to the inhabitants of this building and to the House of Representatives in the light of their shamefully giving in to President Reagan on the Contra vote of $100 million? What would he be saying? To honor him is not to escape his righteous indignation. To honor him is to stand with him and to ask, what does this mean for us? What would King be saying to the leaders of this nation when it becomes clear what everybody really knew and that the direction of the Contras is located very, very close to the center of national power in this country? What would King be saying to Mr. Bush and Mr. Reagan at this point in history concerning his brothers and sisters in Nicaragua who are suffering for no other reason than the fact that an American, organized, mercenary force is killing their children? What would our brother be saying now? What would he be doing now in these precincts? And of course, as someone said, even that is not the central question. The question is, what may *we* be doing now?

Before saying just a few more words I want to suggest to you something that you might be doing. As several people mentioned yesterday, most of you know that four American military veterans, several of them medal winners, are fasting, for life, as they say. And they mean not just their own lives, they mean not just the lives of the Central American people: they are fasting for the lives and the integrity of the American people. They are out on the steps of the Capitol every day between four and seven in the afternoon, including this day when we install the bust of the great peacemaker (along with Gandhi) of the twentieth century. They are there; they have asked us to come join them at any time, and act in solidarity with their concern. They are saying that they are going to fast until they see some change that calls them away from fasting. One of them has been fasting for forty-five days now. Tomorrow has been proclaimed as a national day of fasting among the churches and synagogues in solidarity with these men and their fast. So perhaps there are some things that we can begin to do if we really wish to take seriously this voice, this vision, and this way.

Let me mention a couple of other responses to my brothers and my sisters. Cornel, I want to suggest that when you say that the Gandhian viewpoint that calls for lovingly facing the enemy goes against our common instincts and our moral intuitions, what I trust you really mean is that our instincts have been distorted. Because if you seriously take Jesus as the revealer of what human beings really are like, then Jesus says if you want to be a son or daughter of God, there is no other way than loving your enemy. If that is the true being, then everything else we see in ourselves that goes contrary to that love is really contrary to our authentic selves. So King was indeed calling us, all of us, to be true to ourselves. Not to act like some strange weak person, but to come back to our real self and know that we belong with one another.

And Cornel, about the death of the African gods. I'm not so sure about that. You just talked about the Pentecostals yourself; you just talked about the Holy Spirit. I have a feeling that the least we can say is that the African gods were sleeping for a while, maybe. Or more importantly, perhaps that they have been transformed, like so much else has been transformed. And I would argue that the transformation we brought about in this country is no more creative than the transformation that our sisters and brothers brought about in Latin America and the West Indies. I would not put us above them in what they did in creating an autonomous African-based Christianity. Because when you move among those people you're seeing Christianity, but it's a Christianity unlike anything that we've known in mainstream religions. You walk into some of our Pentecostal churches and you have the same experience. So I would ask us to recognize that God is going to work in all kinds of strange places among all kinds of beautiful people.

My final comment about your paper is that I think that perhaps you attempted too often to work with this idea of the tragic in life. I don't think that Martin defined life as primarily tragic. I think that Martin as a true dialectician saw life as filled with both the tragic and the victorious. Martin was therefore another kind of Jesus man. He saw that cross and understood that the cross is central to our life. But he also understood that the cross is fully connected to the resurrection—and that the resurrection is not tragedy. You don't go to the cross simply because you know that at one time you're going to be raised up. You go to the cross recognizing how horrible it is and how terribly, deathly painful it is to be separated, to seem to be separated, from the love of God. But you also recognize the possibility that there's more than that, and I think that Martin surely recognized that.

So may I say a word or two to my brother Richard King? I thought that some of your comments were of great importance, especially as we explore this matter of what nonviolence was for Martin Luther King. I thought that point was important about presenting black people in the South with the choice, the choice to take a nonviolent direction—and by nonviolent, again I don't mean simply not hitting back or not shooting back, I mean a spirit that engages. A man from Greenwood, Mississippi, said once, "We are not gonna strike back, but we ain't gonna run either. We just gonna keep on working for our rights." Now that's nonviolence put in Greenwood terms. You're not going to strike back because when you strike back you allow the enemy to overcome you with his message. You allow the enemy, the opponent, to take you over because you have given in to the idea that "You can only fight fire with fire; you gotta have the same kind of stuff." Once you do that you are lost. There's no sense fighting anymore because you are becoming that which you oppose. King understood that. This man understood that. So we're not going to fight back the way you fought us, but we're not going to run either. We are going to create new weapons. That's what Martin meant by soul power. We're going to create new weapons and we're going to stand with courage and not be turned around.

Now I think that that's why it is so right to say that in those last years King was indeed out on a tightrope without a safety net. Cornel put it so well in church terms, you know, stepping out onto nothing but knowing at some deep level that there is something. You don't know when you're going to get to that something but still you step out. I think that Martin's understanding of nonviolence—and I want to keep emphasizing nonviolence partly because that's a theme of the morning, as I understand it—Martin's understanding of nonviolence was a way of tremendous faith and courage that did not require a safety net; it made you know that you were indeed an acrobat of the Spirit, that you had to try things that had not been tried before.

That's why I think we must come back to a focus of yesterday's discussion, that this nonviolent method that King and others had worked on through the 1950s and 1960s was playing a very important role for the transformation of our situation up to that time. But then when we got into Chicago with Mayor Daley—and when we got into New York, and when we got into Watts, and we got to talking about coming to Washington, all kinds of different realities were before us. We were trying to figure out how to deal with stopping a war overseas. We were trying to figure out how to deal with the four things that Martin was talking about—racism, poverty, materialism, and militarism. What is called for now is greater creativity and, for some of us, probably walking on an even thinner tightrope than ever before. Because this country has not become less militaristic, it's become more militaristic. The gap between the rich and the poor has not gotten smaller, it's gotten bigger. Racism has taken a variety of different forms. And we have to figure out what it means to live in a society where everything on television tells us, "Want more. Get more any way you can, even by selling drugs at age twelve."

To follow King, it seems to me, is to deal with ways of nonviolent struggle for social change that he had not discovered. Very important. *He had not discovered.* And for me, I'm so glad that my brother didn't discover it before he left, because if he had discovered it, what would we have left to do? He didn't discover it, but we'd better discover it or we aren't going to be around for long. As he said, "The choice is between nonviolence and nonexistence," and he didn't just mean that in terms of nuclear weapons. He was talking about the nonexistence that's being built into our cities every day, that's being built into our White House every day, that's being built into our relationship with the Third World.

What I wanted to stop with was one comment about Professor King and his thoughts about pathology, and then one thought about the wilderness motif. What you're saying, Richard, is that you're not sure about the pathology metaphor. So much depends upon what you mean by sickness and so much depends upon how seriously you take the whole new world and the old world of what we call holistic medicine. Because it is not true that a sick society cannot help itself, just as it is not true that the sick cannot help themselves. What we've learned is that almost all disease is psychosomatic, that the disease of the so-called body is clearly connected to mental processes in many, many ways. Indeed, we say it every day. "He makes me sick." "She gives me a pain in the neck." And it literally happens with some people that we are around. We are around them and we start getting pains in the neck. And some people divorce other people because they stay sick with them for so long.

So it is not that sickness is a helpless condition. I think Martin understood that. The sick can at least open themselves to the possibility of facing their sickness, of recognizing their dis-ease, and then place themselves in a position to be helped and to be healed. And for King, nonviolence was a "sword that heals," as he put it. And then you ask, "How about black people? How about all of us who live in this sick, pathological society; how can we heal?" You know the work of that lovely theologian Henri Nouwen. He has this beautiful essay he calls *The Wounded Healer.* That's us. We ourselves are wounded, but that doesn't mean we can't be healers. We're not dead; we're just wounded. And what we're trying to do is find a way to overcome our own woundedness. And yes, in the process of overcoming our own woundedness, we also overcome the woundedness of the society. As we struggle against the woundedness of society, we become more whole ourselves. Again not either/or but the dialectic, I think, is there.

Now finally the metaphor that Martin loved so deeply—that of the promised land and the wilderness. May I remind you about when that metaphor began—in the Exodus account—because I think it speaks to us at this point in time. The word that was sent to the pharaoh was not, "Let my people go so they can have equal opportunity to press the buttons and to buy the cars." Not "Let my people go so that they can be as rich as everybody else, therefore making many people poor." Not "Let my people go so that they can just be like America as it is." (Oh, that's right, we're talking not about America, we're talking about someplace else, aren't we?) But remember what the statement was. All these wonderful biblical scholars around here can help us out: "Let my people go that they may serve me in the wilderness." The question is, what does it mean to serve in the wilderness now? Because what King was knowing and what those people back there were knowing was that freedom is not an end in itself. Freedom is not an end in itself. We become free not simply *from* something, but *for* something. And what does it mean to serve God in the wilderness of America today? I think that is the magnificent question for us to struggle with.

FOUR

Martin Luther King, Jr., and International Movements of Liberation

George M. Houser

Freedom's Struggle Crosses Oceans and Mountains: Martin Luther King, Jr., and the Liberation Struggles in Africa and America

MY PERSONAL RELATIONSHIP with Martin Luther King, Jr., grew directly out of my involvement with the liberation struggle unfolding in Africa during the 1950s and 1960s, and his sympathy with this historic development. I sought and received his support for many campaigns initiated by the American Committee on Africa (of which I was executive director for twenty-six years) including many of the efforts mentioned in this paper.

I was drawn to and was an admirer of King as soon as he emerged as a national leader with the Montgomery bus boycott. I shared a deep philosophical outlook on life with him. I was an ordained clergyman. Further, I was committed to nonviolence as both a strategy of struggle and as a pattern for life. For more than a decade preceding my work in Africa I was on the national staff of the Fellowship of Reconciliation (FOR). King was a sympathetic supporter of FOR. I was one of the founders of CORE and served as its part-time executive secretary during the last half of the 1940s and the early 1950s. Both of these organizations were committed to nonviolence. I was therefore familiar with nonviolent direct action methods and with civil disobedience, and was thus in full harmony with the tactics King popularized after his emergence as a major leader.

With my vocational transition to work in support of African liberation, it was natural to seek out Martin King and for him to respond as far as he was able to a cause we both enthusiastically supported.

WINDS OF CHANGE IN AFRICA AND AMERICA

It is not by accident that the upsurge against colonialism and imperialism in Africa and the cresting of the civil rights struggle in the United States occurred during the same general period. They were both influenced by the same historical events that were worldwide in scope. The Atlantic Charter, whose chief architect was Franklin D. Roosevelt, proposed freedom for colonial peoples, and this policy was endorsed by the Allied Powers during the Second World War. The United Nations gave organizational reality to these principles through its Charter and its promise of independence for countries under colonial domination. The major colonial administering powers, weakened by the long war, were no longer able to exert uncontested control over their dependent territories in Asia and Africa. The achievement of freedom by India, under the inspired leadership of Gandhi and Nehru, was an unmistakable signal to colonies in the rest of Asia and Africa to quicken their own campaigns for independence. The empires of Britain and France, and the lesser realms of Portugal, Belgium, and Spain, began to feel the strains brought on by pressures for self-determination.

The Bandung Conference in April 1955 epitomized the spirit of the era. "Bandung somehow caught the world's imagination, and early its leaders were conscious that history was looking over their shoulder," wrote Homer Jack, one of the small group of American observers at the conference.[1] Twenty-nine countries sent official delegations, of which twenty-three were from Asia and the Middle East. Of the six African nations represented, two—the Sudan and the Gold Coast (Ghana)—were not yet independent. Fourteen heads of state or government-led delegations attended, including Nehru, Zhou Enlai, Nasser, U Nu of Burma, and Prince Sihanouk of Cambodia. The Bandung Conference heralded the organization of the colored peoples of the world to resist colonialism and racism. It gave rise to the international nonaligned movement and to the Asian-African sub-grouping at the United Nations. Among the American black observers at Bandung were Congressman Adam Clayton Powell and the author Richard Wright.

The Bandung Conference took place at the same time the Montgomery bus boycott was initiated and Martin Luther King, Jr., began his rise to renown. Influenced by the spirit of the times, King, in a 1962 article entitled "The Wind of Change Is Blowing," noted the swift decline of colonialism and imperialism on the international scene, especially in Africa where there were only eight independent countries after Ghana's independence in 1957, but twenty-nine five years later.[2] He overoptimistically forecast that in another five years all of Africa would be independent. King recognized the parallel with the civil rights move-

ment in the United States, where the winds of change were also blowing—150 cities integrating lunch counters since the sit-ins gained
popularity in 1960 and the virtual elimination of segregation in interstate
travel since the freedom rides of 1961—but he warned, "The change
should not be exaggerated. We still have a long way to go."

King was not alone among civil rights leaders to see the relevance of
the struggle for equality in the United States to the momentous events
occurring in the Third World. The heads of all the major movements
were drawn into activities identifying the interconnection of events in
Africa and the United States. Yet the high level of interest and involvement in African developments had not been a long-term concern of
either many American black leaders or the civil rights movement.

Before the post–World War II upsurge in Africa, American blacks
were ambivalent toward that continent. It was difficult to bolster black
self-esteem by identifying with an area that was looked upon as back-
ward and that was ignominiously dominated by foreign powers. Black
Africa, in the popular mind, was too often seen as a land of savages and
heathens; the glories of African empires of the past were known only to
a few scholars. Very few African countries attracted American attention, black or white. The Belgian Congo had received worldwide no-
toriety when King Leopold's atrocities were publicized. Ethiopia was
an area of special attention with Mussolini's invasion and Haile Selassie's
brave resistance, but the ease with which the Italian military devastated
the country made identification difficult for American blacks. A special
relationship existed between the United States and Liberia, but there
was no success story in that part of Africa either, in spite of its being the
place where freed American slaves tried to carve out a home. As the
historian Rayford Logan pointed out, "American Negroes' view of
Liberia vacillates between pride and chagrin."[3] Most of Africa was
simply unknown. The continent, under European domination, offered
little to black Americans already suffering exploitation right here at
home.

BLACK ORGANIZED EFFORTS BEFORE THE AFRICAN UPSURGE

In the pre–World War II era it was not that there were no significant
organized efforts among black Americans making the connection between Africa and the United States, but activities were of a different
order and intensity.

Back to Africa

The "Back to Africa" movement led by Marcus Garvey was a development of major proportions. However, its emphasis was more on

the plight of American Negroes and their need to escape indignities at home than it was on the dynamics of change in Africa. Garvey himself was a Jamaican whose Universal Negro Improvement Association was organized in 1914, several years before he moved his base to the United States.[4]

After World War I Garvey attracted a following among American blacks estimated at six million by 1923.[5] Garvey was a spectacular personality who launched his movement with unusual fanfare at a convention in New York City in 1920 where he was chosen "Provisional President of Africa." His appeal was to the ordinary black American, not to the intellectual. The movement popularized the slogan "Africa for the Africans" and was based on the assumption that justice and equality could not be won in the United States. As W. E. B. Du Bois pointed out, "Garvey proved not only an astonishing popular leader, but a master of propaganda."[6]

Garvey's scheme to transport American blacks back to Africa and to open up commerce through the Black Star Line, for which the movement bought four small ships, failed. Nevertheless, no black leader had ever excited a more spirited following than Garvey. There were lavish parades through Harlem with as many as 50,000 participating, a Black Cross Nurses Corps, a black national church, and a newspaper, all epitomizing the promise of a better life in Africa.

Under Garvey's leadership the movement reached its zenith during its first five years. In 1925 he was convicted of using the mails to defraud and was sentenced to five years in prison. Yet, as Pan-Africanist George Padmore has pointed out, "Garvey most definitely made a marked contribution to the struggle for African awakening." James Weldon Johnson, national secretary of the NAACP during Garvey's era, pointed out that in spite of Garvey's overall failure to realize his practical goals, "He stirred the imagination of the Negro masses as no other Negro ever had."[7] Although the Back-to-Africa approach is not a dominant theme among black Americans today, Garvey's legacy still has its adherents in the United States.

Pan-Africanism

W. E. B. Du Bois was the preeminent exponent of another approach to Africa, Pan-Africanism, which made its mark before the upsurge of the postwar era. Early in his career he wrote, "The problem of the Twentieth Century is the problem of the color line," and he spent his life addressing it. He saw the issue not in parochial American terms but in a worldwide setting. While he appreciated the fact that he was an American, he saw himself in a broader context, although this wider perspective had its complications. "It is a peculiar sensation," he wrote, "this double-consciousness, this sense of always looking at one's self through the eyes of others, of measuring one's soul by the tape of a world that looks on in amused contempt and pity. One feels his twoness —an American, a Negro."⁸ Du Bois conceived of an interracial culture superceding a purely American culture. Pan-Africanism to Du Bois was a universal concept through which he could understand himself. It was also an organized system by which the black world could be protected. During much of his life he felt that American blacks could play a leading role in the establishment of a Pan-African reality.

Africa had a romantic hold on Du Bois. He once wrote, "The spell of Africa is upon me. The ancient witchery of her medicine is burning my drowsy, dreamy blood. This is not a country, it is a world—a universe of itself and for itself."⁹ He made an identification with Africa, not just in a psychological sense, but with the idea of encouraging and supporting the struggle for justice. Fifty-three years before the Belgian Congo became independent, he predicted a day of reckoning for the Belgian colonialists then holding sway. He viewed imperialism as one of the prime causes of world war and urgently called for removing the bases of inequality and discontent in Africa by granting the right of self-determination, advanced education, and land reform. He thought that Afro-Americans, the grandchildren of African slaves, could lead the campaign for the realization of these aims. He was well ahead of his time, not only in his hopes for what his black American compatriots might do but in his vision for the anticolonial struggle in Africa.

In spite of his Pan-Africanist emphasis, Du Bois was no separatist. He believed the main task of the American black was in the United States and opposed the Black Zionism of the Garvey movement. He felt that his Pan-African efforts were hurt by the mistaken identification some people made between Garvey's program and his own. Although he recognized Garvey as "an extraordinary leader of men," and a "hard-working idealist," he criticized him for "bombastic" methods that were "wasteful, illogical, and almost illegal."¹⁰ He felt Garvey's overadvertised schemes retarded the effective development of Pan-Africanism.

To flesh out his movement, Du Bois took the lead in organizing a series of Pan-African congresses. His base was the NAACP, of which he had been a principal founder. As editor of its magazine, *Crisis,* he gave voice to his Pan-African philosophy. Influenced by Du Bois, the NAACP adopted a program after the end of the First World War calling for the internationalization of the former German colonies in Africa. The Association authorized Du Bois to call a Pan-African Congress in Paris in 1919 at the time of the Versailles conference to urge that Wilson's Fourteen Points be extended throughout the world, including colonial Africa. The meeting was small, with only 57 delegates, among which were 16 black Americans, 20 West Indians, and 12 Africans, and it had only limited influence.[11]

Du Bois took the lead in organizing other congresses in 1921, 1923, and 1927. Enough attention was given to his efforts in Washington that President Coolidge appointed him as his representative to the inauguration of Liberia's president following the 1923 Pan-African Congress.[12] Du Bois himself said that the congresses he organized "were chiefly memorable for the excitement and opposition which they caused among colonial imperialists." He noted that their influence might have been lessened by the tendency of the European press to identify the meetings with Garveyism. Du Bois was disappointed by the scant support he received in the United States; "when in 1918 I tried to found a social and spiritual Pan-African movement, my American Negro following was small," he noted.[13] After a fifth Pan-African Congress, planned for 1929, was canceled, he commented, "We are not yet Pan-African minded."[14] Nevertheless, Du Bois's efforts were acclaimed by many African leaders for their historic importance. Dr. Nnamdi Azikiwe, the first president of Nigeria, credited his congresses with giving the "signal for the historic struggle by African nationalists which led ultimately to political emancipation of this continent."[15]

When a fifth Pan-African Congress, organized by a new generation of African leaders, was finally held in Manchester, England, in 1945, Du Bois was invited to serve as its president, although he was then seventy-seven years old. In 1958 he was a specially invited guest to the All African People's Conference held in Ghana, the first representative Pan-African conference on African soil, but he was unable to go because he refused to sign a non-Communist affidavit and therefore was denied an American passport. He later went to Ghana, took out citizenship there, and began work on his ambitious Encyclopedia Africana project. He died in Africa on the eve of the 1963 March on Washington.

Martin Luther King, Jr., extolled Du Bois as "One of the most remarkable men of our time, [who] died at home in Africa, among his cherished ancestors. . . . He recognized the importance of the bonds between American Negroes and the land of their ancestors." He called Du Bois's greatest virtue "his divine dissatisfaction with all forms of injustice."[16]

Council on African Affairs

Very few organizations in the American black community were formed explicitly to address Africa's struggle before the 1960s. One early exception was the Council on African Affairs, which was created in 1939 and went out of existence sixteen years later at about the time the Montgomery boycott was launched. Two key figures in the formation of the council were Max Yergan and Paul Robeson. Yergan had worked as a YMCA executive at several posts in Africa, ending with a fifteen-year tenure in South Africa. In 1939 in London he met Paul Robeson, who was returning from a visit to West Africa. They discussed the need for an American organization devoted to Africa's political liberation as well as its advancement in educational, economic, and social areas. They then founded such an organization, first called the International Committee on African Affairs, with headquarters in New York and Robeson as chairman. The initial sponsoring membership included prominent black as well as white Americans such as Ralph Bunche, Mordecai Johnson, and Channing Tobias; among the whites were Raymond Leslie Buell of the Foreign Policy Association and Mary Van Kleeck, a sociologist associated with the Russell Sage Foundation. In the early 1940s Alphaeus Hunton, who had been a professor at Howard University for twelve years, became the education director and then the staff executive. In 1948, after Du Bois left the NAACP following a rift with its executive secretary Walter White, he became the council's vice chairman with an office at the Harlem headquarters.

During the 1940s and into the early 1950s the council was virtually the only American-based organization programmatically dealing with African affairs. It sponsored public meetings for visiting African leaders and published a magazine and pamphlets on current African issues. The problem of racism in South Africa, even before the Afrikaner Nationalists came to power in 1948 with their policy of apartheid, was a major council focus. During a famine and drought in South Africa in 1946, the council organized a relief program, and thousands of cans of food were sent to South Africa. Thousands of people attended a gathering at the Abyssinian Baptist Church in Harlem and rallies in forty cities around the country. Through communications and deputations, the council attempted to influence the direction of the American government's Africa policy. Numerous mass rallies promoted the anticolonial cause, with Paul Robeson playing a leading role, and Africans studying in the United States, such as Kwame Nkrumah and Nnamdi Azikiwe, were in touch with council programs.

Robeson did a great deal of writing and speaking, especially on racism in South Africa, and gave benefit concerts for the council. He strongly supported the Campaign of Defiance of Unjust Laws in South Africa in 1952, and saw its relevance to the fight against Jim Crow in the United States. He said, "Imagine all sections of the Negro people in the U.S. . . . joining together in a great and compelling action to put a stop to Jim Crowism. . . . Think how such an action would stir the whole of America. . . . A dream? No. Look at the Union of South Africa. See there how the victims of even more savage racist oppression

have solemnly determined that only by establishing a common front
. . . they can escape absolute enslavement by the fascist Malan regime." [17]

The council was plagued during much of its existence with the
"Communist front" label, yet it is quite improbable that the Communist Party in the United States had an important part in its founding.
During the war years, the Soviet Union, in its alliance with the Western
powers, softened its anti-imperialist policy. The council, in spite of the
Marxist leanings of some of its leadership, maintained a hard-hitting
anticolonialist posture. The issue of the degree of Communist influence
came to a head within the council when Max Yergan began an anti-
Communist crusade. Acrimonious internal debates shook the council in
1947 and 1948, with Robeson and Yergan sharply divided. Yergan was
expelled from the council in 1948, and later even testified against it as a
"subversive" organization. Finally the attorney general of the United
States, at the height of the McCarthy era, ordered the council to register
as a Communist front organization under the Internal Security Act of
1950. Faced with resignations of prominent members and an overwhelming financial problem, the council dissolved itself in June 1955
rather than submit to this demand. [18]

The Council on African Affairs never had a mass following. Its
significance lay in the fact that just prior to the anticolonial upsurge in
Africa and the eruption of the civil rights movement in the United
States, it gave prophetic voice to American black concern for freedom
in Africa.

ANTICOLONIAL UPSURGE

Afro-American ambivalence toward Africa changed dramatically in
the late 1950s and 1960s as the liberation struggle expanded in Africa.
The number of independent countries grew phenomenally, African
voices were heard internationally at the United Nations, African culture
was resurrected, and black pride was rejuvenated.

A turning point in Africa might have been the so-called Defiance
Campaign in South Africa, led by the African National Congress
(ANC). In a six-month period in 1952, more than 8,000 apartheid resisters were arrested and jailed for openly and nonviolently disobeying
what they called the unjust laws. The Mau Mau uprising in Kenya
erupted two years later, and Jomo Kenyatta was arrested and confined
for nine years, becoming the country's foremost political leader when
released. At the same time the Algerian people, under the leadership of
the National Liberation Front (FLN), began their seven-year revolution
against French colonial domination. In South Africa the drive against
white minority domination was heightened as the ANC, in a multiracial

gathering in 1955, adopted its Freedom Charter. A year later the government arrested 156 of the top resistance leaders of the country on the charge of "treason." The independence of Ghana—the first African country south of the Sahara to achieve its freedom—under the flamboyant leadership of Kwame Nkrumah, gave an unprecedented lift to the forces for liberation in the rest of Africa. The formation of the All African People's Conference in 1958 in Ghana drew together liberation leaders from all over the continent and particularly strengthened effective nationalist movements in Zambia, Zimbabwe, and Malawi. It inspired the emergence of movements in the Belgian Congo and the Portuguese colonies. The way was paved for the creation of a rash of new, independent African countries in the "freedom year" of 1960 when seventeen nations were born.

And also in 1960 yet another turning point in the African struggle occurred with the Sharpeville Massacre in South Africa: 69 nonviolent protesters were killed and 180 wounded by police fire as they demonstrated against the hated pass laws. The ANC and the Pan-Africanist Congress, the two chief nationalist organizations, were banned, their leadership arrested or driven underground or into exile. In response, the black struggle, which had been basically nonviolent up to this point, added sabotage and occasional violence to its arsenal of tactics. The campaign against white minority control settled in for a protracted conflict. Some easy victories had been won by the early 1960s, but the struggles in Angola, Mozambique, Guinea-Bissau, Zimbabwe, and Namibia turned into guerrilla warfare. Africa was aflame, especially southern Africa. The Organization of African Unity (OAU) was established in 1963 in Addis Ababa to add some cohesiveness to the victories of the decades of struggle against colonialism.

These dramatic developments in Africa not only changed the realities there, but altered the perception of Africa throughout the world, especially for Afro-Americans. In quite a new way, blacks in the United States were able to identify with Africa.

During the same era a political protest movement rose to unprecedented heights in the United States. The Supreme Court decision of 1954 outlawed segregation, the Montgomery bus boycott ushered in a new stage in the civil rights struggle, and federal troops were sent to Little Rock when violence erupted with the desegregation of public schools. Then, the student sit-ins of 1960–61 signaled a broader demand for equality. The NAACP, the Urban League, CORE, SNCC, and the SCLC rose to prominence. The March on Washington in 1963 gave expression to a new unity in the struggle for change. Black anger mounted in the face of the murders of Emmett Till and Charles Mack Parker and violence against the Freedom Riders; dogs and fire hoses were used on demonstrators as Martin Luther King, Jr., and others were marched to jail; black-owned motels and the houses of civil rights leaders in the South were fire-bombed. Riots took place from 1964 to 1966 in major cities around the country as the black community expressed its frustration—in Harlem, Chicago, Philadelphia, Watts, Omaha, Atlanta, and Dayton.

The heightened struggles in both the United States and Africa fostered a new mutual respect for one another by blacks on both continents. During the 1950s many Africans tended to idealize the anticolonial tradition in the United States. The legacy of the Declaration of Independence and the United States Constitution with its Bill of Rights seemed to bolster an image of America among Africans aspiring for freedom that contrasted with their experience of subjugation under colonial regimes. One measure of this was the quickened desire of many African students to attend American colleges. Both Nkrumah of Ghana and Azikiwe of Nigeria, popular heroes of young nationalists in Africa, had studied in the United States at Lincoln University, a predominantly black college. During the twelve-year tenure of Horace Mann Bond as president of the school (1945–57), more than one thousand African students applied annually for admission. Nkrumah was given an honorary degree at Lincoln in 1951 after he had reached national leadership in the Gold Coast, six years before Ghana's independence.

When Tom Mboya, the young labor leader of Kenya, traveled and spoke widely on a trip to the United States during the spring of 1959, one of his objectives was to obtain scholarships to American colleges for students from Kenya. He succeeded. After a four-week speaking tour on campuses all across the country, more than forty scholarships were promised. Out of this grew an unprecedented airlift of East African students to the United States, involving over 300 students in two years.

African students or leaders who lived or traveled in the United States were aware of racial discrimination here. Joshua Nkomo, one of the renowned leaders in the struggle for freedom in Southern Rhodesia (now Zimbabwe) was refused a haircut in a shop only a block from the United Nations in 1959. He later commented in a public speech that this was a "pin prick." Although he felt his experience of discrimination was slight compared to the injustices in Southern Rhodesia, where at that time it was a crime for an African to be in a town without a pass allowing him to be there, he nevertheless gained a new sense of comradeship with those resisting racism in the United States.

The liberation struggle in Africa and the civil rights struggle in the United States each strengthened the other. The Liberian ambassador wrote to Martin Luther King, Jr., after reading about the Montgomery boycott in King's *Stride toward Freedom* and described the nonviolent campaign "as a symbol of greater hope to those of our race who are still struggling for freedom and justice."[19] In their book *Black Power,* Stokely Carmichael and Charles Hamilton wrote, in the same vein, that the struggle in the United States must be seen as "closely related to liberation struggles around the world. We must hook up with these struggles. We must, for example, ask ourselves: When black people in Africa begin to storm Johannesburg, what will be the role of this nation —and of black people here?"[20]

American civil rights leaders began to discover Africa in a new sense. James Farmer, a founder of CORE in the early 1940s and its director during the height of the civil rights movement in the 1960s, described his first trip to Africa as an almost religious experience. He was asked to bring back a bottle of Nile water for one of his associates and an envelope full of Tanzanian soil for another. Speaking at a meeting in West Africa he commented rather plaintively that he had no idea where in Africa his ancestors might have originated. A man from the Ivory Coast spoke to him afterwards and said, "I know where you come from. I know people who look just like you. You are one of my people."[21]

The Mozambican poet Noémia de Sousa wrote a poem during the years of conflict with Portugal attesting to the inspiration of the American struggle to Africans:

> *A warm Mozambican night*
> *and the distant tones of marimba reach me*
> *firm, constant—*
> *coming, I don't know from where.*
> *In my house of wood and zinc*
> *I turn on the radio and let myself drift, lulled . . .*
> *But voices from America stir my soul and nerves,*
> *and Robeson and Marian sing for me*
> *Negro spirituals from Harlem.*
> *"Let my people go"—*
> *Oh let my people go*
> *let my people go—*
> *they say.*
> *I open my eyes and can no longer sleep.*
> *Anderson and Paul sound within me*
> *and they are not the soft voices of a lullaby:*
> *Let my people go.*[22]

BLACK CONSCIOUSNESS AND BLACK POWER

Just as the "wind of change" on the world scene had the effect of quickening the struggle for freedom and equality, especially in South

Africa and in the United States, so did conditions of frustration and resistance to change give rise to a black consciousness on both sides of the Atlantic. The Black Consciousness Movement in South Africa arose in the late 1960s when continued oppression of the African people combined with the outlawing of opposition organizations to create a political vacuum into which stepped new leaders and new tendencies. The Black Consciousness Movement was not a single organization, but rather a whole new realization, especially among younger Africans, that their political salvation lay in their own hands. The leader most closely identified with the rise of black consciousness was a remarkable young man by the name of Steven Biko. He headed the first organization fully embracing this philosophy, the South African Students' Organization (SASO). Later the Black People's Convention (BPC), embracing the same philosophy, was formed.

At first the South African government tolerated the SASO and the BPC as supportive of the separatist doctrine of apartheid, but as the action program of the new organizations identified them as black nationalist in orientation and sympathetic to the liberation struggle in Africa, the government arrested their leadership and banned their activities. In a notorious and tragic case, Biko was killed by beatings and torture while in prison in 1977. The principal leaders were either jailed or escaped into exile.

The counterpart of black consciousness in South Africa was "Black Power" in the United States. The slogan had its beginnings in June 1966 on a march in Mississippi following the shooting of James Meredith on his solitary protest march. SNCC, SCLC, and CORE resolved to continue Meredith's march. At a mass meeting held near Greenwood, Mississippi, Stokely Carmichael proclaimed, in an impassioned speech, "What we need is Black Power!"[23]

King was among those who criticized the black power slogan. He did not use it himself; he felt that it did not come from a sense of strength and would vanish as "Negroes are effectively organized and supported by self-confidence."[24] King saw black power as a call for separatism that he felt was totally unrealistic in the American setting.

Nevertheless the cry of black power in the United States brought a strong sense of identification with Africa. Dashikis, Afro haircuts, and beads and bracelets with an African motif became popular. Just as in South Africa, a new self-awareness arose among many American blacks.

Malcolm X

No one was more important in paving the way toward a new mood among many American blacks than Malcolm X. He aroused an Afro-

American concern with Africa and a new sense of nationalism in the black community that helped inspire an identification with the struggle for freedom in Africa.

Malcolm X rose to prominence through his activities in the Nation of Islam. His brilliance as a street corner speaker in New York's black community, and the publicity he earned as he attracted media attention, gave his message a wide currency. His racial bitterness expressed the frustration of large numbers of American blacks. His leadership of a mosque in New York and the national attention he attracted were major factors in creating the phenomenal growth of the Nation of Islam throughout the country. Tens of thousands joined the Black Muslim ranks by the late 1950s. This growth was enhanced by the colonial revolution at the same time and with it the promise that white supremacy was being eclipsed on a worldwide scale.

Malcolm took three trips to Africa, the first in 1959 and two others in 1964 after he had parted company with Elijah Muhammad and the Nation of Islam. As long as he remained in the Nation of Islam, he accepted the separatist philosophy of Elijah Muhammad, which was grounded in the position that whites and blacks could not live together. His trips to Africa in 1964 broadened his outlook, however. First, he radically changed his views of whites. James Farmer, CORE's director at this time, recorded that Malcolm had been deeply challenged by discussion with the Algerian ambassador whom he met in Ghana. The ambassador had said to Malcolm, "I'm your Muslim brother, but I am not black. I am Caucasian." Second, Malcolm made a connection between the anticolonial upsurge in Africa and the movement against discrimination in the United States. After he returned from his first 1964 trip to Africa, he set up the Organization of Afro-American Unity (OAAU), patterned after the Organization of African Unity, with headquarters in Addis Ababa. He said "the best and most numerous allies of American Negroes . . . were to be found abroad." [25]

The "Basic Unity Program" of the OAAU set forth the absolute necessity for "the Afro-American to restore communication with Africa." This ambitious objective included all people of African descent in the Western Hemisphere "as well as our brothers and sisters on the African continent. . . . Our cultural revolution must be the means of bringing us close to our African brothers and sisters." [26]

In spite of Malcolm's changed outlook, the OAAU membership was not to be opened to whites. "Whites can help us but they can't join us. There can be no black-white unity until there is first some black unity." [27] Malcolm was very much in transition at the time he was killed. He never had the opportunity to bring his program to life, but he had an important effect on the thinking and therefore on the actions of a generation of young Afro-Americans.

King and Africa

Martin Luther King, Jr., responded with excitement to the changes taking place in Africa growing out of the liberation struggle. In a speech he made to a student gathering in May 1962, he spoke of the liberation struggle in Africa as "the greatest single international influence on American Negro students." He remarked that he had frequently heard American black students say that if their African brothers could break the bonds of colonialism, then "the American Negro can break Jim Crow." He proclaimed that "consciously or unconsciously [the American Negro] has been caught up by this [mood of the times] with his black brothers in Africa and his brown and yellow brothers in Asia, South America and the Caribbean [and] is moving with a greater sense of urgency toward the promised land of racial justice."[28]

King's words as well as his deeds testified to the importance he attached to events in Africa. Perhaps he spelled out his approach to Africa most fully in a speech he made in New York in 1965 on Human Rights Day (December 10). The address was delivered before a large audience in the Hunter College auditorium and was one of the few that he devoted entirely to the urgent struggle for freedom in Africa.[29] "The struggle for freedom forms one long front crossing oceans and mountains," King said. "The brotherhood of man is not confined within a narrow, limited circle of select people. It is felt everywhere in the world." In this speech King struck three of his recurring themes on Africa. First, he believed there was a special relationship between the black American and Africa. "Africa is the land of his origin," he said. "The American Negro's ancestors were not only driven into slavery, but their links with their past were severed. . . . Negroes were dispersed over thousands of miles and over many continents, yet today they have found each other again." Second, Africa's liberation struggle, he felt, was an inspiration to those who engaged in the movement for civil rights and equality in the United States. His own words were, "The civil rights movement in the United States has derived immense inspiration from the successful struggles of those Africans who have attained freedom in their own nations." Third, he was deeply convinced that the struggle for freedom was not limited by the boundaries of nations. It was universal. In a 1965 interview King said, "injustice anywhere is injustice everywhere, for we are tied together in a garment of mutuality. What happens in Johannesburg affects Birmingham, however indirectly. Our heritage is Africa. We should never seek to break the ties, nor should the Africans."[30]

Whatever King did or said on African issues was an implementation of one of these basic themes. He felt deeply that the struggle in this country was part of a worldwide struggle, and this awareness made more urgent the success of effort in the United States.[31] Sometimes, in his frustration, King felt the efforts in the American civil rights struggle were lagging behind, and he commented that "the nations of Asia and Africa are moving with jet-like speed toward gaining political independence, but we still creep at horse and buggy pace toward gaining a cup of coffee at a lunch counter."[32]

King's belief in the oneness of the civil rights and the African liberation struggles was brought out clearly in correspondence with Tom Mboya of Kenya. "I am absolutely convinced," he wrote, "that there is no basic difference between colonialism and segregation. They are both based on a contempt for life, and a tragic doctrine of white supremacy. So our struggles are not only similar; they are in a real sense one."[33] Reiterating the same sentiments some time later, King said, "Colonialism and segregation are nearly synonymous, they are legitimate first cousins because their common end is economic exploitation, political domination, and the debasing of human personality." In an article in the *New York Amsterdam News* King wrote about a conversation he had had with Premier Ahmed Ben Bella of Algeria. He was impressed with Ben Bella's detailed knowledge about the civil rights struggle, and wrote that Ben Bella saw "the battle of the Algerians against colonialism and the battle of the Negro against segregation [as] a common struggle."[34]

Martin Luther King, Jr., was not essentially a Pan-Africanist, although his and Du Bois's positions had a great deal in common. Neither was a separatist; both rejected "back to Africa" as a panacea. Both believed their main work was in the United States. King was an integrationist, but only in terms of achieving a just and equal society in this country. Both believed in internationalizing the struggle against colonialism, inequality, and racism. Although there is no basic contradiction between Du Bois's Pan-Africanism and King's belief in the universality of the struggle for racial justice, there is a different psychological emphasis; the understanding of self is different. Pan-Africanism universalizes the concept of one's Africanness. King's starting point was not his African roots, however, but the conviction that the struggle was universal. In terms of anticolonial programs, the two approaches are almost indistinguishable. King reiterated his position in a letter to the African freedom fighters in Rhodesia, "Although we are separated by many miles, we are closer together in a mutual struggle for freedom and human brotherhood . . . we are as concerned about problems of Africa as we are about problems of the United States."[35] This was indicative of his position.

King was mindful, however, of his historic and racial ties to Africa. He expressed himself at times in a way that was reminiscent of Du Bois:

> The Negro is the child of two cultures—Africa and America . . . all too many Negroes seek to embrace only one side of their natures. Some, seeking to reject their heritage, are ashamed of black art and music, and determine what is beautiful and good by standards of white society. They end up frustrated and without cultural roots. Others seek to reject everything American and to identify totally with Africa, even to the point of wearing African clothes. This approach leads also to frustration because the American Negro is not an African. The old Hegelian synthesis offers the best answer to many of life's dilemmas. The American Negro is neither totally African nor totally western. He is Afro-American, a true hybrid, a combination of two cultures.[36]

Although not a specialist on African affairs, King kept a careful eye on events in Africa. At the time of the Nobel Peace Prize ceremony the crisis at Stanleyville in the Congo was at its height. Belgian paratroopers had been dropped on the city where European hostages were in the custody of rebel troops. The emergency was in the headlines and was a matter of first importance in Washington; American planes had been used to transport the Belgian paratroops. When King was asked if he had tried to dissuade the United States government from taking part in the operation, he replied, "No, I haven't gone that far." His position was not as precise as it later became during the Vietnam war. He simply remarked, "The Congo civil war will not be resolved until all foreign elements are withdrawn. The Congo is reaping the violent harvest of injustice, neglect, and man's inhumanity to man across the years."[37]

Despite the recognized urgency of the African liberation struggle, it was difficult for American civil rights organizations and leaders to give this conflict the attention it deserved. They had their hands full with the momentous events occurring as racial segregation and discrimination were being effectively challenged with unprecedented vigor at home. Only as events in Africa reached a crisis proportion were the mainline civil rights organizations able to give more than perfunctory attention to what was happening overseas. A case in point was the NAACP, the oldest and best established American civil rights organization. It had the legacy of the Pan-Africanism of W. E. B. Du Bois, yet African issues remained on the back burner. This writer, as executive director of the

American Committee on Africa, both privately and in correspondence with Roy Wilkins, executive secretary of the NAACP, discussed the possibility of upgrading the African emphasis within the organization when consciousness of Africa was heightened following the independence of Ghana. But while the NAACP cosponsored—with ACOA and the Urban League—a dinner at New York's Waldorf Astoria for Kwame Nkrumah on his first visit to the city as prime minister of independent Ghana, the Association approached more demanding programs with caution. For example, a proposal to join in sponsoring an Africa Freedom Day in April 1959 was laid aside for further discussion.

In an indicative response from the organization, John Morsell, the executive assistant to Roy Wilkins, wrote in January 1959 of an NAACP board discussion on making African affairs a major emphasis: "The matter was referred to a special committee," he recalled. "Ralph Bunche contributed most constructively to the discussion of the Board, pointing out, among other things, that the Africans tended justifiably to regard themselves as reasonably capable of managing their advance toward freedom without outside advice. My reasonably firm guess is that this [that is, an African affairs program] is not too likely an acquisition for the NAACP in the near future."[38] The NAACP has been involved in numerous events related to Africa over the years, but inevitably at a low key.

Martin Luther King, Jr., could be a little more free-wheeling in dealing with African issues than the NAACP, and yet he could give only limited time and attention to the anticolonial and antiapartheid struggles in Africa. He went to Africa only twice, first to Ghana and then briefly to Nigeria, when Nnamdi Azikiwe was made governor-general in 1960. He was invited to attend Ghana's independence celebration in March 1957 at the personal invitation of the prime minister, Nkrumah. Other notable black Americans were also there, including Ralph Bunche (then UN undersecretary), A. Philip Randolph, Mrs. Louis Armstrong, Congressman Adam Clayton Powell, Mordecai Johnson (the president of Howard University), and Lester Granger (the head of the Urban League). King described this as one of the most vivid experiences of his life. Accompanied by his wife, he was honored by being invited to join Nkrumah for lunch at Christianborg Castle, the government house. Later he wrote to thank Nkrumah for his hospitality and a "most rewarding experience at your independence celebration. . . . These things will remain in my thoughts so long as the cords of memory shall lengthen."[39]

That King was impressed by what he saw and felt in Ghana is indicated in notes for a speech in which he alluded to the experience.[40] He proclaimed that "Ghana's diplomats and emissaries will . . . inspire the respect of the world for the culture and traditions of the Negro of Africa." He referred to the "intense democracy of the African Negro deriving from his tribal life." He was impressed in Ghana by the dignity of the position of women and said in these notes that "many nations of advanced scientific technique . . . have much to learn from Ghana's social fabric." Perhaps more than anything else, King was impressed by the fact that Ghana's struggle for independence was characterized mostly by nonviolent methods. He felt that the "aftermath of friendliness and community well-being toward the English and a sense of good will and not bitterness" was testimony to this.[41]

American Negro Leadership Conference on Africa (ANLCA)

The leaders of the principal civil rights organizations made one notable effort in the 1960s to join forces in order to influence American policy on African affairs, and King wholeheartedly supported the effort. In 1962 the American Negro Leadership Conference on Africa (ANLCA) was formed. It was a prestigious body whose primary organizing vehicle was a series of national conferences. The "Call Committee" served as its executive body and was composed of the leaders of the principal civil rights organizations—Martin Luther King, Jr., A. Philip Randolph, Whitney Young, Roy Wilkins, James Farmer, and Dorothy Height of the National Council of Negro Women. Three major conferences were held—in 1962, 1964, and 1967. By the time of the third conference there were twenty-eight sponsoring groups, including many with white as well as black membership, notably several large labor unions such as the United Auto Workers and the Steelworkers. However, the ANLCA had an impact primarily because it represented the main line leadership of the civil rights movement.

The "Big Six," as the Call Committee was dubbed, set a precedent following the first national conference by meeting for more than an hour at the White House with President John F. Kennedy on American policy toward Africa. The agenda recommended for action by the ANLCA included an ambitious Marshall Plan for Africa, beefed-up support for the anticolonial struggle, an increase of black personnel in higher echelons of the State Department and the diplomatic corps, and a closer working relationship with the American mission to the United Nations. The meeting with Kennedy was followed by an extended session with Adlai Stevenson, the American ambassador to the United Nations.

The conference took on limited projects, such as sponsoring James Farmer's speaking tour in Africa. It lobbied to increase foreign aid to Africa. It probably overreached its capabilities when it tried to play a conciliatory role in the Nigerian civil war. Theodore Brown, the executive secretary of the ANLCA, made three trips to Nigeria, but could not find a time when American civil rights leaders were free of their own organizational responsibilities at home to travel together to West Africa.

The conference was probably most successful when it could connect the American civil rights movement to the protest against apartheid in South Africa. Opportunities for this occurred in 1965 and in 1967 over the issue of the potential treatment of black personnel when American naval vessels were due to land at Cape Town. The aircraft carrier *Independence* bypassed that port when, partly as a result of ANLCA pressure, the American public became concerned about the reception black American sailors would receive in the land of apartheid. Similar concerns arose two years later when the carrier *Franklin D. Roosevelt* was scheduled to refuel and to allow its crew of thirty-five hundred—four hundred of whom were black—liberty in Cape Town. This and other incidents led to a government decision to cancel operational calls in South Africa.

ANLCA pressure helped raise the status of blacks in the foreign service. Black ambassadors were appointed to African posts—Franklin Williams to Ghana, Mercer Cook to Niger, Elliot Skinner to Upper Volta (now Burkina Fasso), and Clyde Ferguson to Uganda. ANLCA pressure led directly to the inclusion of a black American (Maurice Dawkins) in the official American delegation to the first anniversary of Algeria's independence in 1963.

Gradually, the ANLCA lost momentum. Its strength was also its problem. It could function in the name of the leaders of the civil rights movement, but it was not able to establish its own base in the black community. Its leaders were primarily concerned for their own organizations and programs. African issues were appealing and important, but also secondary. Fund-raising was critical, and the ANLCA never could find a financial base apart from its constituent groups.

AFRICAN AND AMERICAN STRUGGLES DIFFER

In spite of the fact that the liberation struggle in Africa and the civil rights struggle in the United States were mutually inspiring and supporting, they differed. One was organized to resist domination by a foreign occupying power; the objective was revolution. The other aimed at protesting inequalities and racial injustices within the system; its purpose was reformation. The struggles were more similar for a time in southern Africa, especially in South Africa where resident whites exercised power over blacks in all phases of social, economic, and political life. But even here there was a quantitative difference that became qualitative as well, for blacks in South Africa outnumbered whites more than five to one, with the ratio changing in favor of the blacks every year. The movements on the two continents were influenced by the same forces of history, but the differences led to significant variations in tactics and meant that although the two struggles were conscious of one another, they could not effectively embark on coordinated, joint tactics in a fundamental way. They could maintain at best a fraternal relationship and could influence each other only at a distance.

Some of the tactical measures shared by the movements in both South Africa and the United States were impressive. Martin Luther King, Jr., became a national figure by virtue of his leadership of the nonviolent Montgomery bus boycott in 1955, but such actions were not unique to the United States. Similar bus boycotts had been initiated in the South African township of Alexandra, bordering Johannesburg, twelve years earlier, and were repeated at least three times by 1957. The people who traveled by bus en masse from Alexandra to various places in Johannesburg inaugurated the boycott to protest an increase in bus fares. The confrontation with state power was over the cost of travel, not with seating arrangements on already completely segregated buses; the boycotters won. In Northern Rhodesia, later to become independent Zambia, the nationalist movement organized a boycott of butcher shops in the early 1950s because they discriminated against Africans. Kenneth Kaunda, a leader of the movement (and now president of Zambia) abandoned eating meat and remains a vegetarian to this day. The Defiance Campaign of the ANC was a nonviolent civil disobedience effort that protested the pass laws imposed by the government on Africans; its tactics, which included going into areas prohibited to blacks or openly using facilities reserved for whites, were quite reminiscent of those used by SCLC, CORE, and SNCC.

With the inauguration of sabotage and armed struggle in the early 1960s in the multiracial countries located primarily in southern Africa— Angola, Mozambique, Guinea-Bissau, Zimbabwe, and Namibia—the tactics of the struggles on two continents an ocean apart diverged. While the struggle in the United States was characterized primarily by legalistic and nonviolent methods, violence escalated in southern Africa and in Guinea-Bissau in West Africa. As many as 150,000 Portuguese troops were deployed in Angola, Mozambique, and Guinea-Bissau to try to withstand the guerrilla onslaughts of the liberation movements. Portugal fought a losing war as the movements in her colonies grew in strength and gained international support. Hundreds of thousands of youthful Portuguese went across the European borders to France and Spain to avoid being conscripted to fight in the unpopular African wars. And finally a military coup in Portugal in April 1974 drew this lamentable period to an end, and the former colonies became independent. In the struggle for an independent Zimbabwe an estimated 25,000 died before the conflict ended. On the southern tip of the continent the apartheid regime hung on to its power through draconian tactics, both in South Africa and Namibia, despite the expansion of sabotage, strikes, boycotts, and the escalation of international support for change.

King and South Africa

King gave most attention to the fight against apartheid in South Africa. It was natural for him to do this because the resistance to racism in South Africa most nearly paralleled the experience of combatting segregation in the United States. He was greatly influenced by Mohandas K. Gandhi, renowned primarily for his leadership in the struggle for India's independence. But Gandhi's early experiments with *satyagraha* were in South Africa where he spent over twenty years of his life as a barrister. There Gandhi led his first nonviolent campaigns against the racial restrictions imposed on the Indian minority, long before the Afrikaners came to power with their apartheid policy, and there he first clashed with state power. Gandhi had prepared for his leadership in the nationalist campaign in India through his years of work in South Africa. King traveled to India in 1959 to learn more about Gandhi, the Indian experience, and nonviolence. He spoke of Gandhi with admiration and veneration on his return to Atlanta. "[Gandhi] was able to mobilize and galvanize more people in his lifetime than any other person in the history of this world," King said. "He was able to break the backbone of the British empire. . . . More than 390,000,000 people achieved their freedom and they achieved it nonviolently."[42]

The tradition of Gandhism in South Africa, and the fact that during the 1950s nonviolence was the chosen method of resisting apartheid, made the South African struggle ideologically appealing to King. The fact that American economic relations in trade and investment with South Africa were on the rise gave further impetus to his decision to pay special attention to that country. King enthusiastically backed efforts to gain international support for the antiapartheid cause. In 1957 he was one of the internationally known sponsors of the Declaration of Conscience (serving as vice chairman), which was an appeal for a worldwide protest against South African racism centered on Human Rights Day in that year. "We call upon all men and women to mobilize the moral forces of mankind on this Day of Protest to demonstrate to the Government of the Union of South Africa that free men abhor its policies and will not tolerate the continued suppression of human freedom."[43] More than a hundred prominent men and women around the world supported the call, under the chairmanship of Mrs. Eleanor Roosevelt and sponsored by such persons as Pablo Casals, Alan Paton, Julius Nyerere, Trygve Lie, Toyohiko Kagawa, Martin Niemoeller, and Arnold Toynbee.

In 1962 King joined with Chief Albert J. Luthuli, the president of the ANC, in cochairing an "Appeal for Action against Apartheid." By the time this appeal was launched through the American Committee on Africa, the treason trial had ended in South Africa with the acquittal of all of the 156 originally charged, the Sharpeville Massacre had taken place, the ANC had been declared an illegal organization and its leadership jailed or in exile, and Chief Luthuli had been placed under ban. Over 150 leaders from all parts of the world endorsed the call for action. The central recommendations were for boycotting South African goods and supporting sanctions against South Africa through the United Nations. Specifically, Americans cooperating with the appeal were asked to provide no more dollars to support apartheid, to call on banks to end loans to South Africa, and to demand that business interests support United Nations boycotts and sanctions.[44]

Martin Luther King, Jr., and Albert J. Luthuli were natural allies. Each reached prominence through struggles for racial justice in his own country. Each was primarily motivated by a religious interpretation of history. Each strongly believed in nonviolence. They were both honored with the Nobel Peace Prize, three years apart. They had a mutual respect and admiration for one another, but they never met each other. In 1959 King wrote Luthuli after a friend of his had returned from a visit to South Africa where he talked with the chief: "I have admired you tremendously from a distance. I only regret that circumstances and special divisions have made it impossible for us to meet. But I admire your great witness and your dedication to the cause of freedom and human dignity. You have stood amid persecution, abuse, and oppression with a dignity and calmness of spirit seldom paralleled in human history."[45]

In 1964 a Baptist ministerial colleague of Dr. King wrote him after seeing Luthuli in South Africa and reported, "He is one of the few great men I have met. He is brilliant, of course, but very plain in many ways. His sense of humor is a delight. . . . I asked Chief Luthuli what he would want Americans to know. He said give my highest regards to Martin Luther King. It is not often that we see a clergyman taking a stand on social issues. It means a lot to us here—Martin Luther King is my hero."[46] King responded, "I cannot begin to say to you how delighted I am to hear from Chief Luthuli. I consider him one of the truly great men of our age. So you can see how flattered I am to receive his generous words concerning my work."[47] En route to Oslo for the Nobel Prize, King stopped in London and spoke at a large meeting about his "powerful sense of identification with those in the struggle for freedom in South Africa." In again expressing his admiration for Luthuli he remarked how the chief's nonviolence was met by increasing violence from the state, culminating in the shootings at Sharpeville. "Even in Mississippi we can organize to register Negro voters, we can speak to the press, we can in short organize the people in nonviolent action," he said. "Even the mildest resistance meets with imprisonment in South Africa. We can understand how in that situation people felt so desperate that they turned to other methods, such as sabotage." In his Nobel acceptance speech, King again referred to Luthuli. "So you honor the dedicated pilots of our struggle. . . . You honor once again Chief Albert Luthuli of Africa who struggles with and for his people."[48]

Both King and Luthuli strongly advocated concerted economic action by the international community against South Africa. In 1961 Luthuli said, "I hope the big nations of the world in the interest of world peace will be persuaded to apply economic sanctions on South Africa." King endorsed this tactic many times and especially vigorously in his Human Rights Day speech at Hunter College in 1965. "The international potential of nonviolence has never been employed," he said. He pointed out that the method had been used within the borders of India, the United States, and regions in Africa. "The time has come to utilize nonviolence fully through a massive international boycott which would involve the USSR, Great Britain, France, the United States, Germany, and Japan. Millions of people can personally give expression to their abhorrence of the world's worst racism through such a far-flung boycott."[49]

King would like to have visited South Africa. He received two invitations to lecture there in 1966; one was from a well-established liberal and nonracial student organization, the National Union of South African Students (NUSAS); the second was from the University of Cape Town to give the Beattie Lectures, an annual event of importance. King accepted both invitations, for the events were to come within a few days of one another. He had been told by the inviters that getting a visa from the South African government might be the problem. He wrote to the South African consulate in New Orleans on February 9, 1966, saying that "my visit would be purely as a lecturer." Five weeks later came the response. "I have to inform you with regret that after due consideration your application has not been approved."[50] No one was surprised by the rejection.

The invitations to King received prominent attention in the South African press. Letters from readers poured in to the editors, most of them against the idea of his coming to the country. A typical one read, "It is hoped Dr. King will not be allowed to come to South Africa to stir up trouble and to instruct African extremists (mostly Communists) in the art of freedom marches, organized demonstrations, and sitdown strikes. This is not the way to help Africans or to minimize the evils of racism." Another said, "What is undeniable is that all the groups with which Dr. King is associated, including his civil rights and SCL Movement, have become thoroughly riddled by members of the American Communist Party, one of the most vicious of them all."[51]

A NEW BLACK ACTIVISM

The accelerated liberation struggle in Africa, the intensity of the civil rights campaign in the United States, the new mood of black consciousness—all had the effect of radicalizing black actions in relation to Africa.

The young leaders of SNCC saw the relevance of Africa's liberation struggle to the civil rights movement. James Forman, Stokely Carmichael, Julian Bond, and John Lewis were among those attracted to Africa's challenge. Thirteen SNCC leaders traveled to Africa in 1964 at the invitation of President Sékou Touré of the Republic of Guinea to feel the exhilaration of changing Africa.

As the sense of black power took hold, it even affected the actions of Afro-American scholars. At the annual meeting of the African Studies Association (ASA) held in Montreal in late 1969, a stormy confrontation occurred when black scholars, chafing under a perceived white domination of the organization, revolted. Thirty of the fifty-five seminars were canceled as blacks either refused to participate or disrupted the sessions, and black scholars formed their own organization, the African Heritage Studies Association (AHSA). The pressure of this move was felt by ASA, which instituted reforms, including the decision to have its board composed equally of blacks and whites.

New organizations emerged on the American scene as black awareness of Africa grew and the demand for action quickened. These contrasted with more elite bodies such as the American Negro Leadership Conference on Africa, or the older American Society of African Culture (AMSAC).[52]

Among the most significant new groups was the Africa Liberation Support Committee (ALSC), which grew out of a Pan-African Solidarity Week (May 19–25, 1970) culminating in a Solidarity Day when thousands marched from Harlem to the United Nations for a rally at Dag Hammarskjold Plaza. It was a measure of Malcolm X's influence on the activist leaders of this movement that the week of activity began on Malcolm's birthday. Two years later, on May 27, 1972, a massive black-sponsored African Liberation Day gathering in Washington, D.C., with 50,000 participants, demanded the repeal of the Byrd amendment in Congress—which had lifted United Nations sanctions against the illegal white minority regime in Rhodesia—and support for the liberation struggle in southern Africa. Funds for the African struggle were raised, and a delegation was assigned to deliver the money to African leaders personally. But the ALSC foundered over unresolved internal conflict, primarily between nationalist and Marxist ideological approaches.

Other projects and organizations appeared that were initiated by Afro-Americans. Black lawyer Robert Van Lierop, at one time on the NAACP legal staff, worked with Mozambique's liberation movement, FRELIMO, to make two films on the struggle against Portuguese colonialism, which were widely distributed in the United States. Amiri Baraka founded the Congress of African People, which added a Marxist point of view to its nationalist ideology. A sixth Pan-African Congress, with more than a thousand delegates from all over the world, including strong Afro-American participation, convened in Tanzania in June 1974. The Patrice Lumumba Coalition, based on a Pan-African and nationalist ideology, was formed on November 11, 1975, timed to coincide with Angola's independence under an MPLA government.

In the United States the number of black congressmen grew, with new legislative initiatives as a consequence. The Congressional Black Caucus was formed in 1969 as an informal body consisting of the six black members of the House of Representatives. Charles Diggs, the senior black congressman and chairman of the House Subcommittee on Africa, was also the first chairman of the caucus. A year later the number of black members of the House had doubled, and in 1971 the caucus was formally established with an office in Washington and a full-time executive. African issues were prominent on the caucus agenda. In 1972 it sponsored an African-American National Conference on Africa, giving voice to Afro-American support for the anticolonial, anti-imperialist cause. When the Carter administration came into office in January 1977, Andrew Young was appointed ambassador to the United Nations, with paramount responsibility for African policy. His years as a close associate of Martin Luther King, Jr., and as a member of the Congressional Black Caucus helped prepare him for this assignment.

Campaigns with broad support from the black community had increased in number and intensity over the years. One involved the protest over South Africa Airways flights between the United States and South Africa. The first flight in 1969 was preceded by a well-publicized advertising campaign. Full page advertisements bore headlines saying, "SAA invites 139 distinguished Americans to be among the first to fly the last ocean." An answering ad was created and signed by 139 distinguished black Americans. "We know the welcome of SAA is not meant for us. The tourism which you promote is racist. Racism is not welcome here." Among the signers were: Ralph Abernathy, Muhammed Ali, Arthur Ashe, Harry Belafonte, Count Basie, A. Philip Randolph, Julian Bond, and, from the Congressional Black Caucus, Charles Diggs, Adam Clayton Powell, John Conyers, Shirley Chisholm, and William Clay. A bill was introduced into Congress to stop SAA flights from landing and hearings were held in the House Subcommittee on Africa, headed by Charles Diggs. The *Washington Star* noted the wide support in the black community "from the moderate NAACP to the militant SNCC."[53] A "Black Tourist Guide to South Africa" was issued by the American Committee on Africa detailing the many ways a black visitor would encounter apartheid in South Africa. Feelings were aroused, but SAA flights were not stopped. The campaign served, however, to acquaint a growing segment of the American populace with the nature of apartheid in South Africa.

Another campaign involved South Africa's participation in the Olympics. That nation had been excluded from the 1964 Tokyo Olympics because of its racial practices in sports that violated Olympic principles. The campaign for this exclusion was initiated in South Africa by a nonracial sports body and by a newly formed South Africa Non-Racial Olympic Committee (SANROC). But there was a move in the International Olympic Committee (IOC) to reinstate South Africa for the Mexico City Olympics in 1968 because of some minor reforms instituted by the South African government.[54] The Supreme Council for Sport in Africa, representing the independent African states in international sports, threatened a boycott of the Games.

In the United States Jackie Robinson, the renowned athlete who broke the color bar in professional baseball, took the lead. At a press conference held in the office of ACOA on February 8, 1968, he called for the continued suspension of South Africa because of its violation of Olympic rules. With the IOC still undecided on South Africa's participation in Mexico City, the call for a boycott gathered momentum. Robinson issued a plea for American support of a boycott if South Africa was allowed to participate. An impressive number of top black athletes signed a statement backing a boycott, including Arthur Ashe, Wilt Chamberlain, Lee Evans, John Carlos, Calvin Hill, Oscar Robertson, Maury Wills, and scores of others. Similar efforts were carried on in Britain, in Africa, and in Europe. With a very real threat of a massive boycott, the IOC reestablished the suspension of South Africa.

A third campaign backed economic disengagement from South Africa. This was a major theme for Martin Luther King, Jr., as well as for other black leaders. Perhaps one of the most important efforts endorsing this approach focused on loans to South Africa from American banks. The first targets were Chase Manhattan and Citibank (then the First

National City Bank of New York), the two largest New York banks, both of which had branches in South Africa. A. Philip Randolph, a veteran labor and civil rights leader with great national prestige, gave spirited support to the effort by chairing a newly organized Committee of Conscience against Apartheid, with over 120 prominent sponsors, including labor, church, and entertainment notables, as well as a dozen members of Congress. This Committee of Conscience called on its supporters to withdraw their bank accounts from the offending banks by Human Rights Day in 1966. The initial phase of the campaign ended with a large demonstration on Friday, December 9, the day before the deadline, at Citibank headquarters in the Wall Street area, where Randolph made an impassioned appeal to end American economic support of South Africa. Some 22 million dollars were withdrawn, almost equal to the size of the loans of the two banks to South Africa.

The public debate on corporate investment in South Africa and its role in strengthening apartheid, or its potential as a force for change, became increasingly urgent. The issue was highlighted by the case of the Polaroid Corporation. In late 1970 a group of black workers at Polaroid's headquarters in Cambridge, Mass., protested the company's involvement in South Africa. The main protest centered on the fact that Polaroid materials were used in preparing the pass books Africans were required to carry. The workers called for a boycott of Polaroid products, and representatives of the black workers appeared at hearings at the United Nations. Enough controversy was aroused for Polaroid directors to initiate a campaign to justify their position of remaining in South Africa. Through full-page ads in seven leading daily newspapers and twenty-eight black weeklies Polaroid announced a "Polaroid experiment." They would stay in South Africa to work for change and would assure that Polaroid equipment was not used for the pass system. They would train African employees for leadership, earmark profits for black education, raise black wages, and in other ways encourage reform.

The black workers disagreed with this "enlightened" position, and those who opposed attempts to implement change in South Africa through investment continued their boycott. The experiment ended rather abruptly in 1977 when incontrovertible evidence came to light that South Africa was indeed by subterfuge using Polaroid materials for African passes. Polaroid, true to its promise, thereupon closed its operation in South Africa. On November 22, 1977, the *Boston Globe* gave front-page headlines to the story, "Polaroid Halts Its South African Shipments."

In the late 1970s a black lobby organization was established in Washington called TransAfrica. It combined the best features of its black-oriented predecessors, such as the American Negro Leadership

Conference on Africa and the American Society of African Culture, but had an independent base. Its close working relationship with the Congressional Black Caucus gave it additional strength.

TransAfrica achieved prominence when it fathered the South Africa Freedom Movement in support of the mass resistance to apartheid in South Africa in late 1983. Thousands of Americans, black and white, were arrested in protest gatherings at the South African Embassy in Washington, D.C., and at South African consulates in various cities around the United States.

THE KING LEGACY

Who knows what role Martin Luther King, Jr., might have played, not only in the continuing struggle for racial justice in the United States, but in relation to American policy on the escalating crisis in South Africa —had he lived. That he would have been deeply involved is indisputable. His close coworkers have been drawn into the controversy. Jesse Jackson, Andrew Young, Coretta Scott King, Harry Belafonte, and many others who were inspired by him are actively involved in supporting the antiapartheid struggle in South Africa.

A whole new generation that did not know King is influenced by him and takes action in his name. Every spring a series of antiapartheid projects are initiated, especially on college campuses, in answer to the call for "Days of Action against Apartheid." The period of this annual event stretches from the anniversary of the Sharpeville Massacre on March 21 to the date of King's assassination on April 4.

The headline in a *New York Times* story on the culmination of the "Days of Action" for 1985 gives an indication of the King legacy: "Dr. King Honored by Wide Protests." The article summarized events of the day: 4,000 arrested outside the South African Embassy in Washington, D.C.; at Columbia University in New York "protesters . . . wrapped a silver-link chain around the handles of the main door of Hamilton Hall and 250 students massed at the steps of the building, [proclaiming they] would not leave until Columbia's board of trustees issued a statement that it would divest itself of $33 million of holdings in companies that do business in South Africa"; at a rally of 4,000 at Harvard University, Jesse Jackson spoke against investment in South Africa; and at the University of California in Berkeley, Rosa Parks, whose refusal to move to the back of the bus sparked the Montgomery boycott thirty years earlier, was the featured speaker.[55] The legacy of Martin Luther King, Jr., is still very much alive today in support of racial justice both here and in South Africa.

James H. Cone

Martin Luther King, Jr., and the Third World

MY EXISTENTIAL AND RE-search interest in Martin Luther King, Jr., cannot be separated from my vocation in the Christian ministry and participation in the civil rights movement. I was born in Arkansas and received my college education at Shorter and Philander Smith colleges, located respectively in the twin cities of North Little Rock and Little Rock. My theological education was taken at Garrett-Evangelical Theological Seminary in Evanston, Illinois, and I received the M.A. and Ph.D. degrees in religion (systematic theology) at Northwestern University (1963 and 1965). Like many others, I was challenged by Martin King's work as a civil rights activist and his commitment as a Christian minister, relating the Gospel of Jesus to the black struggle for justice in the United States.

My teaching career began as an assistant professor of religion at Philander Smith College, and I later accepted a similar position at Adrian College in Adrian, Michigan. I began my teaching at Union Theological Seminary (New York City) in 1969 and now serve as the Charles A. Briggs Distinguished Professor of Systematic Theology. My theological research has been in the area of black liberation theology, seeking to analyze the meaning of religion in the black struggle for justice. This concern naturally led me to a study of Martin King because of his outstanding contribution in this area. My publications include eight books, among which are: *Black Theology and Black Power* (1969); *A Black Theology of Liberation* (1970); *God of the Oppressed* (1975); and *Speaking the Truth* (1986). I am currently writing a book titled, *Martin and Malcolm on America: A Dream or a Nightmare?*

At the time Martin Luther King, Jr., achieved international fame as the leader of the Montgomery bus boycott in 1955–56, no African country below the Sahara had achieved political independence from the colonial regimes of Europe. When he was assassinated twelve years later in 1968, the great majority of African countries had gained their independence. Since 1968 black Africans have continued their "stride toward freedom," overcoming the political domination of Europeans in every country except South Africa. Today black South Africans and their supporters, under the leadership of Archbishop Desmond Tutu, Alan Boesak, Nelson and Winnie Mandela, and a host of others in the African National Congress and similar organizations are currently engaged in a protracted life-and-death struggle against apartheid.

Similar struggles for freedom have occurred in Asia and Latin America. The struggles of the poor in all societies remind us that the fires of freedom are burning, and nothing short of justice for all will bring about peace and tranquility in the world.

As we reflect upon the significance of the life and thought of Martin Luther King, Jr., for the people of America, it is important to remember that the meaning of his life is not bound by race, creed, or nationality. Speaking of the international significance of his son, Daddy King was correct when he said: "He did not belong to us, he belonged to the world."[1] I would add that Martin Luther King, Jr., belonged particularly to the Third World, the world of the poor and the disinherited. It is therefore important for us to ask about his significance for the peoples of Africa, Asia, and Latin America and about their significance for him. What impact did the liberation movements in the Third World, particularly in Africa, have upon the actions and ideas of Martin Luther King, Jr.? What influence did his life and thought have upon Third World people struggling for freedom?

To answer the first question, I will examine King's writings, published and unpublished, and his actions regarding liberation movements in Africa, Asia, and Latin America. As to the second, I will use personal interviews with leaders and workers from the grassroots, mostly members of the Ecumenical Association of Third World Theologians (EATWOT), in which they give their impressions of his influence in their communities.[2] My assessment will also include interviews with Third World university and seminary students. Lastly, my interpretation will consider comments about King in the writings and speeches of Third World people, especially theologians, political leaders, and other informed persons. With this, I hope to provide a meaningful interpretation of the image of King that is emerging in the Third World.[3]

THE IMPACT OF THE THIRD WORLD ON MARTIN LUTHER KING, JR.

Martin King's thinking on the Third World and other questions can be divided into two periods.[4] The first begins with the Montgomery bus boycott in December 1955 and ends with the enactment of the Voting Rights Bill in August 1965. The second begins in the fall of 1965 as King began to analyze more deeply the interrelationship of racism, poverty, and militarism in the policies of the United States government. In both periods his ideas were defined by his faith in the God of justice, love, and hope. The difference between the two periods was his shift of emphasis as he sought to develop a nonviolent philosophy of social change that would eliminate racial and economic exploitation and establish peace in America and the world.

During the first period, King's thinking was defined by an optimistic belief that justice could be achieved through *love,* which he identified with nonviolence. The Third World liberation movements reinforced his liberal optimism about the certainty of the rise of a new world order of freedom and equality. In the early months of the Montgomery bus boycott, Martin King began to interpret the black struggle for justice in America as "a part of [an] overall movement in the world in which oppressed people are revolting against . . . imperialism and colonialism."[5] He believed that the black people's will to fight against segregation in America was identical with the spirit that led Africans, Asians, and Latin Americans to revolt against their European colonizers. Both revolts—that of the blacks in America and of the poor in the Third World—signified to King "the birth of a new age." Using that phrase for the title of an address to the Alpha Phi Alpha fraternity in August 1956, he said: "Third World people have lived for years and centuries under the yoke of foreign power, and they were dominated politically, exploited economically, segregated, and humiliated."[6] Because King saw little difference between colonialism in Africa and segregation in America, he employed the same language to describe both experiences. Speaking of the impatience of black and Third World peoples with continuing oppression, he said:

> There comes a time when people grow tired, when the throbbing desires of freedom begin to break forth. There comes a time when people get tired of being trampled over by the iron feet of the tramper. There comes a time when people get tired of being plunged across the abyss of exploitation, where they have experienced the bleakness and madness of despair. There comes a time when people get tired of being pushed out

of the glittering sunlight of life's July and left standing
in the pitying state of an Alpine November.[7]

With this and many statements like it, King emphasized that black
and Third World people had become fed up with segregation and colonialism. "In the midst of their tiredness," something happened to them.
They began to reevaluate themselves and, as a result, they "decided to
rise up in protest against injustice."[8] The protests of the oppressed
throughout the world, King believed, were a signal that "the time for
freedom has come."[9] No resistance from the oppressors could abort
freedom's birth because, as King often said, quoting Victor Hugo,
"there is no greater power on earth than an idea whose time has
come."[10]

Martin King's travel to the independence celebration of Ghana in
1957, the rapid achievement of independence by other Third World
nations, and his study-tour of India in 1959 increased his optimism that
freedom would soon be achieved.[11] Analyzing the motivations of students in the sit-in movements, King saw them as reflecting his own
views. He wrote: "Many of the students, when pressed to express their
inner feelings, identify themselves with students in Africa, Asia, and
South America. The liberation struggle in Africa has been the greatest
single international influence on American Negro students. Frequently
I hear them say that if their African brothers [and sisters] can break the
bonds of colonialism, surely the American Negro can break Jim
Crow."[12]

King's optimism regarding the prospect of such an achievement derived partly from the success of the civil rights movement in America
and liberation movements in the Third World. The Montgomery bus
boycott, sit-ins and freedom rides, Birmingham, the March on Washington, the Selma March, and other less publicized civil rights victories
throughout the South—all were linked with the success of anticolonialist movements in the Third World. King believed that freedom's time
had come because oppressed peoples all over the world were demonstrating that they would no longer passively accept their exclusion from
the material riches of God's creation.

In Martin King's view, segregation in America and colonialism in
the Third World were a denial of the dignity and worth of human
beings. Both the segregator and the colonialist were asserting by their
actions that blacks and other colored peoples were inferior beings, incapable of governing themselves or of living in a relationship of equality
with white Americans and Europeans. Without strong resistance from
black and Third World peoples, the old order of segregation and colonialism would remain unchanged. The new age of freedom could only

break forth when a "New Negro" was born in America and a "New Human Being" could rise up from among the ragged and hungry masses of the world. Armed with a new sense of dignity and self-respect, these new people would march together toward the promised land of freedom.

Martin King's optimism about the new world order was articulated with passion and excitement in his early speeches. "Those of us who live in the Twentieth Century are privileged to live in one of the most momentous periods of human history. It is an exciting age filled with hope. It is an age in which a new social order is being born. We stand today between two worlds—the dying old and the emerging new."[13] King was aware that not everyone shared his euphoria about the coming of this new age, especially the guardians of the vanishing old order. "I am aware of the fact that there are those who would argue that we live in the most ghastly period of human history. They would argue that . . . the deep rumblings of the discontent from Asia, the uprisings in Africa . . . and the racial tensions of America are all indicative of the deep and tragic midnight which encompasses our civilization. They would argue that we are retrogressing instead of progressing."[14]

To answer the critics of Third World liberation and civil rights movements, King employed the liberal theological perspective dominant in the social gospel movement in the late nineteenth and early twentieth centuries.

> Far from representing retrogression or tragic meaning-lessness, the present tension represents the necessary pains that accompany the birth of anything new. Long ago the Greek philosopher Heraclitus argued that justice emerges from the strife of opposites, and Hegel, in modern philosophy, preached a doctrine of growth through struggle. It is historically and biologically true that there can be no birth and growth without birth and growing pains. Whenever there is the emergence of the new we confront the recalcitrance of the old. So the tensions which we witness in the world today are indicative of the fact that a new world order is being born and an old order is passing away.[15]

Naturally Martin King was aware that oppressors do not voluntarily grant freedom to the oppressed. He was also aware that white segregationists and European colonists had much more military power than their victims. Yet he contended that the coming of a new world order of freedom was inevitable. How could he be so sure? The answer is found in his faith in the biblical God of justice, love, and hope. No idea or strategy that King advocated can be accurately understood apart from his deep faith in the Christian God as defined by the black Baptist and liberal Protestant traditions. The new age was coming and could not be stopped, because God, who is just and loving, wills that the oppressed be liberated. That was why King could say:

> Oppressed people cannot remain oppressed forever. The urge for freedom will eventually come. This is what happened to the American Negro. Something within has reminded him of his birthright of freedom; something without has reminded him that he can gain it. Consciously and unconsciously, he has been swept in by what the Germans call the *Zeitgeist,* and with his black brothers of Africa, and his brown and yellow brothers of Asia, South America, and the Caribbean, he is moving with a sense of cosmic urgency toward the promised land of racial justice.[16]

The German word *Zeitgeist* was often employed by King to refer to his belief that "the universe is under the control of a loving purpose, and that in the struggle for righteousness [we have] cosmic companionship."[17] This is what he had in mind when he said that Rosa Parks "had been tracked down by the *Zeitgeist*—the spirit of the times."[18] He made a similar statement about himself when he offered his resignation to Dexter Avenue Baptist Church in Montgomery: "I can't stop now. History has thrust something upon me which I cannot turn away."[19] King was referring to a historical movement of freedom that was rooted in ultimate reality, and thus was not exclusively dependent on human decisions.

The role of God in King's concept of the coming new age is also reflected in his use of the striking image of the "dream." Although he often spoke of the "American dream," referring to the idea of equality in the Declaration of Independence, the Constitution, and the Judeo-Christian scriptures, King's dream was not limited to racial equality in the United States but was defined chiefly by its universality and eternality. To say that the dream is universal means that it is for all—blacks and whites, men and women, the peoples of Africa, Asia, and Latin America, as well as the United States and Europe. To say that it is eternal means that equality is not a right conferred by the state; it is derived from God, the creator of all life.[20]

When Martin King urged people to "make the dream a reality" or to "face the challenge of a new age," he almost always told them to "develop a world perspective." "All life is inter-related" because God is the creator of all. "No individual . . . [or] nation can live alone" because we are made for each other. No people can be who they ought to be until others are who they ought to be. "This is the way the world is made."[21]

When Martin King received the Nobel Peace Prize in 1964 it deepened his commitment to global justice and peace and reinforced his belief that God willed it. "I have the audacity to believe," he said in his acceptance speech, "that people everywhere can have three meals a day for their bodies, education and culture for their minds, and dignity, equality, and freedom for their spirits."[22] For King, the Nobel Prize was an "unutterable fulfillment," given in recognition of those fighting for freedom all over the world.[23] His dream of a coming new age of freedom was eloquently expressed in his Nobel lecture.

> What we are seeing now is a freedom explosion. . . .
> The deep rumbling of discontent that we hear today is
> the thunder of disinherited masses, rising from dun-
> geons of oppression to the bright hills of freedom. . . .
> All over the world, like a fever, the freedom movement
> is spreading in the widest liberation in history. The
> great masses of people are determined to end the ex-
> ploitation of their races and land. They are awake and
> moving toward their goal like a tidal wave. You can
> hear them rumbling in every village street, on the
> docks, in the houses, among the students, in the
> churches and at political meetings.[24]

Because God is involved in the freedom struggles, King believed that they could not be halted. Victory was inevitable. Success in the civil rights and Third World liberation movements, combined with his deep faith in God's loving justice, gave King an optimistic hope that freedom was not too far away.

Many persons have misunderstood Martin King's commitment to nonviolence because they have separated it from his faith in God. It is true that he encouraged persons who lacked his faith to endorse nonvio-lence for the practical reason that neither black nor Third World people had the military technology to wage a violent fight for freedom. But King's *own* commitment to nonviolence was derived from his faith in a loving and just God who created us for each other and for eternity. He did not believe that one could participate with God in the creation of the beloved community and at the same time use violent methods. Violence is derived from hate, and hate contradicts God. People who use violence have lost faith in the God of love and thus have lost hope that a beloved community can be created.

Nothing is more central to King's philosophy than the idea that oppressed people must use moral means to achieve just ends. Whether he spoke of the civil rights struggle in the United States or of Third World liberation struggles, he was certain that nonviolence was the "only road to freedom."[25] He was pleased that Ghana and other African nations had achieved their independence with little or no violence. Gandhi's success in India had an even greater impact upon King. "I left India," he said, "more convinced than ever before that nonviolent resistance is the most potent weapon available to oppressed people in their struggle for freedom."[26]

But much more important than the success of nonviolence in India or Ghana or even the civil rights movement was Martin King's faith in a God of justice and love. King's faith and theology enabled him absolutely to reject violence while granting him the conviction that a new order of justice was coming into being. His affirmation of nonviolence was derived from his deep conviction that there is a personal, creative, divine power at work in the world establishing freedom in and through the nonviolent actions of the weak and helpless.

Turning to the second period of King's thought, 1965–68, I want to emphasize that certain of his bedrock ideas did *not* change. He did not change his mind regarding the basic principles of his faith or the goal of freedom in the civil rights movement. In fact, his convictions regarding God's will to inaugurate a new age of freedom were deepened in the last years as he gave himself totally to the world struggles for justice and peace. His faith in nonviolence remained completely unshakable. What, then, was new or newly emphasized in the later period?

First, there was his great disappointment over the failure of the majority of white moderates in the North and South, in government, labor, church, business, and even the civil rights movement, to support the goal of genuine equality for blacks and other poor people. For several years he thought that he could win the support of the decent, "white majority" in America through a moral appeal to religion and the democratic traditions by which they claimed to live. But as early as his *Playboy* interview in January 1965 he acknowledged his great letdown regarding government officials and white moderates:

> I have been dismayed at the degree to which abysmal ignorance seems to prevail among many state, city and even Federal officials on the whole question of racial justice and injustice. . . . But this white failure to comprehend the depth and dimension of the Negro problem is far from being peculiar to Government officials. . . . It seems to be a malady even among those whites who like to regard themselves as "enlightened." . . . I won-

der at [persons] who dare to feel that they have some paternalistic right to set the timetable for another [person's] liberation. Over the past several years, I must say, I have been gravely disappointed with such white "moderates." I am inclined to think that they are more of a stumbling block to the Negro's progress than the White Citizen's Counciler or the Ku Klux Klanner.[27]

When summer riots became a regular occurrence during the second half of the 1960s, King became impatient with whites who withdrew their support of the civil rights movement and began to say that "law and order" ought to be the highest priority of government. "I say to you," proclaimed King, "the riots are caused by nice, gentle, timid white moderates who are more concerned about order than justice."[28]

Martin King's disappointment with moderate whites reached a peak during his preparations for the Poor People's campaign, only a few weeks before his death. According to King, racism was a disease, a cancer in the body politic, but many whites seemed unconcerned about it as he developed his analysis of the "sickness of America."[29] White indifference to racism puzzled him. "The thing wrong with America is white racism. White folks are not right. Now they've been making a lot of studies about the Negro, about the ghetto, about slums. It's time for America to have an intensified study on what's wrong with white folks. . . . Anybody that will go around bombing houses and churches, it's something wrong with him."[30]

Another disappointment for Martin King was his failure to convert the majority of blacks to nonviolent direct action as the primary method for gaining their freedom. The Watts riot in August 1965 and the others that followed in other urban centers, along with "Black Power," revealed the great gap between his optimism about nonviolence and the despair evidenced in the random acts of violence in the ghettos of American cities.

During the period from 1955 to 1965, Martin King and others in the southern-based civil rights movement had assumed that the blacks of the North would benefit in a derivative fashion from the victories gained in the South.[31] The Watts riots and the subsequent rise of Black Power during the Meredith March in June 1966 showed that King badly miscalculated the self-esteem that northern blacks would receive from the rights gained in the South. When he went to Watts he was surprised that many blacks there had never heard of him and even more astonished when he heard a group of young blacks boasting, "We won." "How can you say you won," King asked, "when thirty-four Negroes are dead, your community is destroyed, and whites are using the riots as an excuse for inaction?" "We won because we made them pay attention to us," they answered.[32] When King thought about that response and the hostile reactions his message of nonviolence received from Chicago street gangs and young Black Power advocates during the Meredith March, he began to realize that the Civil Rights Act (1964) and the Voting Rights Bill (1965) did not significantly affect the problems of racism and poverty, especially among northern blacks.

To Martin King's further dismay, some black preachers and theologians began openly to support the rise of Black Power by interpreting the Christian gospel in its light.[33] No longer willing to endorse King's absolute commitment to nonviolence, they began to move toward the black nationalism of Malcolm X and even to talk about the revolutionary writings of Frantz Fanon, especially *The Wretched of the Earth,* in an affirmative manner.

Martin King experienced a third disappointment. He expected the success of American blacks with nonviolence to help persuade the majority of the oppressed of Africa, Asia, and Latin America to adopt a similar method in their struggles for freedom. But instead of adopting the creative method of nonviolence, many Third World people were openly advocating armed revolution. King was aware that even some theologians in Latin America were joining revolutionary groups in their efforts to overthrow oppressive governments.

All of this caused him to reevaluate in a global manner, *not* the efficacy of nonviolence, but the degree of the problem of injustice. When King began to analyze global injustice in depth, he concluded that the three evils of racism, poverty, and militarism were interrelated and deeply rooted, both in the sociopolitical life of America and in the international economic order. His focus on the global implications of racism in relation to poverty and war led him to the conclusion that the slums in American cities are a "system of internal colonialism" not unlike the exploitation in the Third World by European nations.[34] "I am appalled that some people feel that the civil rights struggle is over because we have a 1964 civil rights bill with ten titles and a voting rights bill. Over and over again people ask, What else do you want? They feel that everything is all right. Well, let them look around at our big cities."[35] King's global vision enabled him to see that the sociopolitical freedom of blacks was closely tied to the liberation of their sisters and brothers in Africa, Asia, and Latin America. Token integration (that is, a few professionals moving into the existing mainstream of American society) could not be considered true freedom. "Let us not think of our movement," King wrote in *Where Do We Go from Here?,* "as one that seeks to integrate the Negro into all the existing values of American society."[36]

The economic exploitation of the Third World nations and the deepening poverty of the poor in the United States led King to the conclusion that there was something desperately wrong with America. "Why are there forty million poor people in a nation overflowing with such unbelievable affluence? Why has our nation placed itself in the position of being God's military agent on earth, and intervened recklessly in Vietnam and the Dominican Republic? Why have we substituted the arrogant undertaking of policing the whole world for the high task of putting our own house in order?"[37] These questions led him to call "for a radical restructuring of the architecture of American society" so that it could serve the needs of humanity throughout the world.[38] That was why he said: "However deeply American Negroes are caught in the struggle to be at last at home in our homeland of the United States, we cannot ignore the larger world house in which we are also dwellers. Equality with whites will not solve the problems of either whites or Negroes if it means equality in a world society stricken by poverty and in a universe doomed to extinction by war."[39]

The later years of Martin King's theology were also defined by a shift in emphasis and meaning for the themes of love, justice, and hope. Except for his great Holt Street address on December 5, 1955, with its powerful focus on justice, the first period of King's spiritual and intellectual development was centered on love, with justice and hope flowing from love.[40] But as a result of his later, more somber reflections, *hope* became the center of Martin King's thinking, with love and justice interpreted in its light. There was a difference between his early and later years regarding the idea of hope. In the early period, it was similar to a naive optimism, because it was based in part on the progress of the freedom movements in America and the Third World and the support this received from both the oppressed (by their active commitment to nonviolence) and the majority in the dominant classes (by their apparent commitment to formal equality). In contrast, his hope in later years was not founded on the backing he received from blacks and whites in the United States or from the international community. Rather, it arose almost exclusively from his faith in the God of the biblical and black traditions, who told him during the early months of the Montgomery bus boycott: "Stand up for righteousness. Stand up for justice. Stand up for truth. And lo, I will be with you, even until the end of the world."[41]

Instead of trusting human allies to produce a victory over the forces of organized evil, King's hope was now a transcendent one, focusing on the biblical God of the oppressed who "put down the mighty from their thrones, and exalted those of low degree" (Luke 1:52). This came out in his opposition to the Vietnam War, which he knew would alienate his former allies.

Nothing pained Martin King more than America's military involvement in Vietnam and the criticisms he received from his white and black friends, in government, the media, and the civil rights movement, for opposing it. America's escalation of the war, along with a de-escalation of the war on poverty at home and an indifference toward massive poverty in the Third World, motivated King to become one of the most severe critics of the domestic and foreign policies of his government during the second half of the 1960s. He began to speak like a prophet, standing before the Day of Judgment, proclaiming God's wrath and indignation upon a rich and powerful nation that was blind to justice at home and indifferent to world peace. Instead of talking about the American dream, as he had done so eloquently in the first half of the 1960s, he began to refer, over and over again, to an American nightmare, especially in Vietnam.[42]

Martin King did not enjoy criticizing his government. He loved America deeply, particularly its democratic and religious traditions of equality and justice as articulated in the Declaration of Independence, the Constitution, and the Judeo-Christian Scriptures. But he could not overlook the great contradictions of racism, poverty, and militarism. For King there was no greater inconsistency between creed and deed than America's military adventure in Vietnam. He frequently referred to Vietnam as a small nation that quoted our Declaration of Independence in its own declaration of freedom from the French in 1945. "Yet," he said, "our government refused to recognize them. President Truman said they were not ready for independence. So we fell victim as a nation at that time of the same deadly arrogance that has poisoned the international situation for all these years."[43]

The arrogance that King was referring to was racism. "I don't believe," he wrote in a *Playboy* essay, "we can have world peace until America has an 'integrated' foreign policy. Our disastrous experiments in Vietnam and the Dominican Republic have been . . . a result of racist decision making. Men of the white West . . . have grown up in a racist culture, and their thinking is colored by that fact. . . . They don't respect anyone who is not white."[44] King also felt that the vehement criticisms he received from the white community for his opposition to the Vietnam War were motivated by racism. He spoke against his white allies in government and the media who had supported his stand on nonviolence during the sit-ins and freedom rides and in Birmingham and Selma and then rejected his position on Vietnam.

> They applauded us in the sit-in movement when we nonviolently decided to sit in at lunch counters. They applauded us on the freedom rides when we accepted blows without retaliation. They praised us in . . . Bir-

mingham and Selma, Alabama. Oh, the press was so
noble in its applause and . . . praise when I would say
"Be nonviolent toward Bull Connor," . . . "Be
nonviolent toward Jim Clark." There is something
strangely inconsistent about a nation and a press that
would praise you when you say, "Be nonviolent toward Jim Clark," but will curse you and damn you
when you say, "Be nonviolent toward little brown
Vietnamese children!" [45]

Many blacks in the civil rights movement joined the chorus of criticism against King's views on Vietnam. There were even sharp disagree-
ments about Vietnam within SCLC. King often found himself alone
and isolated. In one of the most agonizing periods of his life, he turned
to the God of the prophets and Jesus as he took his stand for humanity.
"It is just as evil," he proclaimed in a sermon at Ebenezer, "to kill
Vietnamese as it is to kill Americans, because they are all God's children." [46]

Martin King refused to accept the idea that being an American citizen
obligated him to support his country in an unjust war. He refused to
equate "dissent with disloyalty," as many of his critics did. On the
contrary, he contended that he was the true patriot, because in his
opposition to the war he was in reality defending America's tradition of
freedom and democracy. Furthermore, as a Nobel Laureate, King believed that he was obligated to transcend nationalism and thereby take a
stand for world peace. But much more important than his obligation as
a citizen of America or of the world was his vocation as a minister of
God, the creator of the universe. When people queried him about the
wisdom of mixing peace and civil rights, King responded: "Before I
was a civil rights leader, I answered a call, and when God speaks, who
can but prophesy? I answered a call which left the spirit of the Lord
upon me and anointed me to preach the gospel. . . . I decided then that
I was going to tell the truth as God revealed it to me. No matter how
many people disagreed with me, I decided that I was going to tell the
truth." [47]

For Martin King, telling the truth meant proclaiming God's judgment upon America for its failure to use its technological resources for
the good of humanity. "Here we spend thirty-five billion dollars a year
to fight this terrible war in Vietnam and just the other day the Congress
refused to vote forty-four million to get rid of rats in the slums and the
ghettoes of our country." [48] "The judgment of God is on America
now," he said. [49] He compared America to the rich man, Dives, who
passed by the poor man, Lazarus, and never saw him. And, like Dives,

who went to hell because he refused to use his wealth to bridge the gulf that separated him from Lazarus, "America," King said, "is going to hell too, if she fails to bridge the gulf" that separates blacks from whites, the United States and Europe from the Third World.[50]

Because Martin King believed that America's war in Vietnam violated its own democratic values and the moral principles of the universe, he could not keep silent. There comes a time "when silence is betrayal."[51] A nation that spends 500,000 dollars to kill an enemy soldier in Vietnam and only fifty dollars to get one of its citizens out of poverty is a nation that will be destroyed by its own moral contradictions, he said.[52] "If something doesn't happen soon, I'm convinced that the curtain of doom is coming down on the U.S."[53] The more the American government and its citizens tried to ignore King, the more forcefully he proclaimed his message:

> America, I don't plan to let you rest until that day comes into being when all God's children will be respected, and every [person] will respect the dignity and worth of human personality. America, I don't plan to allow you to rest until from every city hall in this country, justice will roll down like waters and righteousness like a mighty stream. America, I don't plan to let you rest until from every state house . . . men will sit humbly before their God. America, I don't plan to let you rest until you live it out that "all . . . are created equal and endowed by their creator with certain inalienable rights." America, I don't plan to let you rest until you believe what you have read in your Bible that out of one blood God made all [people] to dwell upon the face of the earth.[54]

Although King was often depressed about his government's refusal to stop the war in Vietnam and to eliminate poverty at home and in the Third World, he did not lose hope. In "A Christmas Sermon on Peace," he proclaimed that despite the nightmare of racism, poverty, and war, "I still have a dream, because . . . you can't give up on life. If you lose hope, . . . you lose that courage to be, that quality that helps you to go on in spite of all."[55]

It was Martin King's hope that sustained him in the midst of controversy, enabling him to achieve solidarity with the victims of the world, even though he failed to win the justice for which he gave his life. King's hope was grounded in the saving power of the cross of Jesus Christ, and it enabled him to see the certainty of victory in the context of an apparent defeat. "When you stand up for justice, you never fail.

The forces that have the power to make concession to the forces of justice and truth . . . but refuse to do it . . . are the forces that fail. . . . If there is no response from the federal government, from the Congress, that's the failure, not those who are struggling for justice." [56]

KING'S SYMBOLIC INFLUENCE ON THE THIRD WORLD

No black American or American church official, and few Americans of any profession, have made an international impact in the area of justice and peace comparable to that of Martin Luther King, Jr. This is particularly true in Africa, Asia, and Latin America where the vast majority of the people are colored and poor. Martin King's influence may be described as both symbolic and substantive.

His symbolic influence can be seen in four areas: (1) as a symbol of the black struggle for justice in the United States; (2) as a symbol of the Third World peoples' struggles for justice against colonialism and neo-colonialism; (3) as a symbol of the best in the American democratic and Christian traditions; and (4) as a symbol of the struggle for world peace through nonviolence.

The name Martin Luther King, Jr., is widely known in Africa, Asia, and Latin America for its connection with the American civil rights movement of the 1950s and 1960s. He is thought of as the leader of the black people's successful struggle for constitutional rights, emphasizing that Americans of all races must learn to live together in a beloved community, defined by justice and love, or they will perish together.

Martin King's international prominence began with the Montgomery bus boycott. People admired his commitment to justice and his courage to stand up to white bigots of the American South with intelligence, dignity, and Christian love. Many Third World people wrote to King informing him of the inspiration they received from his leadership. "What you are doing," wrote a person from Singapore, "is a real inspiration to us here in the part of the world where the struggle between democracy and communism is raging." [57]

In addition to the Montgomery bus boycott, King is recognized for his success in gaining constitutional rights for blacks and his solidarity with the black poor, even to the point of giving his life. It is also well-known that King has been elevated to the status of a national symbol of America with his birthday honored as a federal holiday.

During the 1950s and 1960s and, to a large degree, throughout much of the 1970s and 1980s, most people in the Third World thought of King almost exclusively as a symbol of the black struggle for equality in the United States. Now that he has been made a national symbol, some leading Third World theologians and scholars say that many in their countries mistakenly conclude that full freedom has been won by black Americans. As evidence of this, they not only point to Martin King's name as a national symbol of the country, they also refer to the electoral success of many of his well-known disciples, like Jesse Jackson and Andrew Young. Other highly visible black personalities in politics, business, the media, movies, sports, and music are often cited to demonstrate that racism is a thing of the past in the United States.

The assumption that Afro-Americans have achieved equality in American society has led to an alienation between Afro-Americans and Third World peoples struggling for freedom. Consequently, when the United States is criticized for its military excesses or for stifling democratic change in the Third World, many do not make distinctions between white and black Americans.

While some Third World peoples see Martin King primarily as a black leader of the civil rights movement, others view him as transcending race, nation, and religion. For them, King is a symbol of poor people on all continents who are fighting racism, poverty, and political oppression. Four things served to make Martin King's name an important symbol of the poor fighting for justice in the Third World: (1) his association with the black freedom songs of the civil rights movement, especially "We Shall Overcome"; (2) his devotion to the life and teachings of Gandhi, a prominent figure in the Third World; (3) his interpretation of the Nobel Peace Prize as identifying him with "two-thirds of the people who go to bed hungry at night";[58] and (4) his passionate opposition to the war in Vietnam, defending the right of self-determination of a small colored nation.

The theme song of the civil rights movement, "We Shall Overcome," is widely used by oppressed groups in Africa, Asia, and Latin America. I have heard it sung in many countries on all continents; in particular I will never forget my first hearing it in South Korea.[59] It was in May 1975, in the context of the infamous "Presidential Emergency Measure No. 9" of the Park regime. I had been invited to lecture on a black theology of liberation. The situation was filled with tension as the Korean CIA agents carefully proctored the occasion. I was fearful that I might say something that would cause some of my Korean friends to be arrested. I spoke about the black struggle for justice in the United States, hoping that my frequent use of the black spirituals of slavery would camouflage (for the KCIA) the political implications of my talk for the current struggle for democracy in Korea. I was greatly moved when the Korean audience responded by enthusiastically singing "We Shall Overcome."

Third World nations have paid tribute to Martin King's memory in many ways. The most popular has been to recognize his birthday with special programs, recalling his words and deeds on behalf of the poor. Governments also frequently recognize him with the issuance of commemorative postage stamps. Still another way is to give his name to streets, libraries, parks, and other public properties.[60]

A special session of the United Nations' Special Committee against Apartheid was held in Atlanta in January 1979 to pay an international tribute to Martin Luther King, Jr. Most of the participants were representatives of nations of Africa, Asia, and Latin America who used the occasion to define King as "one of the most courageous freedom fighters of our times" who "fought for the liberation of the oppressed all over the world."[61]

Because King is viewed as "an inspiring example to the liberation struggle the world over," some Third World people resent the use of his name as a symbol of the nation that they regard as the major enemy of Third World initiatives toward freedom.[62] Tissa Balasuriya, director of the Centre for Society and Religion in Colombo, Sri Lanka, and Asian coordinator of EATWOT, caustically stated: "America kills him, and then makes a hero of him in order to neutralize his true meaning. To attack the leaders for justice during their life-time and then, after killing them, incorporate them into the value system is to perform a contradiction far greater than the ones that King spoke out vehemently against."[63]

As one who appealed to the moral conscience of America, King became known as a person who represented the best in the Christian and democratic traditions of freedom in the United States. With his frequent references to the Declaration of Independence, the Constitution, and the Bible in his sermons and addresses, he presented a compelling perspective on American culture and its people, about which Third World people have rarely been aware.

Third World people mainly are poor and colored, and are followers of faiths other than Christianity. The people of the United States chiefly are affluent and white, and are adherents of the Christian faith. Since King was a Christian black and identified with the poor everywhere, he helped many Third World people to make a distinction between the American government's foreign policy and the desires of its people. This has especially been true for the peoples of Southeast Asia, Southern Africa, and Central America. With the Bible in one hand and the Declaration of Independence in the other, King challenged the American government to use its great technological resources for good and not evil. In the *La Nueva Biblia Latinoamerica* (1972), King's photo is appropriately placed among the prophets of the Old Testament, opposite one of Don Helder Camara, with the comment that he was a pastor and freedom fighter who was assassinated like other prophets.

Nothing established King as a symbol of peace in the Third World more than his devotion to nonviolence and his heroic opposition to the war in Vietnam. He is a dominant personality in many peace organizations in Africa, Asia, and Latin America. In some instances, his image is more widely used among non-Christian groups than among Christians in the Third World. This is especially true in Asia where Gandhi and King often appear together as symbols of achieving peace through nonviolence.

The Christian identity of Martin King has made it possible for a few Christians to work for world peace in societies that are predominately non-Christian and in which Christian churches seem essentially white, Western, and indifferent to peace. It is ironic that King is often not as influential among Christian groups as he is among student, peace, and left-oriented intellectuals interested in developing a methodology of social change.

KING'S SUBSTANTIVE IMPACT ON THE THIRD WORLD

By "substantive impact" is meant those instances in which Third World people have seriously studied King's ideas and actions for the purpose of assessing their usefulness in their own struggles for freedom. His life and writings have been examined primarily in the context of a small number of Third World Christians who are interested in the role of the church in societies defined by poverty, racism, and political oppression. Like King, they have asked: What tactics are ethically appropriate or inappropriate for Christians who are fighting for social justice? In their debate about Martin King, the issue, as most would expect, has focused on his absolute commitment to nonviolence, with some Third World Christians agreeing with King and others seriously questioning the applicability of his perspective for their situation.

It is probably accurate to say that most Third World theologians, who are actively engaged in the struggle against poverty, racism, and political repression, disagree with Martin King's absolute commitment to nonviolence. During the 1950s and early 1960s, Third World activist Christians and theologians shared his optimism about the coming of a new age, a time when colonialism and imperialism would be no more. African and Asian nations were rapidly gaining political independence from their European colonizers, and the United States and Latin American nations were making an "Alliance for Progress." But by the middle of the 1960s it had become clear to many of the Third World analysts that what the United Nations had called the "decade for development" —the 1950s—was in fact a decade of dependence. The economic gap between the rich nations of Europe and North America and the poor nations of Africa, Asia, and Latin America was growing wider instead of narrowing. When Third World activist Christians and theologians began to study history and the social sciences, they discovered that their economic deprivation was a logical development of their dependent relationship with rich nations. Analysis of the political situation of their countries and of the international economic order convinced them that poverty in the Third World is created by unfavorable trade relations between rich and poor nations and unjust economic relations between haves and have-nots within nations. Since oppressors do not give up their privilege through an appeal to morality, it is questionable whether nonviolence is always the most appropriate method for dislodging privileged classes. This perspective on ethics naturally placed these activist Christians in sharp disagreement with King's philosophy of nonviolence.

The first major international discussion about the relevance of King's views on nonviolence for the Third World happened at the World Council of Churches' (WCC) well-known World Conference on Church and Society in Geneva, Switzerland, in July 1966. There were 420 participants from 80 nations and 164 churches, with almost half from Africa, Asia, and Latin America. According to the "Official Report," "the Conference was charged with advising the churches and the WCC on their ministry in a world undergoing revolutionary change." [64] Martin Luther King, Jr., was invited to address the conference but could not attend because of the riots in Chicago. However, he "was seen by millions of viewers on the European television network, and his voice was heard in the service in the Cathedral of St. Pierre in Geneva, since a film of his sermon had been flown to Switzerland." [65] Entitled "A Knock at Midnight," it reflected his mood and that of others at the conference.

> It is . . . midnight in our world, and the darkness is so
> deep that we can hardly see which way to turn. . . . On
> the international horizon nations are engaged in a colos-
> sal and bitter contest for supremacy. Two world wars
> have been fought within a generation, and the clouds of
> another war are dangerously low. . . . In the terrible
> midnight of war, [people] have knocked on the door of
> the Church to ask for the bread of peace, but the Church
> often disappointed them. . . . Those who have gone to
> the Church to seek the bread of economic justice have
> been left in the frustrating midnight of economic depri-
> vation. . . . The Church today is challenged to pro-

claim God's son, Jesus Christ, to be the hope of [people] in all of their complex personal and social problems.[66]

Although many Third World participants were deeply impressed by Martin King's solidarity with the poor and his commitment to establish justice on their behalf, they openly challenged the usefulness of his philosophy of nonviolence in liberating their countries from the "remaining vestiges of old western colonialism, which keeps one people subject to another, and of neocolonialism, which keeps peoples from the right to determine their own political and economic life."[67] In a preparatory essay, entitled "Awakened Peoples, Developing Nations, and the Dynamics of World Politics," M. M. Thomas of India, chairman of the Church and Society Conference, referred to a "kind of conversion from nonviolence to violence [that] is taking place every day" in South Africa, Rhodesia, Angola, and other Portuguese territories of that period.[68] In some situations, Thomas contended, the liberation of the oppressed could only be achieved through violence. Thomas supported his point by quoting from the report of the consultation on race relations in South Africa that was held in Mindolo, Zambia, in 1964 and sponsored by the WCC and the South African Institute of Race Relations. "The urgency of the situation in South Africa is further increased by the conviction of leading Africans that, as all peaceful measures tried by African political organizations over a period of many years to bring about an ordered change have proved abortive, only one avenue remains open—that of violence. . . . For many Christians involved in the struggle for a just solution, the question of possible violence as the only remaining alternative has become an urgent and ever-pressing one."[69]

Much of Thomas's essay analyzed the question of whether King's philosophy of nonviolence was appropriate for the developing societies in Africa and Asia. Many European and white North American participants strongly promoted King's philosophy of nonviolence as the only option for Third World Christians engaged in political activity. Thomas and other Third World Christians agreed that King's nonviolent direct action was most appropriate for a racial minority seeking constitutional rights in a nation founded on democratic values like the United States, but they denied that it would be applicable in all situations, especially in many countries in the Third World. In a sharp critique of liberal humanism, and with King's philosophy in mind, Thomas said: "There still seem to be some theologians who have not learned the necessity of dealing with the relativities of politics and society. There is no evidence that the forces of liberal humanism, Christian humanism, or even nonviolent militancy have fully understood the working of the political, economic and social powers that are seeking to consolidate white extremist elements, especially in Africa. [People] are thus left struggling for their rights, with the path of violence their only choice."[70]

The Geneva Conference represented a major turning point in Protestant thinking on the role of "Christians in the Technical and Social Revolutions of our Time."[71] For the first time, Third World Protestants began to search for a radical commitment to social change in their societies that did not depend upon the approval of the dominant theologians of Europe and North America. A similar turning point occurred in Catholic thinking at Vatican II during the same period. Following Vatican II, the famous Second General Conference of Latin American Bishops was held in Medellín, Colombia, in 1968 and gave support to an emerging Latin American liberation theology.[72] Both Catholic and Protestant Christians of the Third World began to develop a perspective on the church and society that did not exclude violence as a method for achieving justice. While Martin King's life and writings continued to influence their thinking in Christian ethics, they contended that the sociopolitical situation of the Third World required a different option of them than the one chosen by King. C. S. Banana, the president of Zimbabwe and an ordained Methodist minister, made this distinction in a Martin Luther King Lecture at Wesley Theological Seminary in 1981.

> In pursuing our goals we might have differed from him [Martin King] as we had to use tactics adapted to the realities of our country and to the nature of the colonial situation. We fully agreed with him in the goals and motivations. The goals were exactly the same—the freedom and fulfillment of the people. The motivation could only be one: the great love that Jesus showed us when he chose "to lay down his life for his friends" (John 15:13). To a great extent the methods and tactics to follow in any revolutionary process are determined by the historical context. By analysing the circumstances in which the Civil Rights Movement developed and the circumstances which press for armed solutions in the Third World countries, one may be able to prove that there are not "prefabricated" answers which may be applied to any existing situation. Answers have to be found in the process of liberation by the very people involved in it.[73]

Despite the many Third World Christians who reject Martin King's commitment to nonviolence as being inapplicable to their situation,

there are many others who strongly endorse it. The two most prominent Third World representatives of the nonviolent approach to social
change are Allan Boesak and Desmond Tutu of South Africa. Like
King, both view the gospel as a demand for justice and refuse to separate
the salvation of the soul from the health of the body. Like King, Boesak
and Tutu are black leaders in a society sharply defined by white racism.
Both characterize, as King did, the problem of racism as a moral issue.
But unlike King, who could appeal to the moral demands of democracy
and Christianity existing in American history and culture, Boesak and
Tutu are struggling against a South African white government that is
openly defiant of any demand for the sociopolitical equality of blacks
and whites. The idea of a beloved community is anathema to most
whites in the government and the churches.

Although there are differences between Boesak and Tutu of South
Africa and King of America, they are minor when compared with their
similarities. In taking their stand against racism, all three have based
their resistance to it upon moral values derived from the Christian gospel. According to this gospel, all people were created by God for each
other. Therefore any government that gives privileges to a few at the
expense of the necessities of the many must be passionately and
nonviolently resisted.

Allan Boesak, who has devoted a great deal of study to the life and
thought of Martin King, has adopted fully King's views on nonviolence. For Boesak, as it was for King, it is not a matter of what is
practical but rather what is Christian. He contends that the gospel, as
defined by the cross of Jesus Christ, demands a love that is both powerful and nonviolent. Boesak's perspective on nonviolence has evolved
over a period of years, beginning with his studies on King and Malcolm
X in graduate school, continuing with the publication of his first book
on black theology, and now being refined in the struggle against apartheid in South Africa.[74] In his first book, seeking to express insights from
both King and Malcolm X, Boesak reluctantly acknowledged that the
retaliatory violence of the oppressed is sometimes unavoidable.

> Whereas we do not deny that a situation may arise
> where retaliatory violence is forced upon the oppressed
> and no other avenue is left open to them, we do so with
> a clear hesitancy, knowing full well that it will probably
> prove a poor "solution" and that violence can never be
> "justified." Furthermore, the questions of King . . .
> haunt us still. Behind these questions lies the deeply
> disturbing theological question for any Christian,
> namely this: Is it not the essence of discipleship that the

> Christian is required to react on a completely different
> level in order to create and keep open the possibilities
> for reconciliation, redemption, and community?[75]

However, when Allan Boesak discussed the issue of violence and nonviolence in 1985 with a group of theologians from the United States and South Africa, there was no hesitation as he advanced an absolute commitment to nonviolence, explicitly identifying his view with Martin King's perspective.[76]

Unlike Allan Boesak, Desmond Tutu's commitment to nonviolence is not absolute.

> People are making a big mistake. I am not in the same
> league as he [King]. He was quite outstanding, and I am
> not trying to be falsely modest. When you think of him
> as an orator, I don't even get anywhere near that. He
> was more than anything else a pacifist. I am not a paci-
> fist; I am a peace-lover. He believed firmly and abso-
> lutely in non-violence and never going to war. There
> may be situations where war is justifiable, like when
> you are fighting Nazism; that is to say there is such an
> evil existing that you have to use a lesser evil to over-
> throw it.[77]

While Tutu believes that "apartheid is as evil and as vicious as Nazism," he has been careful not to condone violence in South Africa.[78] Rather, he has endorsed a deep commitment to nonviolence with the hope that the white people of South Africa will see the wisdom of his view. But as the white South African government continues to turn a deaf ear to him, Tutu is finding it more difficult to continue to advocate nonviolence. In a *Winnipeg Free Press* interview in 1986 he said that "if sanctions [economic and diplomatic] fail to persuade South Africa to abandon its repressive system of apartheid, 'the church would have no alternative but to say it would be justifiable for Christians to use violence and force to overthrow an unjust regime.' "[79]

Although Desmond Tutu differs slightly from Martin King regarding the nature of his commitment to nonviolence, the spirituality that undergirds his struggle for justice is very similar. Like King, his deep love for his people and country shows in everything he does and says. Like King, he initially expressed much optimism in dismantling apartheid by appealing to the moral conscience of whites in government and the churches. But, like King, he, too, was greatly disappointed with the failure of whites to experience enough moral outrage to cause them to join with blacks in the struggle against apartheid.[80] Tutu became bitterly angry when Western governments, especially those of the United States, Britain, and West Germany, refused to support his nonviolent initiative by instituting tough economic sanctions against South Africa. In response to President Reagan's speech on South Africa, and the support he received from Prime Minister Margaret Thatcher of Great Britain and Chancellor Helmut Kohl of West Germany, Tutu, sounding like King during the Vietnam War and the deepening crisis in America's cities, angrily expressed his frustrations with white Western governments that apparently place little value upon the lives of black people. He referred to the president's speech as "utterly racist and totally disgusting" because it tells black South Africans that "we are completely dispensable and can forget about help from them." "The West," Tutu said, "as far as I am concerned can go to hell."[81]

In the midst of the daily killing of black children, women, and men by the white government, Tutu, again in the spirit of King, refuses to lose hope. Despite the evil that people do, Tutu still believes that God, not white South Africans, is in charge of the world. "As a human being, I just say, 'Look at these guys. Do they have any sense at all?' As a human being, I feel hopeless sometimes. But as a Christian I hold on to the belief that this is God's world and He is in charge. It may not always seem so. One also believes in the resurrection of Our Lord Jesus Christ, and I end up being a prisoner of hope. Sometimes I hold on to that by the skin of my teeth."[82]

INSIGHTS FROM MARTIN KING AND THE THIRD WORLD

There are several insights about humanity that we can derive from the life and thought of Martin King and from the fighters for freedom in the Third World:

"There is nothing in all the world greater than freedom."[83] Martin King gave his life for it. South African blacks, endowed with the same liberating spirit, are facing death daily because they do not believe that whites have the right to determine the conditions and the date of their freedom. Poor people throughout the world are demonstrating with their bodies that one cannot begin to live until one is ready to die for freedom. Freedom is that quality of existence through which a people recognize their dignity and worth by fighting against the sociopolitical conditions that limit their participation in society.

Martin King's foremost contribution as a moral thinker was his penetrating insight into the meaning of justice during his time. No one understood justice with more depth or communicated it with greater clarity in the area of race relations in the United States and the world than Martin Luther King, Jr. Because of King, the world is not only more aware of the problem of racial injustice but equally aware of its interrelatedness with poverty and war. "Injustice anywhere is a threat to justice everywhere."[84]

The "anemic democracy" to which King pointed is still present in America and around the world; the dream is still unfulfilled. Whether we focus on the relations between nations or the relations between persons within nations, the distinction between the few rich and the many poor is still widening. To incorporate the true meaning of Martin King's beliefs into American national policies would mean using our technological resources to bridge the huge economic gap that separates rich and poor nations.

Martin King's greatest contribution was his ability to communicate a vision of hope in extreme situations of oppression. No matter how difficult the struggle for justice became, no matter how powerful were the opponents of justice, no matter how many persons turned against him, King refused absolutely to lose hope, because he believed that ultimately right would triumph over wrong. He spoke of this hope to the masses throughout the world, inspiring them to keep on struggling for freedom and justice even though the odds were against them. "I am not going to stop singing 'We shall overcome,' " he often said,

> because I know that "truth crushed to the earth shall rise again." I am not going to stop singing "We shall overcome," because I know the Bible is right, "you shall reap what you sow." I am not going to stop singing "We shall overcome," because I know that one day the God of the universe will say to those who won't listen to him, "I'm not a playboy. Don't play with me. For I will rise up and break the backbone of your power." I'm not going to stop singing "We shall overcome," because "mine eyes have seen the glory of the coming of the Lord. He's trampling out the vintage where the grapes of wrath are stored. Glory hallelujah, his truth is marching on."[85]

Shun P. Govender

"We Shall Overcome"

WHY DOES ANYONE GET IN-volved in peace work? Why in a country like South Africa? Perhaps the easiest answer is that it is the most obvious thing to do. In truth, I think that there are various reasons that motivate people to get "involved." All of them are personal, some altruistic, many selfish. Mine are existential, religious, and political.

I am personally motivated by the twin factors of fear of violent men and the challenge which the striving for peaceful options presents, precisely because it is such a difficult one. Perhaps that is the spirit of the gambler I inherited from my father. Secondly, from a very early age, my view on life in South Africa has been fundamentally influenced by the fact that I believe in Jesus Christ and have been trained to think theologically. I was born in Germiston, Transvaal, in 1949, received my high school education in Newcastle,

Natal, and then attended the University of Durban-Westville (1967–72), where I was awarded the B.A. and B.D. degrees. For six years I served a congregation in Durban of the Reformed Church in Africa, and I was subsequently (1983–88) general secretary of the Belydende Kring (Confessing Circle) of the Dutch Reformed Churches. I received my Th.D. in 1987 from the University of Kampen in Holland.

From my intitial upbringing in a tradition of piety, I learned to become sensitive to taking people seriously as human persons; from my study and practice of liberation theology I am learning to take the life situation, the context of suffering, in which our people find themselves, absolutely seriously. So I find myself moving between the pole of spirituality, on the one hand, and the pole of a strict analysis of the roots of oppression in South Africa, on the other. Third, out of a faith commitment comes my political commitment to the liberation struggle. Here I work to resist the temptation of stereotyping the "Struggle" and of losing my freedom within it. Like so many others, I, too, am engaged in a daily battle to "find my place" in this national project.

Since delivering my lecture at the United States Capitol Historical Society's symposium on Martin Luther King, Jr., much has happened in South Africa that impels us to a more earnest search for peaceful solutions to the country's problems. In the last few years we have been plunged into greater, not less, violence. The lesson to be learned from all this bloodshed is that violence is not and will not bring about the desired ends, namely, a more humane and just society where the rights of every individual, regardless of race, gender, or social status will be protected.

The catalog of our social sins is well documented. South Africa is into its fourth term of emergency rule. The security establishment has virtually taken over control of the country, operating as it does behind the facade of a multiethnic, tricameral parliamentary democracy. The political rhetoric of "broadening the base of democracy" goes hand-in-hand with the axiomatic belief in "law and order," the former always giving way to the latter whenever there are signs of increased popular unrest.

The politics of reform is in a shambles. Its architects, P. W. Botha and Co., have finally been forced into retirement. The legacy they leave behind is nothing more than a refined form of white minority domination. The vagueness with which the "new deal" was announced and implemented since 1983 when the New Constitution was unleashed upon the nation is now seen to have been a deliberate exercise in the political chicanery typical of the last number of years.

Politics in South Africa revolves around the twin issues of race and money. These are the two requirements, the one an internal and the other a Western necessity, that any white ruler must satisfy if he is to survive. The preservation of the white political future in South Africa is what the new leader of the Nationalist party, Frederik W. de Klerk, has inherited from the Botha era. He can do no other than try to improve on the performance of his predecessors, which so far has been nothing more than inventing a new political language to describe old racial realities. However, the political future belongs to those who can guarantee the survival and expansion of the capitalist enterprise in South and southern Africa. In the end this is what politics in South Africa is and will be all about. The Nationalist party has feverishly generated an image of championing the ideals of the free market system by promoting economic deregulation and privatization of major state-owned interests. The new Democratic party, which enshrines the white liberal tradition in its better guise, is hammering home the message that only a more tolerant and non-racial society can promote economic recovery, reassure foreign capital, bring back the much needed multinationals, and return South Africa to the international forum with her honor restored. Whatever the shape or hue of white politics will be when the time comes to do real negotiating with the acknowledged leadership of the majority, there is no doubt that these two economic and racial policies will determine the agenda and the choice of violent or nonviolent options in the search for solutions.

The myth that South Africa is the only African country with a free press has finally been shattered. The liberal press has been curbed by the state of emergency in what it can report. Foreign journalists who refused to be cowed into submission soon felt the wrath of the ministry of internal affairs, if not its boot. The home-grown type have simply been incarcerated, repeatedly or indefinitely. The state media conducts its regular barrage of manipulated reporting, while the alternative press has been mercilessly hounded and persecuted. A nation that is guilty of killing the reasonable word is on the verge of giving up civilized standards.

Peaceful, nonviolent protest has been proscribed, and the mobilization of mass democratic forces to oppose the government's illegitimate rule by force has been declared illegal. Worker organizations, trade unions, students, com-munity organizations, even the churches and clergy have been subjected to banning orders, water cannons, and *sjambok* whipping by the police and army.

But we have also seen the resistance to apartheid-based rule grow to maturity over the last few years in the face of overwhelming odds. Minimum demands have been put forward to achieve a climate amenable to negotiating a settlement. These demands—which have remained constant—are: an end to the state of emergency, a lifting of the bans on all political organizations, the release of all political detainees, the unimpeded return of exiles, and the establishment of structures for negotiating a settlement with the acknowledged leaders of the people. To date, none have been met. We would be naive to imagine that Mr. de Klerk, as the new state president after the general elections of September 6, 1989, might suddenly give in to any one of them unconditionally. Indeed, it has become abundantly evident that "the liberation" is not just around the corner. Not even the release of Nelson Mandela would herald the end of apartheid rule. Mr. Mandela would have to take up where he left off more than a generation ago.

The fundamental question that every South African faces is whether peace is still a possibility in a society as violently deformed as ours and to which violence is endemic. Are we doomed to the historical inevitability of a future filled with violence and counter-violence? Is what lies just ahead for us so predictable? How can we do all those ordinary things like marry, have children, and work to better our personal and collective lots when we know that we have already been robbed of our future? These are some of the questions that middle-class and professional folk in the country agonize over. In the black townships the reality of violence is confronted from a totally different perspective. There life is nothing other than violence —abnormal human relations, squalid and overcrowded living conditions, perpetual poverty, unemployment, disintegration of educational, welfare, and health facilities, and the absence of any escape from such personal and social entrapment. There is anxiety all around, even in the laughter.

In such a situation, we should not decry the option of violence too quickly. It is a weapon, a powerful weapon for survival. On the one hand, it may preserve an ordered and decent way of life; on the other, it may be the only way out of hell. Besides, we are long past the academic debate on violence or nonviolence. The option for violence has already been taken by both sides. And both sides have developed powerfully plausible arguments to justify their choice.

Yet the challenge for peace in South Africa remains. The fact that people are being killed on both sides of the great divide—directly in combat situations and indirectly as a result of the evil effects of apartheid—limits the weight that can be attached to the moral argument as to who is right and who wrong. Obviously, the present rulers are misguided and morally reprehensible. Obviously, apartheid is justly decried as theological blasphemy, and white Christianity is guilty of a heinous sin in its uncritical support of oppressive social structures. Obviously, given the present set of disastrous political and economic circumstances, the African National Congress constitutes a viable alternative to white Nationalist rule.

Yet winning the moral argument does not in itself produce a mentality of peace. Haranguing the oppressor on every possible occasion may be a politically strategic and necessary move, but it has not led to a change of heart. Producing a Kairos Document to expose the disobedience of Christians in South Africa has done very little to transform the traditional churches into havens of human reconciliation and fountains of peace. A change of government may bring political peace and a cessation of hostilities, even economic recovery, but can it overcome generations of human hostility, suspicion, and alienation? Are we not already witnessing the emergence of a revolutionary elite who, after the waves of popular uprisings have died down, will take over the reins of government? The language would certainly have changed, this time converted into a radical rhetoric, but would the reality and its foundations of violence have changed any?

That is the dilemma of everyone who is consciously engaged in the struggle for a new South Africa and committed to achieving a peaceful end by peaceful means. We understand the logic of violent options only too well. All of our analyses of the root causes of oppression force upon us the conclusion that violence is the only realistic option available if an end is to be made of this miserable domination. Short of armed resistance, political solutions are bound to favor those already in power or to promote an elitist class of new rulers; there is just too much evidence in liberation struggles that points in this direction.

Furthermore, we are faced daily with the debilitating awareness of ourselves as members of a violent way of life. Much to our shame, we contribute to its daily increase. With a superior attitude we claim to be disciples of peace, but time and time again we show how much we lack faith in its efficacy.

But despite all of this cowardice, we cannot let go of an overriding conviction that peace is a possibility available to us South Africans. Precarious as it may be to create, and fragile as it may be to hold onto, peace is within our reach. Despite all the suggestions that we as a people are beyond the pale, we must refuse to let go of the conviction that deep within our national soul lie untapped reservoirs of goodwill and the ability to make a genuine peace with ourselves, our neighbors, our country, our continent, and our God. Be-

fore the violence gets out of hand, and after the violence has erupted, the only option we have is that of peace.

We will have to begin reading our history in a nonviolent manner, searching for and highlighting the traditions of peace, peacemaking, and peaceful ways of existing and coexisting. The stories of persons and communities who patiently suffered adversity and loss will have to be resurrected and become part of the collective memory of the nation.

We will have to develop lifestyles of peace that are not escapist or resignatory in the face of violence, or that consist of comfortable noninterference in the plight of those who suffer in our society. Instead, we will have to develop techniques to root out the inbuilt and ingrained violent tendencies affecting every facet of our lives. Justice is what we want and must work for with heart and soul. But peace is no less a goal to be striven for.

We will have to become peacemakers, both inside this divided country and as a regional power. The international community and our friends who are in solidarity with our liberation struggle can help us up to a point, but we will have to take the baton and finish the race. God forbid that we should be found wanting then. Given our internal demographic structure, our regional geopolitical position, our technological advantage, and our natural resources, we have a perfect recipe to become the most aggressive force to be reckoned with by the rest of southern Africa. That will have to change radically —our liberation movements, the churches, and our leaders have the responsibility to take us beyond the struggle for the possession of political and economic power.

I am delighted to be here with you. This is my first visit to the United States, but I can now go back home and say, "On my first try, I made Capitol Hill. Even though I've never voted in my life." First impressions are usually the most lasting ones, and I shall have the treasured memory that my first physical encounter with the greatness that constitutes America was in the context of peace and of the memory of Dr. Martin Luther King, Jr.

What we are talking about here and what we are calling to mind at this conference, to receive light for our mission in life, actually comes from the underside of American history. It comes from beneath the pillars holding these overwhelming symbolic edifices together. For people like myself, America is its foreign policy. To us from South Africa, America is a reminder that we are not free, that perhaps *because* of America we shall not be free for a long time to come. America is a reminder to us that black life is expendable. From the viewpoint of the mighty of this world, who are determined to preserve the Western world order, black history, black culture, and black humanity will always come after white priorities. But you call us here at this conference to join hands with you in remembering the life and the work and the death of Dr. Martin Luther King, Jr. In this we hear you say to us, "There is another America. There is an America where the people who were yesterday openly oppressed as slaves are still the victims of exploitation today, but where these oppressed of yesterday and today refuse to become the oppressors of tomorrow." This is what we hear you say to us. There are people here whose struggle for peace with justice in America makes them reach out in solidarity to those who suffer in the world from which I come.

So I am here, and I bring you greetings from our charismatic leaders and from our people, and from our movement for peace and justice. And we thank you for telling us, in the life and death of Martin Luther King, Jr., that peace and justice are possible. History is not fate. We shall not be humiliated and suffer forever. Keep the hope alive for we, too, are acting on your behalf.

I remind you of what King called for in 1962 when he called for disengagement from apartheid; this became a law in the United States only in 1986. We waited a full generation for that voice to be heard by the American people. We waited a full generation for them to take the option of nonviolent direct action on our behalf. And now they have. I believe that such a determination could become law the way it did, could stand the test of a presidential veto, only because of the quality of the suffering that has gone into the struggle for peace and justice in America during the civil rights movement.

I would like, with your permission, to reflect on what it means when we, in our context, say "We shall overcome." We are now in the last quarter of the twentieth century, and yet South Africa has not changed. The dream has not yet been realized. We are beyond the first and second world wars, in which blacks fought to preserve the ideals of freedom, and yet darker skinned people—and we in South Africa—are still standing outside of history. The legacies of decolonization and the birth of nation states in the rest of the poorer world have turned into a nightmare of twisted reality for us in South Africa. For us decolonization came to mean the rebellion of white Afrikaner tribes from British hegemony, that those who were oppressed yesterday have become the managers of the capitalist world order today. The birth of the nation state for us in South Africa actually means the constitutional trick of replacing one white minority group with another, with white apartheid republicanism and all its historical and political and economic manipulations. The oppressed black majority has been left out.

I don't wish to bore you, but I must ask the question this afternoon: What is apartheid? The truth about South Africa today emerges when the nature of its historical contradiction becomes apparent. As a nation we are caught in a kind of time warp that goes deeper than the conflict between the first and the third world. We are all of the contradictions contained in the east–west and north–south divides, and yet we are more than these. As a nation, if we are that yet, we have inherited the legacy of everything that is bad or has become bad in this world— racism, economic avarice, cultural arrogance, political selfishness. And we have converted these evils into greater evils. In a bad world, South Africa is worse. Our propensity for evil and for wreaking havoc in the world is just beginning to become clear. But let me go on to say that we have also taken what is considered good and worthy and noble in history, what other nations have fought for and defended jealously— such as democracy, individual and social freedom, freedom of speech and thought, and cultural, ethnic, and racial variety—we have taken these good things and corrupted them to serve the evil ends of the mighty. For behind the glitter of gold and the sparkle of silver, the humanity of our people lies in rot. The stench of visible and subtle oppression seeps through the order and efficiency of a highly industrialized capitalist democracy.

We should realize what an historical monstrosity that thing called apartheid is. It is not just race relations gone sour. It is not just a temporary ailment afflicting the body politic. It is not just some arrogant white racist holding the black majority to ransom. It is not just the legal separation of the races. It is not just the exclusion of poor black people from the benefits of modern society. Apartheid is all of these things and much more. Apartheid is yet another example of the arrogance and destructiveness of Western man. It must be seen in the context of that tradition of willful disobedience that has dogged Western man ever since his historical origins. It is the most modern expression of the barbarity of civilized man and his awesome power to turn light into darkness, truth into an active lie, life into death. Apartheid is the historical expression of the most antihistorical and antihuman primeval impulses of man, which have gained control of the social, political, economic, military, ideological, and religious instruments of power. Apartheid is modern man going on the rampage.

While there is general agreement today about the evil of apartheid, there is radical disagreement about how to eradicate it. Today even the architects and managers of this policy have declared their willingness to change. Mr. Botha and his government now openly commit themselves to a policy of reform. Being antiapartheid has become respectable, even fashionable. Support for the cause of black people is now being declared from the most unexpected sources. Thus the Pretoria regime demands appreciation for removing what it considers discriminatory measures and regulations. Apartheid is now officially dead, they tell us proudly.

It seems that they have convinced Mr. Reagan and Mrs. Thatcher and Mr. Kohl of this. These Western leaders now believe that Pretoria's reform program includes the unbanning of the ANC—the African National Congress—the release of Mr. Nelson Mandela, and the dismantling of the homelands policy. They believe it means the abolition of segregated residential life and unrestricted equal opportunities in all the institutions of civic society. From their point of view, these Western leaders seem to believe that it is just a question of speeding up the process. They believe that the rulers in Pretoria really want to do all these things.

But apartheid cannot be reformed. It cannot be humanized. The policies of persuasion and change from within have failed dismally. This has been proved beyond any shadow of a doubt on two fronts—from the failures both of the white liberal and the black moderate oppositions in South Africa. The white liberal opposition to Afrikan Nationalist rule is in its death throes. It will die as a political force because it is incapable of achieving fundamental political and economic power for the majority. The liberal tradition has been sapped of all its political relevancy because its program of ideological administration over the civic institutions of the nation, such as education, the courts, the democratic process of parliament, and labor relations, has been taken over by the Nationalists. The attitude of tolerance and accommodation, the middle-of-the-road policies that yesterday were the characteristic hallmark of the liberals, have today become the political stance of the once racist Nationalist party.

Paralleling this development has been the co-option and the consequent crippling and silencing of all black moderate opposition. These range from the Hendrikses to the Rajbansis to the Gatsha Buthelezis. The ideology of political compromise has inevitably led to political corruption. These ethnic leaders of minorities have today become more enthusiastic defenders of the status quo than Pretoria itself. The minor concessions so begrudgingly granted us by the Nationalists have not come as a consequence of pressure from the opponents of apartheid. Rather, they are part of the overall strategy of the regime itself.

I must say this to you. It is a painful fact that today blacks in South Africa actively participate in the direct oppression of our people. They sit in government and as junior partners in the exercise of oppressive power. They sanction the presence of police and the army in our townships. They laud the introduction of emergency rule and greater militarization. They condemn the revolt of our pupils against apartheid education. The petit bourgeois elitist rulers that Pretoria created in the homelands some years ago have now become a reality in the metropolitan, urban, and industrialized centers as well. What is happening is that apartheid politics is actually managing to shed its racist appearance, and in that act, to gain a new lease on life. Having adopted a liberal political image to enhance their power and their control, the Afrikaner Nationalists have now adopted some blacks into the system of control and have thereby relinquished their overtly racist image.

I think there are some lessons to learn from this. First, this program of change is part of the strategy for survival by the ruling class in South Africa. Reform in the eyes of Pretoria is the ability to shift the emphasis of control in such a way that the fundamental basis of power is not dislodged. Apartheid cannot be reformed; however, it can and will change its complexion from time to time.

Second, it has become abundantly clear that apartheid is essentially a system of racial capitalism with a distinctly South African form. This system of oppression must be seen in the context of both race and class. From the perspective of the victims, from the arrogant political exhibitionism of those who hold power, and from the ideological perspective of the black consciousness movement, it would appear that the racist attitude of whites toward blacks is the dominant characteristic of the policy. But from the viewpoint of a radical leftist democratic analysis or from the Afrikaner Nationalists' present defense of the capitalist order, it would appear that class oppression is the sole essential conceptual category and that race is a less important consideration. Our analysis, therefore, must include both emphases. Whites and blacks today are joining hands in an unholy political alliance to oppress the majority of poorer blacks.

The third lesson is that the strategies of Western governments, which aim at dismantling apartheid in the hope that the capitalist economic structure will be preserved, are a calculated policy of mischief. Critical questions that need to be put in the context of any international involvement in South Africa, political or economic, are: What do these people want to achieve through their involvement? Do they want to recreate their political and economic image all over again in South Africa in a neocolonial era? Do they really believe that once sufficient numbers of blacks have been technically and academically trained, placed in the role of managing the vacant positions, and ultimately taken over the system, that more justice will result and peace become a reality? Are they sure that capitalist bourgeois democracy in South Africa has the potential to employ the millions of black unemployed, feed, clothe, and house them, educate and keep them healthy, and appreciably enhance their life expectations?

The present crisis of apartheid is actually a crisis of racial capitalism. The adjustments that it has made to date have led to more direct and overt repression. The small benefits that the big business corporations are now making in favor of blacks by way of housing subsidies, scholarships, and nurseries, are beneficial and are welcome, but they are potentially divisive and damaging to the overall cause of emancipation for the majority of our people. What in this respect may appear to be a strategy for nonviolent evolutionary change may actually contain the seeds of violent conflict due to the polarization and the unbridgeable gap created between rich and poor. We in South Africa have to rid ourselves of naïveté in this matter. All international involvement in South Africa has economic, political, military, and ideological strings attached to it. We have to make up our own minds about how to deal with such associations in the light of the ideals, goals, and objectives we set ourselves within our struggle for liberation.

I would like to say something about the people's struggle against apartheid. Allow me to get right to the issue by posing this question: What is it that we blacks want to achieve in and with our struggle? What are we struggling for? Surely it is not enough for us to be haranguing the whites for their racist behavior toward us. However eloquently formulated, isn't this cataloging of the evils of apartheid becoming inadequate? Even if being antiapartheid is fashionable, isn't it time that we began saying what it is that we want? I believe that it is vital for us in the South African struggle to understand the dynamics operating in history. Without insight into what is happening and why it is happening, without a conceptual framework in which the events occurring around us are gathered, analyzed, and given logical coherence, we run the grave risk of letting all strategies for change, even the so-called progressive ones, fall into the quagmire of subjective confusion, emotional shortsightedness, and eventual defeat.

Since we here at this conference are attempting to come to grips with the struggle of the Afro-American for liberation and human dignity in the context of the American dream, and since we blacks in South Africa have been influenced in a special way by things American, starting with Coca-Cola, it can only be helpful for us to gain some understanding of the Afro-American interpretation of history and the Afro-American models of engagement for change. I would like to link what I am saying to the comments of Cornel West and my understanding of the four traditions he mentions in his book *Prophesy Deliverance: An Afro-American Revolutionary Christianity*. He states that there is an Afro-American exceptionalist tradition, an Afro-American assimilationist tradition, a marginalist tradition, and a humanist tradition. West makes the important point that our understanding of Afro-American perspectives on the world should go deeper than mere political categorization. For, quoting Gramsci, he says: "Any political consciousness of an oppressed group is shaped and molded by the group's cultural resources and resiliency as perceived by individuals in it. So the extent to which the resources and resiliency are romanticized, rejected, or accepted will deeply influence the kind of political consciousness that individuals possess."

I must say that it comes as a surprise to me as someone uninitiated and unschooled in the Afro-American struggle to learn from West's analysis that the philosophy of nonviolence fits into the exceptionalist tradition. According to West the exceptionalist doctrine of nonviolence tends to assume tacitly that Afro-Americans have acquired, as a result of their historical experience, a peculiar capacity to love their enemies, to endure patiently suffering, pain, and hardships, and to thereby teach the white man how to love. King seems to believe that Afro-Americans possess a unique proclivity for nonviolence, more so than other racial groups, and that they have a certain bent toward humility, meekness, and forbearance, and are naturally disposed toward nonviolence. King's positive contribution to the Afro-American struggle is that he mobilized support from the black church, and he harnessed the potential for resistance inherent in black spirituality to force the American legal, political, and constitutional apparatus to reckon with and redress the plight of the Afro-American in the face of institutionalized American racism. He did this by means of a nonviolent strategy for achieving change in favor of the oppressed.

All of this is pertinent to the black struggle for liberation in South Africa. We, too, are confronted with the historic undertaking of gaining our freedom. We, too, have to make the historical choices of the means to be used. We, too, have to assess the spiritual, material, and ideological resources that are available to us. We, too, are confronted with the choices of what it is that we want and what sacrifices we are prepared to make in order to achieve our ideals. We, too, must decide whether acquiring civic freedoms within the context of the present capitalist order in South Africa or struggling to replace that order with a socialist form of society is the historically more acceptable and just choice. This is what *we* are confronted with. These are precisely the issues King was grappling with and talking about toward the end of his life, and they are now the center stage issues confronting us in South Africa. The question for us is, are we struggling for civic freedoms or for national liberation?

This has to do with our fundamental historical understanding of the future. It is unmistakable that all South Africans are concerned about the future. Reactionary forces like the government are feverishly making moves today to preserve tomorrow and to be present in it. In their frenzy to remain in power, the powers that be are stage-managing a grandiose act in counterfeit democracy that can only buy time but will not ultimately deliver peace and justice.

Big business, too, is deeply worried about the increasing political instability overtaking the country. This has occurred not only because their profits are going to be threatened, but also because they have lost faith in the ability of Mr. Botha to carry through his proposed reforms. After the president's Rubicon speech, big business realized that they would be the biggest losers because the Nationalists are too divided among themselves and too divisive when it comes to the issue of the black man's future in the country. Business cannot completely trust the Afrikaner politicians to protect the interests of capital. They must find another alternative. Maybe an alliance of white opposition liberalism and black ethnicity of the Inkatha-Buthelezi type, given enough international respectability, media coverage, and financial backing, could become politically attractive to the profit seekers. What is very clear is that the powerful want to remain in place after the upheaval, and they want to be there enjoying the power that they hold today.

But the future is also the fundamental historical category of the struggle for liberation. It informs and sustains the will to stay committed and involved even against overwhelming odds. It is the historical watchword of all progressive forces inside and outside the country, of large and sophisticated liberation organizations as well as tiny backroom-based community groups of political activists. It is a concept based on the deeply held belief that the oppressed peoples of South Africa will ultimately triumph. No amount of arbitrary white-based rule will ever succeed in eliminating the dream of a free future that has sustained all those engaged in our struggle for freedom. The vision of a free, united, democratic, nonracial society is the key that interprets and unlocks the past of the oppressed. The history of the oppressed cannot be truly understood in the categories of modern-day reform apartheid, but must be considered in terms of an unshakeable commitment to what lies ahead.

For good or ill, therefore, South Africans are locked in a struggle for tomorrow. We have no other historical perception of reality. By choice and circumstance we are being inexorably driven to our fate somewhere in the future. The nature of our gamble with time is to make right choices today and bear the consequences tomorrow—and to see which side will capitulate first. Whites in colonial Africa have consistently collided with history in their "nevers" and their "over my dead body" and their "not in another hundred years." They'll have to pay dearly for such obstinacy. So, too, the decolonized Afrikaner in South Africa has yet to make his historical peace with the black man, and there is every sign that there will be an explosive collision. But even the oppressed have to learn that an overflow of utopian euphoria about ultimate victory is not enough to bring about peace and justice on the continent tomorrow.

What we decide about what we want influences the efforts we make to develop strategies for change. What is clear is that at this stage the oppressed majority is not making an either/or choice. We do not need to choose between the options of peace and violence. Our history of resistance shows clearly that we have selected peaceful change. We have developed a tradition of resistance that incorporates the insights of Calvin, of Gandhi, of Martin Luther King, of Biko, of Mandela, and also of Marx. At no point have we said that we engage in resistance to apartheid because we refuse to talk. All our strategy has been used to make the point that we will and want to talk, but on the basis of an agenda that is mutually acceptable and that can be arrived at on the basis of certain conditions. We have said that very clearly inside our country. From both within the church and outside it, we have said that the ANC and other political organizations must be unbanned. We have said that Mandela and other political prisoners must be released unconditionally.

We have said that there must be a commitment on the part of the authorities to dismantle apartheid and to be *seen* dismantling it so that a credible basis for negotiation could be created, not to improve race relations or to open the way for blacks to participate in white privileges, but to change South Africa fundamentally. Maybe you would say that that is a pipe dream. But then today we are the dreamers.

I close by asking the question: What is peace for us? Peace is a fragile yet precious gift that we South Africans will give to one another. It can exist only when we who are caught in the unending spiral of violence and counterviolence, with its million and one justifications, realize that the time has finally come for us to do a truly great deed—to make peace. It is not there until we create it in the act of selfless love. Being such a tender thing, our peace lives in different measures, at the behest of the powerful and the powerless alike. For the powerful, peace can become a new weapon in an arsenal of modern weaponry; for the lowly, peace is more powerless than the powerless of this planet. Only in making peace do violent men and women again become human beings. Only in the preservation of peace, as an act of submission to its powerless yet perfect rule, will we here in South Africa become Africans. We will *become* our future. Africans are peacemakers given wholly to the task of establishing peace within structures of justice. More than the absence of visible violence and war, peace is the opportunity to give to the weakest and neediest and the most-sinned-against people a chance to live their lives.

Diplomats, politicians, generals, businessmen—and sadly now, also clergymen—do not usually congregate on behalf of the oppressed. It is usually for themselves. They ask, are we ready to do a great deed in Africa? It does not seem so. But we are trying. Indeed, maybe we will be remembered in South Africa as being of Africa's most violent children. Maybe we ourselves are responsible for the raping of Africa, our mother. Our question to you is whether *you* will become part of *our* tomorrow.

I close by saying you may have your bust of Martin Luther King. You may have your national holiday. You may even have the White House. We have King as our tomorrow.

CONCLUSION

Clayborne Carson

Reconstructing the King Legacy:

Scholars and National Myths

THE MODERN BLACK FREE-dom struggle transformed my life, as it did the lives of many other young people. Because of it I became aware that young black students such as myself might transform America and assume new, previously unimaginable social roles. This awareness inspired my own political activism and altered my sense of racial identity and destiny. My understanding of the black struggle changed as I absorbed its emergent values and became aware of a rich African-American protest tradition I knew little about.

I am sometimes asked whether my previous participation in the struggle interferes with my ability to write about it. The question seems meaningless to me because the struggle revealed the kind of history I wanted to write. The experiences that brought me to the Capitol Historical Society's conference on Martin Luther King, Jr., can be traced back to another day more than two decades ago when I participated in my initial civil rights demonstration and saw King for the first time.

In August 1963, after completing my freshman year in college, I joined the multitudes at the March on Washington. It was a wonderful introduction to the struggle, culminating in a major historical event —King's "I Have a Dream" speech —but also punctuated with those unrecorded occurrences that forever separate history as lived from history as reconstructed by historians. My initial encounters, a few days earlier, with the brash young activists of SNCC heightened the March's impact on my undeveloped political consciousness. Participating in the March was the most politically unconventional thing I had ever done, but Stokely Carmichael of SNCC reshaped the meaning I attached to my involvement when he gratuitously informed me that the event was only a sanitized, middle-class version of the real black movement, which was occurring in places such as Albany, Georgia, Cambridge, Maryland, Danville, Virginia, and the Mississippi Delta.

Having just emerged from the racial isolation of growing up in New Mexico, I was not yet ready to venture into the battlefields of the deep South where Carmichael and other SNCC workers confronted racist authorities. For me the Washington "picnic" was an epiphany. During that one day I saw more black people than I had seen in my life. Exposed to the constantly widening range of views among activists, I saw black politics differently from before. I will never forget King's oration, but the militancy of the SNCC workers, exhibited at the March in John Lewis's caustic warm-up to King's speech, tempered my enthusiasm. That SNCC existed revealed to me that King was only one aspect of a multifaceted social movement.

Today, after years of political activism and ivory-tower reflection, I have now come full circle, returning to the nation's capital to take part in another occasion dominated by King's ideas. After spending the first years of my professional life studying SNCC, I have now—as editor of King's papers—turned my scholarly attention to the person who was the antithesis of SNCC's notion of leadership from the bottom up. Having once sympathized with the young SNCC militants who were my age when they challenged King (who was then fifteen years my senior), I find my sympathies have shifted somewhat as I study King, who, when he died, was younger than I am now.

During the last half of the 1960s, my own youthful impatience and a measure of arrogance led me to agree with some of SNCC's criticisms of King's moderation and firm commitment to integration and nonviolence as a way of life. In later years, acknowledgment that the black power movement failed to achieve the power, or even the racial unity we anticipated, has fostered a greater degree of humility in my assessment of King's alternative course. For me and for many of his youthful critics, King became wiser as we grew older. My changing views of the modern black struggle have continued to reflect the enduring tension between the ideas of King and those of its little-known shock troops.

M artin Luther King's status as the main symbol of the modern African-American freedom struggle has now been sanctioned by the creation of a federal holiday honoring his birth. Given this formal recognition of his historical importance, it becomes more difficult, yet also more necessary, for those of us who study and carry on his work to counteract the innocuous, carefully cultivated image that we honor in these annual observances. The historical King was far too interesting to be encased in simplistic, didactic legends designed to offend no one —a black counterpart to the static, heroic myths that have embalmed George Washington as the Father of His Country and Abraham Lincoln as the Great Emancipator. King was an exceptionally gifted, fascinating, and courageous individual who challenged authority and took such controversial stands as opposing American intervention in Vietnam and mobilizing the Poor People's Campaign of 1968. He was also a leader best understood in the context of African-American history and as the product of the social movements that he has come to symbolize.

Serious students of Martin Luther King and of the black struggle have recognized their responsibility to understand, on the one hand, the nature and sources of his ideas and, on the other, the historical significance and social impact of his life. Contemporary biographers, theologians, political scientists, sociologists, philosophers, social psychologists, and historians, a number of whom participated in this symposium, are in the process of constructing a more balanced, comprehensive assessment of King. The recent works of David J. Garrow and Taylor Branch have illustrated the benefits of studies that combine thorough biographical investigation with efforts to understand larger issues of social and historical context.[1] These and other contemporary writers may benefit from and stimulate the popular interest in King spurred by the national holiday, but their probing research and critical analyses serve as a necessary corrective to the mythmaking. This volume provides a valuable opportunity to acknowledge and assess this outpouring of reflective and critical works about King and allows us to place them within the broader literature of African-American freedom struggles.

The initial King biographies were, for the most part, laudatory accounts written by his acquaintances. Although they benefited from their authors' firsthand knowledge of the man, these early accounts were not based on extensive research in primary documents.[2] More recent biographies have taken on the task of critically assessing King's leadership and intellectual qualities. August Meier's 1965 essay on King and David Lewis's *King: A Critical Biography,* published in 1970, broke new ground in their acknowledgment of King's limitations as well as his achievements as a civil rights leader. Both scholars saw him as part of a broader social movement that included important factions forcefully challenging his leadership.[3]

Neither Meier nor Lewis placed much emphasis on King's intellectual orientation—the latter explicitly derided his intellectual credentials —but their inattention has been more than rectified by numerous studies focusing on King's religious and political ideas. One line of research has focused on his contribution to Christian thought. Although he received his doctorate in systematic theology, he published no significant writing in this field, and most scholars recognize that his main intellectual contribution was in the area of Christian social practice. That King saw himself primarily as a religious leader is clearly evident in his graduate school and later religious writings, which have been closely examined in the pioneering work of Kenneth L. Smith and Ira G. Zepp, published in 1974, and in later efforts by Harold L. DeWolf (King's advisor at Boston) and John Ansbro.[4] Recently, even scholars who seek primarily to explicate King's thought have recognized that it was not shaped simply by his academic training but derived as well from the emergent ideas of social movements. In addition, rather than solely emphasizing King's graduate school experiences and readings, scholars have begun to acknowledge his indebtedness to African-American sources and, in particular, to the tradition of black Christian activism. James P. Hanigan's work, for example, marked an important departure in this respect.[5]

The essays in this volume by Richard H. King and Cornel West provide interesting and contrasting approaches to the study of King's thought. Professor King's explication of the meaning of freedom for Martin Luther King is, from one point of view, narrowly conceived intellectual history, locating the sources of King's ideas in his earlier readings. But while viewing Martin Luther King as an intellectual, Professor King also shows an awareness that these ideas should be evaluated in light of other strategies of struggle, such as SNCC's anticharismatic model. Although Cornel West is similarly concerned with King's intellectual life, his emphasis on the African-American church as a source for King's ideas suggests a promising area of research for other scholars moving beyond the internalist—ideas as sources for other ideas—approach of traditional intellectual biography and history. The relationship between King's Christian ministry and black religious traditions and practices has attracted the attention of other scholars as well, including Lewis V. Baldwin, James H. Cone, and David J. Garrow.[6]

The danger is that studies linking King to African-American religious thought may underestimate the extent to which, as a religious liberal, he departed from the mainstream of that tradition. Although, like many black clergymen, King used his well-developed oratorical skills to strengthen his appeal to blacks, he set himself apart from other black preachers through his use of traditional black Christian homiletics to advocate unconventional political ideas and to extend the boundaries of African-American religious thought. King's autobiographical writings reveal that early in his life he became disillusioned with the unbridled emotionalism associated with his father's religious fundamentalism. As a thirteen-year-old, he questioned the bodily resurrection of Jesus in his Sunday School class and subsequently struggled to free himself from "the shackles of fundamentalism."[7] King's search for an intellectually satisfying religious faith stemmed from his reaction against the emphasis on emotional expressiveness that he saw in Christian evangelicalism. His preaching manner derived from the traditions of the black church, while his subject matter, which often reflected his wide-ranging philosophical interests, distinguished him from other preachers who relied on rhetorical devices that manipulated the emotions of their listeners. A religious liberal and pioneering proponent of what is now called liberation theology, King carried on a long and determined—though unsuccessful—struggle against the conservative leadership of the National Baptist Convention. Instead of viewing himself as the embodiment of widely held African-American racial values, he willingly risked his popularity among blacks as well as whites through his steadfast advocacy of Christian social activism and militant nonviolent strategies to achieve radical social change.

Recent scholarship of King's leadership has displayed a growing understanding of the interplay between his exceptional oratorical abilities and the expectations and understandings of his various audiences. Aldon D. Morris notes in his essay in this volume that the type of leadership exercised by King and other black leaders developed within the institutional context of the black church, where charismatic ministers "occupied strategic positions which enabled them to become extremely familiar with the needs and aspirations of blacks."[8] It is misleading, however, to explain King's unique role in the black struggle simply by referring to the supposedly charismatic qualities he displayed in the pulpit. The term "charisma," which once referred to the godlike, magical qualities of an "ideal" leader, has now, in our more secular age, lost many of its religious connotations and refers to a wide range of leadership styles that involve the capacity to inspire—usually through oratory—emotional bonds between leaders and followers. Arguing, therefore, that King was not a charismatic leader in the broadest sense of the term is akin to arguing that he was not a Christian, but emphasis on his charisma obscures other important aspects of his role in the black movement. To be sure, King's oratory was exceptional, and many people saw him as a divinely inspired leader, but he did not receive and did not want the kind of unquestioning support associated with charismatic leaders. He was a profound and provocative public speaker, not simply an emotionally powerful one. Emphasis on his charisma conveys the misleading notion of a movement held together by spellbinding speeches and blind faith rather than by a combination of rational and emotional bonds.

Not only did King's supposed charisma fail to place him above criticism, but he was never able to gain mass support for his notion of nonviolent struggle as a way of life, rather than as simply a tactic. Most movement activists saw him not as their unquestioned commander but as the most prominent among many influential movement strategists, ideologues, theologians, and institutional leaders. King used charisma as a tool for mobilizing black communities, but always in the context of other forms of intellectual and political leadership that reflected his academic training and that were appropriate for a movement containing many strong leaders. He undoubtedly recognized that charisma could not provide the only basis for leadership of a modern political move-ment, one which enlisted the efforts of many other self-reliant leaders. Moreover, he rejected aspects of the charismatic model that conflicted with his sense of his own limitations.

King was a leader full of self-doubts, keenly aware of his own limi-tations and weaknesses. He was at times reluctant to take on the respon-sibilities suddenly and unexpectedly thrust upon him. Scholars have only begun to understand the significance of his evolving religious be-liefs as a foundation for his leadership abilities and political attitudes. David Garrow's paper, for example, stresses the importance of the "kitchen experience" in 1956 during the Montgomery bus boycott, when King was overcome with fear as a result of threats to his own life and to the lives of his wife and child. Rather than feeling confident and secure in his leadership role, he was able to continue only after acquiring an enduring understanding of his dependence on a personal God who promised never to leave him alone.[9]

Although King biographies and King-centered studies of the black struggle continue to appear, serious writers have moved beyond ha-giography and have challenged the notion of King as the modern black struggle's initiator and indispensable leader. This reflects a general his-toriographical trend away from the notion of Great Men either as deci-sive elements in historical processes or as sole causes, through their unique leadership qualities, of major historical events. Because the King myth emphasizes personality rather than social context, it exaggerates his considerable contribution to black advancement without acknowl-edging his indebtedness to other organizers and activists who set the stage for his appearance in a leading role. Robert Moses's apt metaphor of the movement as "an ocean of consciousness," which he offers in his commentary, provides a useful framework for understanding the surging wave that was King's leadership.

The historical significance of King's political ideas, furthermore, especially his contributions to the Gandhian and African-American traditions of nonviolent resistance, cannot be fully understood without a determination of the extent to which activists adopted his tactics and strategies.[10] The importance of James H. Cone's essay on Martin Luther King and Third World liberation movements is enhanced by his decision not only to describe what King said about those movements, but also to explore the impact of King's ideas on Third World activists and leaders. Cone only begins to study an issue that requires much further research, both abroad and at home: To what extent did King's ideas actually guide the mass struggles he sought to influence? Implicitly assuming that King's role in the southern black movement was indispensable or at least crucial to its success, King-centered scholarship has unfortunately contributed to the popular but misleading notion that most movement activists adopted his philosophy of nonviolence. Such scholarship has also reinforced the tendency of many Americans to see him not only as the exemplar of the modern black leader, at least in the pre–Jesse Jackson era, but as a charismatic figure who single-handedly directed the course of the civil rights movement.

Even the most perceptive King-centered studies will have limited value unless they acknowledge that the black struggle was a locally-based mass movement rather than simply a reform movement led by national civil rights leaders.[11] King was certainly not the only significant leader of the civil rights movement, for sustained protest campaigns developed in many southern communities with which he had little or no direct involvement. In Montgomery, for example, local black leaders such as E. D. Nixon, Rosa Parks, and Jo Ann Robinson started the bus boycott before King became the leader of the Montgomery Improvement Association. Thus, although he inspired blacks in Montgomery, and black residents recognized that they were fortunate to have such a spokesperson, talented local leaders other than King played decisive roles in initiating and sustaining the boycott. Similarly, the black students who initiated the 1960 lunch counter sit-ins admired King, but they did not wait for him to act before launching their own movement. The sit-in leaders who founded SNCC became increasingly critical of his leadership style, seeing it as the cause of feelings of dependency that often characterize the followers of charismatic leaders.[12] The essence of SNCC's approach to community organizing was to instill in members of local communities the confidence that they could lead their own struggles. A SNCC organizer had failed if local residents became dependent on his or her presence; as the organizers put it, their job was to work themselves out of a job. Though King influenced the struggles that took place in the Black Belt regions of Mississippi, Alabama, and Georgia, self-reliant local leaders guided those movements. They occasionally called on King's oratorical skills to galvanize black protesters at mass meetings, but they refused to depend on his presence.

If King had never lived, the black struggle would have followed a course of development similar to the one it did. The Montgomery bus boycott would have occurred, because King did not initiate it. Black students probably would have rebelled—even without him as a role model—for they had sources of tactical and ideological inspiration besides King. Mass activism in southern cities and voting rights efforts in the deep South were outgrowths of large-scale social and political forces rather than simply consequences of the actions of a single leader. Though perhaps not as quickly and certainly not as peacefully or with as universal a significance, the black movement probably would have achieved its major legislative victories without King's leadership, for the southern Jim Crow system was a regional anachronism and the forces that undermined it were inexorable.

To what extent, then, did King's presence affect the movement? Answering that question requires us to look beyond the usual portrayal of the black struggle. Rather than seeing an amorphous mass of discontented blacks acting out strategies determined by a small group of leaders, we should recognize King as a major example of the emergent local black leadership that developed as African-American communities mobilized for sustained struggles. Directing attention to the other leaders who initiated and emerged from those struggles should not detract from our appreciation of King's historical significance; such movement-oriented research reveals him to be a leader who stood out in a forest of tall trees.

King's major public speeches—particularly the "I Have a Dream" speech—have received much attention, but his exemplary qualities were also displayed in countless strategy sessions and in meetings with government officials. His success as a leader was based on respect for his intellectual and moral cogency and his skill as a conciliator among movement activists who refused to be simply his "followers" or "lieutenants."

The success of the black civil rights movement required the mobilization of black communities as well as the transformation of attitudes in the surrounding society, and King's wide range of skills and attributes prepared him to meet both these internal and external demands. He understood the black world from a privileged position, having grown up in a stable, prominent family within a major black urban community; yet he also learned how to speak persuasively to the surrounding white world. Alone among the major civil rights leaders of his time, King could not only articulate black concerns to white audiences, he could mobilize blacks through his day-to-day involvement in black community institutions and through his access to the regional institutional network of the black church. His advocacy of nonviolent activism gave the black movement invaluable positive press coverage, but his success as a protest leader derived mainly from his ability to mobilize black community resources.

Analyses of the southern movement that emphasize its nonrational aspects and expressive functions explain the black struggle as an emotional outburst by discontented blacks, rather than as a sustained, politically effective mobilization of black community institutions, financial resources, and grass-roots leaders.[13] The values of southern blacks were profoundly and permanently transformed not only by King, but also by their own involvement in sustained protest activity and in community-organizing efforts, mass meetings, workshops, citizenship classes, freedom schools, and informal discussions. Rather than merely accepting guidance from above, many southern blacks became leaders in their communities as a result of their movement experiences.

Although the literature on the black struggle has traditionally paid little attention to the intellectual content of black politics, movement activists of the 1960s made a profound, though often ignored, contribution to political thinking. King's own most significant leadership attributes did not derive from his academic training, his philosophical readings, or even his acquaintance with Gandhian ideas. Instead, his influence on the black struggle resulted mainly from his immersion in, and contribution to, the intellectual ferment that has always been an essential part of African-American freedom struggles. Scholars are only beginning to recognize the extent to which his attitudes and those of many other activists, white and black, changed as a result of their involvement in a movement in which tactical and strategic ideas disseminated from the bottom up as well as from the top down.

Although such a movement-centered perspective on King's role in the black struggles of his time reduces him to human scale, it also increases the possibility that others may recognize his qualities in themselves. Idolizing King lessens one's ability to exhibit some of his best attributes or, worse, encourages one to become a debunker, emphasizing his flaws in order to avoid embracing his virtues. Undoubtedly fearing that some who admired him would place too much faith in his ability to offer guidance and overcome resistance, King often publicly acknowledged his own limitations and mortality. Near the end of his life, he expressed his certainty that black people would reach the Promised Land whether or not he was with them. His faith grew from an awareness of the qualities that he knew he shared with all people. When he suggested his own epitaph, he asked not to be remembered for his exceptional achievements—his Nobel Prize and other awards, or his academic accomplishments; instead he wanted to be remembered for giving his life to serve others, for trying to be right on the "war question," for trying to feed the hungry and clothe the naked, for trying to love and serve humanity.[14] Those aspects of King's life did not require charisma or other superhuman abilities.

If King were alive today, he would doubtless encourage those who celebrate his life to recognize their responsibility to struggle as he did for a more just and peaceful world. He would prefer that we remember the black movement not as the scene of his own achievements, but as a setting that brought out extraordinary qualities in many people. If he were to return, his oratory would be unsettling and intellectually challenging rather than confining itself simply to comforting diction and soothing cadences. He would probably be the unpopular social critic he was on the eve of the Poor People's campaign rather than the object of national homage that he became after his death. His basic message would be the same as it was when he was alive, for he did not bend with the changing political winds. He would talk of ending poverty and war and of building a just social order that would avoid the pitfalls of competitive capitalism and repressive communism. He would give scant comfort to those who condition their activism upon the appearance of another King, for he recognized the extent to which he was a product of the movement that called him to leadership.

The notion that appearances by Great Men (or Great Women) are necessary preconditions for the emergence of major movements for social change reflects a poor understanding of history and contributes to a pessimistic view of the possibilities for future social change. Waiting for the Messiah is a human weakness that is unlikely to be rewarded more than once in a millennium. Studies of the modern black freedom struggle offer support for a more optimistic belief that participants in social movements can develop their untapped leadership abilities and collectively improve their lives.

THOUGHTS AND
REFLECTIONS

Coretta Scott King

Thoughts and Reflections

CORETTA SCOTT KING, THE widow of the late Martin Luther King, Jr., has been a major force in the civil rights movement for over a quarter of a century. Born in Marion, Alabama, she received her B.S. from Antioch College in 1951 and her Mus.B. from the New England Conservatory of Music in 1954; she married Martin Luther King in 1953. With her husband she was a participant in the black freedom struggles of the 1950s and 1960s, and she has continued her activities in the movement since his death. A recipient of hundreds of awards, Mrs. King is a noted lecturer, writer, and diplomat.

I must begin by saying that all of you here, and thousands and even, we may think, millions of people throughout our nation and other parts of the world have contributed significantly to bringing us to where we are today. I think Martin Luther King, Jr., would be the first to say that.

Some of us are privileged to be a part of history. We have been given an opportunity to engage in work that is meaningful and that brings fulfillment. We are inspired by that work. I feel that I was one of those privileged persons who had an opportunity that few people have in their lives. It was not something that I specifically chose. I didn't know my opportunity was going to be at the side of a man who would change the course of the nation's history and have an impact upon the thought of Western civilization to the extent that the most renowned scholars still have not determined what that impact really is or will finally be. But I knew when the movement started that something very, very significant was occurring in history that had not happened before. We were a part of a great unfolding of what seemed to be a divine plan, one that connected us to other victims of oppression throughout the world. Martin used to talk about having cosmic companionship. When you were in Montgomery, Alabama, in 1956, you realized it. It started in 1955, but it was 1956 when we really understood that there was a movement in progress. It was the first time that black people in this country had stood up in one particular area as a united force.

I think the solidarity of that effort inspired people in many other communities as far away as South Africa. The press reported during 1956 that there was a boycott in Johannesburg, South Africa, and they linked it to the inspiration of Martin Luther King, Jr. I believe that it really was linked to Martin because when I met with Winnie Mandela on my trip to South Africa, she said to me that she and her husband had been inspired by what Martin Luther King, Jr., had done and what I had done. And I said, what you have done all these years—separated from your husband, raising a family, during the time when I suppose you were most lonely, being held in isolation with only a few people allowed to visit you—you reached out to me and sent me one of the most beautiful expressions of love and concern. I was very moved by that. I was impressed with the fact that she had no bitterness, and I thought, "How do they do this?"

I thought that this movement was so important that its history had to be documented, so I started collecting material during the Montgomery struggle. I knew it was important history, and I knew that there would be a time in the life of our nation and the world when scholars would be researching this period and that they would need to have the basic documents preserved so that they could interpret what it meant and be able to tell the story to succeeding generations. So I saved all the papers and letters that came in and filed them and organized them, and I found a young student to clip newspapers. It was very important to me.

Martin's time in the struggle lasted twelve years and four months—a relatively short time to accomplish so much change. When you think about how slowly positive social change comes about, that is a *very* short time. It was a nonviolent civil rights revolution that always encompassed the whole human rights struggle. Martin always understood that, and he always linked the two, if you listened to him carefully.

Throughout that whole struggle I realized that here was a moment in history unfolding, something very important that was far beyond us, that we did not understand. To be a part of it—that was part of my life also. I had been preparing myself for that moment and I did not know it. But when it started unfolding I knew that this is why my life had taken the course that it had.

I want to say that what has happened here in these last two days, and just the fact that it was thought of in the first place, is terribly meaningful to me and my family and I'm sure to all the persons who have been working and struggling and hoping that the time would come when the nation would begin seriously to grapple with the meaning of Martin Luther King, Jr.,—both his meaning in history and what we can learn from him that will help us to continue our nonviolent struggle to complete the democratization of our nation.

Democracy means equal justice, equity in every aspect of our society. I think Martin understood from the very beginning that this goal could not be accomplished all at once. He knew he could not take a people who were largely uneducated and unrepresented and suddenly transform them into political activists who could immediately change the system. And he also knew that the basic problem in our society had to do with economic injustice or, as someone has said here, the contrast of wealth between the haves and the have-nots. Believe it or not, he spoke those words to me when I first met him. It wasn't something that he learned later and developed. He was practical enough, he had enough understanding of the realities of politics and of human nature, and an appreciation of how you can change people. He also understood how to influence people. He did not understand it from having had the experience of doing it when I first met him, but somehow his words conveyed that to me. At the time I couldn't understand how he could be that mature and that sophisticated at twenty-three years of age— that's how old he was when I met him. I had had enough training and background myself to appreciate where he was in his thinking at that time and to realize that, since he had been in school all those years, he hadn't had a chance to actually test any of these theories. He somehow knew that they could all come together.

He knew all this, and knew, too, at the time of his death, that only the physical body could be destroyed, not the spirit and the love that he embraced. Love *is*—we don't create it, we discover it and we embrace it. That's one of those absolutes. I thought as one of the speakers talked about Martin's power and influence and his difference, that this came from the fact that he responded in an obedient way to the loving force in the universe, which is God. He believed in a personal God. He believed in a God of justice and a God of peace.

I want to thank all of you because I think each presentation has made a real contribution to an assessment of Martin. I said to Sam DuBois Cooke, who was a classmate of Martin's, now president of Dillard University, during the funeral period or shortly after, "It may be twenty-five, it may be fifty years, before this nation really realizes and appreciates the important contribution that Martin has made to our nation and to the world." I knew it would take time for us to catch up spiritually, before we could understand someone of the magnitude of Martin Luther King, Jr.

I saw him as the man I fell in love with and got married to, but I could also be objective when it came to knowing whether or not he was a good Christian. I knew he was because I lived with him. I had the greatest respect for his ability to discipline himself to do what he knew was right to do. He was almost constrained to try to do the right thing, and his conscience—his own conscience—haunted him when he thought he had mistreated anyone. I saw that throughout the struggle. He was not just out there doing something, he was thinking about it, and he agonized over it. He questioned his own motivation time and time again. He was one of the most selfless persons I have ever known, and yet at the time I met him he was what we call "secure," secure with himself. He knew who he was. He knew that he had something to offer, and he knew how he was going to get to his goals.

He said, "I am going to be a Baptist preacher and I will preach from a black Baptist pulpit in the South," because he knew that's where he had to preach in those days. He said: "I'm going to preach from the black Baptist pulpit, and I am going to conduct my ministry from the church. I won't be at a college campus, because I think that's where I can be most effective. And I have problems with the organized church, but I'm going to stay in it and try to work from within and change it. I have problems with America not living up to what she can be, but I'm going to work within the system. I don't think we can trade it off for a new system, but I have problems with it." And he talked about working within the framework of democracy to move us toward a kind of socialism. I say this very advisedly because I think that people misunderstand the word "socialism," but in the sense that Martin used it—he said a kind of socialism has to be adopted by our system because the way it is, it's simply unjust. He looked at the poor and the fact that so many people were in ill health with no way for them to pay for their medical expenses. He asked, how do you catch up on all these things? There's got to be some kind of concern within the nation. "But," he said, "I could never be a communist."

Now this was within the first month or so of our meeting. He had already figured out a lot of things and certainly he grew and developed and evolved, as someone has said, but I think his basic value structure was there from the beginning, and also his ability to articulate what it was. He was already living it. I want to say that he did not always espouse total nonviolence. I think he had achieved a kind of relative nonviolence in his earlier life, but as he thought about it and went back and restudied Gandhi and other persons in history who shared those views, he said, "There was a time when I saw violence as a negative good where a force like a Hitler could be stopped and somehow, if you could stop a Hitler, then you could create some negative good. But I finally came to feel that violence and certainly violence of that magnitude and war could not serve any positive good. And that's why I have to oppose all war and all violence." He said, "You may win temporary victories, but never permanent peace. Because the nature of it is that it keeps on; it sows the seeds of its own destruction."

I want to finish now. There are some things that we've got to do in terms of getting the whole picture. Martin spoke about everything. There was nothing he did not have a view on as expressed in his writings and speeches. This will be clear when his papers are published, with Clay Carson as the editor in chief. But we have yet to deal with how Martin Luther King, Jr., saw women and how he dealt with women and women's roles. The next time we have a conference on him I want to see more women scholars. He allowed me to be myself and that meant that I always expressed my views; he always sought my views because he valued them and so I felt an equal to Martin. Equal in my own context; he was superior to a whole lot of people in his development, but I always felt that equality. Martin had a way of helping everybody feel that way, no matter what the difference was.

I don't think enough has been said about—not taking anything away from the black struggle and the efforts of black people—but Martin continued to say and would be the first to say that it could not have been done without the support of allies in the white community and people of good will, that we could not have done it without them. Now that may be well understood, but I don't think so. I think it is important to say that, and not to be labeled "Tom." Because there were white people who gave their lives, even during the civil rights period, in the struggle. So I think something needs to be said about how Martin dealt with that and viewed that, and not just as an integrationist. It was much more than that. It was incorporated in his whole philosophy and ideology about life, about people and human beings, and sacredness of personality, no matter what the race.

Another point I want to make is the importance of coalition building as we move on to what he called the most difficult phase of the struggle, the achievement of economic justice. He knew it wasn't going to be easy. He understood that resistance would be greater, and he said "that's why we've got to engage in studying the discipline and philosophy of nonviolence so that we can be prepared to overcome." If he had the belief—and he did—that somehow there was a God of justice and that God working through history and working through people in history could bring about the Kingdom, then it was because he also believed that people had the capacity to develop their inner powers sufficiently to overcome any form of oppression. So that's why he called for serious study and experimentation with nonviolence in every field of human endeavor. That is what he has charged us with. He completed his work in thirty-nine years, in twelve years and four months of public life. So it has been left to us, although he left the blueprint for us to follow.

In talking to young people today on college campuses, they say to me, "I respect Dr. King. That worked back then, but it just won't work now." And I have to say to them it doesn't work because people don't understand it. They either don't understand it or they haven't tried it. It hasn't worked because not enough people have tried it. Nonviolence *will* work and *has* worked because it's based on those absolutes of eternal truths that have lasted throughout history. Martin found a way to develop them into a program of action because he had studied Gandhi. When he said, "I got my motivation and inspiration from Jesus and my techniques from Gandhi," that's what he meant. I've heard a lot about colonialism, how it shapes a whole mentality. Yes, but Gandhi made nonviolence work. I'm sure colonial oppression in India was pretty bad; if you talk to Indian people they will tell you how bad it was. But Gandhi did it; that's an example in that part of the world. King did what he did in a different part of the world—in the context of Western culture, Western materialistic culture. And more recently—in the Philippines—it was through *nonviolent* political action that one of the world's worst dictators was removed from power. Don't forget that. So I say that there's hope for South Africa, there's hope.

Notes

DAVID J. GARROW: "MARTIN LUTHER KING, JR., AND THE SPIRIT OF LEADERSHIP"

1. For the WPC's crucial role, see David J. Garrow, "The Origins of the Montgomery Bus Boycott," *Southern Changes* 7 (Oct.-Dec. 1985):21–27, and Jo Ann Gibson Robinson's autobiographical memoir, *The Montgomery Bus Boycott and the Women Who Started It* (Knoxville, 1987), as well as the author's interviews with both Mrs. Robinson (5 Apr. 1984, Los Angeles) and the WPC's first president, Mary Fair Burks (29 July 1984, Salisbury, Md.).

2. For fuller accounts of King's selection see David J. Garrow, *Bearing the Cross: Martin Luther King, Jr., and the Southern Christian Leadership Conference* (New York, 1986), 20–22, and Ralph D. Abernathy, "The Natural History of a Social Movement: The Montgomery Improvement Association"(M.A. thesis, Atlanta University, 1958), 29–32, as well as the author's interviews with Rufus Lewis (16 Sept. 1979, Montgomery), E. D. Nixon (15 Sept. 1979, Montgomery), and Abernathy (14 Sept. 1979, Atlanta), and the additional oral histories with all three interviewees listed in Garrow, *Bearing the Cross*, 749,757,759.

3. Peter C. Mohr, "Journey Out of Egypt: The Development of Negro Leadership in Alabama from Booker T. Washington to Martin Luther King" (B.A. thesis, Princeton University, 1958), 54, and Martin Luther King, Jr., *Stride toward Freedom: The Montgomery Story* (New York, 1958), 55–58.

4. Martin Luther King, Jr., Address at Holt Street Baptist Church, 5 Dec. 1955, Martin Luther King, Jr., Papers, Martin Luther King, Jr., Center for Nonviolent Social Change, Atlanta, Ga. Also see *Montgomery Advertiser*, 6 and 7 Dec. 1955, and *Birmingham World*, 13 Dec. 1955.

5. *Alabama Journal* (Montgomery), 7 Dec. 1955. Also see Garrow, *Bearing the Cross,* 14–16 and 23–25. On the WPC's earlier efforts, see Garrow, "Origins," and particularly Mrs. Robinson's extremely significant 21 May 1954 letter to Montgomery Mayor W. A. Gayle, in the boycott-related "Complaint File," Montgomery County District Attorney's Office, Montgomery County Courthouse, Montgomery, Ala., which is reprinted in Clayborne Carson et al., eds., *Eyes on the Prize: America's Civil Rights Years, A Reader and Guide* (New York, 1987), 41–42.

6. Ralph Abernathy in Dorothy Cotton, "A Conversation with Ralph Abernathy," *Journal* (United Church of Christ) 9 (Nov.-Dec. 1970): 26; Jo Ann Gibson Robinson in Steven M. Millner, "The Montgomery Bus Boycott: A Case Study in the Emergence and Career of a Social Movement," (Ph.D. diss., University of California, Berkeley, 1981), 199, and King, *Stride toward Freedom,* 113.

7. King, *Stride toward Freedom,* 120. Also see *Montgomery Advertiser,* 20 Dec. 1955, and Garrow, *Bearing the Cross,* 30–31.

8. King, *Stride toward Freedom,* 121–23; Garrow, *Bearing the Cross,* 51–52.

9. *Montgomery Advertiser,* 19 Jan. 1956.

10. William Peters, "The Man Who Fights Hate with Love," *Redbook,* 117 (Sept. 1961): 96. Also see King, *Stride toward Freedom,* 127–31, and Garrow, *Bearing the Cross,* 55–56.

11. Martin Luther King, Jr., "Thou Fool," 27 Aug. 1967, Mt. Pisgah Missionary Baptist Church, Chicago, 11–14, King Papers, King Center. Also see idem, *Stride toward Freedom,* 134–35, and idem, *Strength to Love* (New York, 1963), 106–7, as well as James H. Cone, "Martin Luther King: The Source for His Courage to Face Death," *Concilium* 183 (1983): 74–79, and David J. Garrow, "Martin Luther King, Jr.: Bearing the Cross of Leadership," *Peace and Change* 12 (1987): 1–12, for additional commentary on the centrality of this experience in King's life.

12. *Montgomery Advertiser,* 31 Jan. 1956. Also see *Afro-American,* 11 Feb. 1956; Coretta Scott King, *My Life with Martin Luther King, Jr.* (New York, 1969), 127–32; and Garrow, *Bearing the Cross,* 59–61.

13. Transcript of Martin Luther King, Jr., press conference, 23 Mar. 1956, quoted in Garrow, *Bearing the Cross,* 75.

14. *Montgomery Advertiser,* 28 Jan. 1957; *Pittsburgh Courier,* 9 Feb. 1957.

15. Martin Luther King, Jr., to Dwight Loder, 5 Aug. 1958, author's files; Fred Shuttlesworth to King, 24 Apr. 1959, Martin Luther King, Jr., Papers, Drawer 1, Mugar Library, Boston University; *Jet,* 17 Dec. 1959, 12–17. Also see King to Harold DeWolf, 4 Jan. 1957, Drawer 2, and King to Mordecai Johnson, 5 July 1957, Drawer 1, King Papers, Boston University. Garrow, *Bearing the Cross,* 96, 116, 120–25. Given the exceptionally poor conditions under which the King collection at Boston University has been maintained over the years, citations to the locations of specific documents within it can only be approximate at best, as experienced King scholars have come to realize.

16. Andrew Young interview with Milton Viorst (1 May 1975, Washington, D.C.), Moorland-Spingarn Research Center, Howard University, Washington, D.C. Also see my interview with Young (27 July 1982, Atlanta), and comments of Young in Howell Raines, *My Soul Is Rested* (New York, 1977), 425–27.

17. Martin Luther King, Jr., briefcase notes, n.d., King Papers, King Center; Martin Luther King, Jr., "The Three Dimensions of a Complete Life," 14 Mar. 1965, Chicago Sunday Evening Club, Chicago, Ill., 5–6, Chicago Sunday Evening Club Papers, Chicago Historical Society; Andrew Young, "Bill Moyers' Journal," 2 Apr. 1979, Show 409, transcript, 7.

18. *New York Times,* 15 Oct. 1964; Garrow, *Bearing the Cross,* 354–55.

19. Martin Luther King, Jr., "Why I Must March," 18 Aug. 1966, Greater Mt. Hope Baptist Church, Chicago, Ill., 8, King Papers, King Center.

20. Idem, "Beyond Discovery, Love," 25 Sept. 1966, Dallas, Texas, 8, King Papers, King Center.

21. Garrow, *Bearing the Cross,* 394, 422–30, 436–61, 469–70, 472, 485, 502, 538–44; William F. Pepper, "The Children of Vietnam," *Ramparts* 5 (Jan. 1967): 44–68.

22. U.S. Federal Bureau of Investigation, New York office file serial 100-111180-9-1254, 25 Mar. 1967, 12. This wire-tapped phone conversation transcript, or "log," is one of hundreds of such items from the numeric sub-files ("9") in the Bureau's New York office file (100-111180) on Stanley Levison, which were the product of the Bureau's long-standing electronic surveillance of Levison. See, generally, David J. Garrow, *The FBI and Martin Luther King, Jr.: From "Solo" to Memphis* (New York, 1981).

23. SCLC board meeting tape, 30 Mar. 1967, King Papers, King Center; Garrow, *Bearing the Cross,* 552–53.

24. Martin Luther King, Jr., "Beyond Vietnam," 4 Apr. 1967, Riverside Church, New York, King Papers, King Center; *Pittsburgh Courier,* 15 Apr. 1967; *Washington Post,* 6 Apr. 1967; *New York Times,* 7 Apr. 1967; King to Stanley Levison, FBI New York 100-111180-9-1268A, 8 Apr. 1967.

25. *Cleveland Press,* 26 Apr. 1967; Martin Luther King, Jr., "Why I Am Opposed to the War in Vietnam," 30 Apr. 1967, Ebenezer Baptist Church, Atlanta, Ga., King Papers, King Center; Garrow, *Bearing the Cross,* 542, 557–59, 562.

26. Martin Luther King, Jr., "To Charter Our Course for the Future," 22 May 1967, Penn Community Center, Frogmore, S.C., King Papers, King Center.

27. Coretta Scott King interview with Charlotte Mayerson (31 July 1968, Manchester, N.H.), 26: 29–30; King, *My Life with Martin King,* 61–62, 171, 274; King, "To Charter Our Course."

28. Martin Luther King, Jr., "The Crisis in Civil Rights," 11 July 1967, Chicago, Ill., King Papers, King Center. Also see Vincent Harding,

"The Land Beyond," *Sojourners* 12 (Jan. 1983): 18–22; David J. Garrow, *Martin Luther King: Challenging America at Its Core* (New York, 1983); Robert Weisbrot, "Celebrating Dr. King's Birthday," *New Republic*, 30 Jan. 1984, 10–16; David J. Garrow, "The King We Should Remember," *Focus* 14 (Jan. 1986): 3–7.

29. Levison interview with Jean Stein, 21 Nov. 1969, New York, N.Y., author's files.

30. King, *My Life with Martin King*, 61–62, 171; Coretta King interview with Mayerson, 27: 51–52; Garrow, *Bearing the Cross*, 571.

31. Martin Luther King, Jr., "To Take Possession of Society," 1 Sept. 1967, Washington, D.C., 14, King Papers, King Center, which also appears in large part as "The Role of the Behavioral Scientist in the Civil Rights Movement" in the *Journal of Social Issues* 24 (1968): 1–12, see p.11, and in the *American Psychologist* 23 (1968): 180–86, see p.185; idem, "Address at Mt. Moriah Baptist Church," 18 Sept. 1967, Atlanta, Ga., 5–6, King Papers, King Center; idem, "Mastering Our Fears," 10 Sept. 1967, Ebenezer Baptist Church, Atlanta, Ga., King Papers, King Center.

32. Idem, "The State of the Movement" (also known as "A New Sense of Direction"), 28 Nov. 1967, Penn Community Center, Frogmore, S.C., King Papers, King Center.

33. Idem, "Prelude to Tomorrow," 6 Jan. 1968, Operation Breadbasket, Chicago, Ill., 8–9; idem, "The Meaning of Hope," 10 Dec. 1967, Dexter Avenue Baptist Church, Montgomery, Ala., 17; and idem, "In Search for a Sense of Direction," 7 Feb. 1968, Vermont Avenue Baptist Church, Washington, D.C., 10, King Papers, King Center.

34. Ralph Abernathy's testimony, 14 Aug. 1978, U.S. Congress, House of Representatives, Select Committee on Assassinations, *Hearings —Investigation of the Assassination of Martin Luther King, Jr.*, 95th Cong., 2nd sess., vol. 1, 25–26; Martin Luther King, Jr., "Unfulfilled Dreams," 3 Mar. 1968, Ebenezer Baptist Church, Atlanta, Ga., 2, King Papers, King Center.

35. Jesse Jackson interview with the author (3 Mar. 1985, Atlanta, Ga., and Montgomery and Selma, Ala.); Andrew Young interview with the author (27 July 1972, Atlanta, Ga.).

36. Dorothy Cotton interview with the author (8 Sept. 1979, Atlanta, Ga.).

37. Ralph Abernathy in Lerone Bennett, Jr., "The Martyrdom of Martin Luther King, Jr.," *Ebony* 23 (May 1968): 174–82, see p. 180; Coretta King interview with Mayerson, 28: 30; King and Levison in FBI New York 100-111180-9-1624A, 28 Mar. 1968. On Memphis generally, see Garrow, *The FBI and King*, 188–201, and idem, *Bearing the Cross*, 604–6, 609–24.

38. *New York Times*, 30 and 31 Mar. 1968; Garrow, *Bearing the Cross*, 616–18.

39. Martin Luther King, Jr., "I've Been to the Mountaintop," 3 Apr. 1968, Memphis, Tenn., King Papers, King Center.

ALDON D. MORRIS: "A MAN PREPARED FOR THE TIMES: A SOCIOLOGICAL ANALYSIS OF THE LEADERSHIP OF MARTIN LUTHER KING, JR."

1. Carroll Green, "A Man for All Nations," *American Visions* 1 (1986): 36–37.

2. Aldon D. Morris, *The Origins of the Civil Rights Movement: Black Communities Organizing for Change* (New York, 1984).

3. E. Franklin Frazier, *The Negro in the United States* (New York, 1949), 204.

4. Anthony Oberschall, *Social Conflict and Social Movements* (Englewood Cliffs, N.J., 1973); William Gamson, *The Strategy of Social Protest* (Homewood, Ill., 1975); Charles Tilly, *From Mobilization to Revolution* (Reading, Mass., 1978); Doug McAdam, *Political Process and the Development of Black Insurgency, 1930–1970* (Chicago, 1982); Morris, *Origins of Civil Rights Movement.*

5. SCLC, Constitution and By-Laws of the Southern Christian Leadership Conference (Atlanta, n.d.).

6. Morris, *Origins of Civil Rights Movement.*

7. Benjamin Mays and Joseph Nicholson, *The Negro Church* (New York, 1933); McAdam, *Political Process.*

8. McAdam, *Political Process,* 99.

9. Gunnar Myrdal, *An American Dilemma* (New York, 1944), 873.

10. McAdam, *Political Process,* 101–2.

11. W.E.B. Du Bois, *The Souls of Black Folk* (1953; reprint ed., New York, 1973), 108.

12. Benjamin Mays, *Born to Rebel* (New York, 1971), 186, 188.

13. Genna Rae McNeil, *Groundwork: Charles Hamilton Houston and the Struggle for Civil Rights* (Philadelphia, 1983).

14. Daniel C. Thompson, *A Black Elite: A Profile of Graduates of UNCF Colleges* (New York, 1986), 6.

15. Ibid., 150.

16. Mays, *Born to Rebel,* 172, 83.

17. Andrew Billingsley, *Black Families in White America* (Englewood Cliffs, N.J., 1968), 97.

18. Ibid., 94, 98.

19. Martin Luther King, Sr., with Riley Clayton, *Daddy King: An Autobiography* (New York, 1980), 24.

20. Lawrence D. Reddick, *Crusader without Violence: A Biography of Martin Luther King, Jr.* (New York, 1959), 42.

21. John F. Kennedy, *The Strategy of Peace* (New York, 1961), 30.

22. Ibid., 110–11.

23. Ibid., 178–79.

24. Ibid., 165.

25. Henry F. Jackson, *From the Congo to Soweto: U.S. Foreign Policy toward Africa since 1960* (New York, 1984), 121–68.

26. Robert Ivanov, *Blacks in United States History* (Moscow, 1985), 207.

27. Arthur M. Schlesinger, Jr., *A Thousand Days* (Boston, 1965), 556–57, 583.

28. Ibid., 583, 564.

29. Harris Wofford, *Of Kennedys and Kings* (New York, 1980), 166.

30. Ivanov, *Blacks in United States History*, 236.

31. Christopher H. Sterling and John M. Kittross, *Stay Tuned: A Concise History of American Broadcasting* (Belmont, 1978), 535.

32. Erik Barnouw, *Tube of Plenty: The Evolution of American Television* (New York, 1975), 288–89.

33. Ibid., 309–10; Sterling and Kittross, *Stay Tuned*, 379.

34. Lerone Bennett, Jr., *Confrontation: Black and White* (Baltimore, 1965); Joanne Grant, ed., *Black Protest: History, Documents, and Analyses, 1619 to the Present* (New York, 1967); Vincent Harding, *There Is a River: The Black Struggle for Freedom in America* (New York, 1983).

35. Stephen B. Oates, *Let the Trumpet Sound: The Life of Martin Luther King, Jr.* (New York, 1982), 6.

36. Lerone Bennett, Jr., *What Manner of Man? A Biography of Martin Luther King, Jr.*, 3d ed. (Chicago, 1968), 5–8.

37. Bennett, *Confrontation*, 18.

38. Ibid.; Oates, *Let the Trumpet Sound*.

39. Maurice Isserman, "Black Protest Movements," *Dissent* 33 (1986): 116.

40. Oates, *Let the Trumpet Sound*, 4.

41. King, Sr., *Daddy King*, 27.

42. Bennett, *What Manner of Man?*, 17.

43. Andrew Young, "Andrew Young Remembers Martin Luther King," Bill Moyers' Journal (transcript), 1979, 6.

44. Martin Luther King, Jr., *Stride toward Freedom: The Montgomery Story* (New York, 1958), 91.

45. Bennett, *What Manner of Man?*, 26.

46. Oates, *Let the Trumpet Sound*, 17.

47. Mays, *Born to Rebel*, 265, 184.

48. Interview with Wyatt Walker, 29 Sept. 1978.

49. Barnouw, *Tube of Plenty*, 207.

50. Letter from Stanley Levison to Aldon Morris, 21 Mar. 1979.

51. Barnouw, *Tube of Plenty*, 20.

52. Interview with Walker.

53. Interview with James Lawson, 2 and 6 Oct. 1978.

54. Martin Luther King, Jr., *Why We Can't Wait* (New York, 1964), 20–21.

55. Martin Luther King, Jr., *Where Do We Go from Here: Chaos or Community?* (New York, 1967), 169–70.

56. King, *Why We Can't Wait*, 21.

57. Schlesinger, *A Thousand Days*, 558.

58. King, *Why We Can't Wait*, 20.

59. Alan F. Westin and Barry Mahoney, *The Trial of Martin Luther King* (New York, 1974), 153–54.

60. King, *Why We Can't Wait,* 112.

61. Oates, *Let the Trumpet Sound,* 5.

62. King, *Daddy King,* 104–5, 100.

63. Bennett, *What Manner of Man?,* 10–11.

64. King, *Stride toward Freedom,* 100.

65. John J. Ansbro, *Martin Luther King, Jr.: The Making of a Mind* (Maryknoll, N.Y., 1982), 22.

66. Young, "Andrew Young Remembers," 5–6.

67. King, *Where Do We Go from Here?,* 160.

LOUIS R. HARLAN: "THOUGHTS ON THE LEADERSHIP OF MARTIN LUTHER KING, JR."

1. Richard M. Dalfiume, *Desegregation of the U.S. Armed Forces: Fighting on Two Fronts, 1939–1953* (Columbia, Mo., 1969).

2. August Meier and Elliott Rudwick, *CORE: A Study in the Civil Rights Movement, 1942–1968* (New York, 1973), 3–39.

3. C. Vann Woodward early recognized the relationship between the Cold War and the American racial dilemma. See *The Strange Career of Jim Crow,* 3d rev. ed. (New York, 1974), 130–32.

4. Richard Kluger, *Simple Justice: The History of Brown v. Board of Education and Black America's Struggle for Equality* (New York, 1976); J. Harvie Wilkinson III, *From Brown to Bakke: The Supreme Court and School Integration, 1954–1978* (New York, 1979).

5. See Numan V. Bartley, *The Rise of Massive Resistance: Race and Politics in the South during the 1950s* (Baton Rouge, 1969).

6. Aldon D. Morris, *The Origins of the Civil Rights Movement: Black Communities Organizing for Change* (New York, 1984), 17–25.

7. Meier and Rudwick, *CORE,* 6–7, 11–15.

8. Martin Luther King, Jr., *Stride toward Freedom: The Montgomery Story* (New York, 1958) is still the best narrative account of the bus boycott. For historical perspective, see David L. Lewis, *King: A Critical Biography* (New York, 1970), 46–84. J. Mills Thornton III is at work on a major historical study of the boycott.

9. Clayborne Carson, *In Struggle: SNCC and the Black Awakening of the 1960s* (Cambridge, Mass., 1981), 19–30.

10. August Meier, "On the Role of Martin Luther King," *New Politics* 4 (1965), 1–8, reprinted in Meier and Elliott Rudwick, *Along the Color Line: Explorations in the Black Experience* (Urbana, Ill., 1976), 174–85.

11. Carson, *In Struggle,* 164, citing interview with Stokely Carmichael, 18 Oct. 1977.

12. Meier and Rudwick, *Along the Color Line,* 176.

13. David L. Lewis, "Martin Luther King, Jr., and the Promise of

Nonviolent Populism," in John Hope Franklin and August Meier, eds., *Black Leaders of the Twentieth Century* (Urbana, Ill., 1982), 277–303.

14. Martin Luther King, Jr., *Why We Can't Wait* (New York, 1964), 146–47, 151–55.

15. This essay was written before the publication of the biography by David J. Garrow, *Bearing the Cross: Martin Luther King, Jr., and the Southern Christian Leadership Conference* (New York, 1986).

16. Harvard Sitkoff, *The Struggle for Black Equality, 1954–1980* (New York, 1981), provides a good survey and guide to further reading. See also Juan Williams, *Eyes on the Prize: America's Civil Rights Years, 1954–1965* (New York, 1987).

John Hope Franklin: "Martin Luther King, Jr., and the Afro-American Protest Tradition"

1. Martin Luther King, Jr., *Where Do We Go from Here: Chaos or Community?* (New York, 1967), 65.

2. For a delineation of the protest tradition, together with the documents, see Joanne Grant, ed., *Black Protest: History, Documents, and Analyses, 1619 to the Present* (New York, 1967).

3. Numerous examples of the resort to violence are provided by those who planned revolts—such as Denmark Vesey and Nat Turner—as well as those who poisoned their owners, burned their owners' property, and even mutilated themselves. See Raymond Bauer and Alice Bauer, "Day-to-Day Resistance to Slavery," *Journal of Negro History* 27 (1942): 388–419; Kenneth Stampp, *The Peculiar Institution: Slavery in the Ante-Bellum South* (New York, 1956), 86–140.

4. Massachusetts Historical Society *Collections*, 5th ser., 3 (Boston, 1877), 436–37.

5. Lamont D. Thomas, *Rise to Be a People: A Biography of Paul Cuffe* (Urbana, Ill., 1986), 9–12.

6. *United States Constitution*, Art. 4, Sec. 2.

7. I *U.S. Statutes*, 302.

8. *Annals of the Congress of the United States*, 4th Cong., 2d sess., 6 (Washington, 1849), 2015–18; Herbert Aptheker, *A Documentary History of the Negro People in the United States* (New York, 1951), 40–44.

9. II *U.S. Statutes*, 514–16.

10. Virginia Writers Project, *The Negro in Virginia* (New York, 1940), 175–76.

11. King, *Where Do We Go from Here?*, 65, 68–69.

12. Ibid., 72.

13. Quoted in Merle A. Richmond, *Bid the Vassal Soar: Interpretive Essays on the Life and Poetry of Phillis Wheatley . . . and George Moses Horton. . . .* (Washington, D.C., 1974), 110–11.

14. The complete text of Walker's *Appeal* is in Herbert Aptheker, *One Continual Cry: David Walker's Appeal to the Colored Citizens of the World*

(1829–1830): Its Setting and Its Meaning (New York, 1965), 61–147. The quotations may be found on pp. 101–2, 108.

15. Martin Luther King, Jr., *Why We Can't Wait* (New York, 1964), 85–86.

16. Earl Ofari, "Henry Highland Garnet," in Rayford W. Logan and Michael R. Winston, eds., *Dictionary of American Negro Biography* (New York, 1982), 252–53, and Leon F. Litwack, *North of Slavery: The Negro in the Free States, 1790–1860* (Chicago, 1961), 118–20.

17. Aptheker, *Documentary History of the Negro People,* 230–31.

18. Philip S. Foner, ed., *The Life and Writings of Frederick Douglass,* 5 vols. (New York, 1950–75), 2:181–204.

19. Although Douglass sympathized with Brown, he regarded his scheme to free the slaves as impracticable. But, he said, "Let every man work for the abolition of slavery in his own way" *(The Life and Times of Frederick Douglass, Written by Himself,* facsimile edition [Secaucus, N.J., 1983], 316).

20. Ibid., 282.

21. Benjamin Quarles, *Frederick Douglass* (Washington, D.C., 1948), 204–7.

22. For a discussion of the postwar vestiges of slavery, see Leon F. Litwack, *Been in the Storm So Long: The Aftermath of Slavery* (New York, 1979), especially "How Free Is Free?," 220–91.

23. John Hope Franklin, *Reconstruction after the Civil War* (Chicago, 1961), 49–53.

24. Aptheker, *Documentary History of the Negro People,* 534–47.

25. It was during the controversy in 1820 over the admission of Missouri that Jefferson remarked that in slavery Americans had a "wolf by the ears, and we can neither hold him, nor safely let him go. Justice is in one scale, and self-preservation in the other" (Paul L. Ford, ed., *The Writings of Thomas Jefferson,* 10 vols. [New York, 1892–99], 10:157–58).

26. Franklin, *Reconstruction,* 62–65.

27. Aptheker, *Documentary History of the Negro People,* 551.

28. Ibid., 562–63.

29. Allen W. Trelease, *White Terror: The Ku Klux Klan Conspiracy and Southern Reconstruction* (New York, 1971).

30. *Congressional Record,* 43d Cong., 2d sess., pt. 2, 947.

31. John Hope Franklin, "The Enforcement of the Civil Rights Act of 1875," *Prologue* 6 (1974): 225–35.

32. Alfreda M. Duster, ed., *Crusade for Justice: The Autobiography of Ida B. Wells* (Chicago, 1970), 35–59.

33. Ibid., 115–31.

34. Ida B. Wells-Barnett, *A Red Record: Tabulated Statistics and Alleged Causes of Lynchings in the United States, 1892–1893–1894* (Chicago, 1894), 12.

35. John Hope Franklin, *From Slavery to Freedom: A History of Negro Americans,* 5th ed. (New York, 1980), 274–80.

36. Ibid., 318–20.

37. King, *Where Do We Go from Here?*, 74.

38. Ibid., 76–77.

RICHARD H. KING: "MARTIN LUTHER KING, JR., AND THE MEANING OF FREEDOM: A POLITICAL INTERPRETATION"

1. Niccolò Machiavelli, *The Prince and The Discourses,* introduction by Max Lerner (New York, 1950); J.G.A. Pocock, *The Machiavellian Moment* (Princeton, 1975); Hanna Fenichel Pitkin, *Fortune Is a Woman* (Berkeley, Cal., 1984).

2. Georg Wilhelm Friedrich Hegel, *The Philosophy of History* (New York and London, 1900), 30, 31. In *Hegel's Theory of the Modern State* (Cambridge, 1972), Shlomo Avineri notes that Hegel never really made up his mind about the degree of self-consciousness possessed by the historical hero.

3. Ralph Waldo Emerson, "Fate," in *Selected Writings of Ralph Waldo Emerson* (New York, 1981), 670, 680, 682, 686.

4. Ibid., 688.

5. Machiavelli, *The Prince,* 92.

6. See particularly Kenneth L. Smith and Ira G. Zepp, Jr., *Search for the Beloved Community: The Thinking of Martin Luther King, Jr.* (Valley Forge, Pa., 1974), for a thorough analysis of King's theological and philosophical background.

7. Quoted in David L. Lewis, *King: A Critical Biography* (Baltimore, 1971), 109.

8. Martin Luther King, Jr., *Chaos or Community* (Harmondsworth, U.K., 1969), 98–99. This is the British edition of *Where Do We Go from Here?*

9. Lerone Bennett, Jr., *What Manner of Man? A Biography of Martin Luther King, Jr.,* 2d ed. (London, 1966), 75–76; Elie Landau, *King: A Filmed Record, Montgomery to Memphis* (1970), reel 3.

10. Quoted in Lewis, *King,* 236.

11. Erik Erikson, *Gandhi's Truth* (New York, 1969), 144.

12. Gary Wills, "Dr. King on the Case," in *Lead Time* (Garden City, N.Y., 1984), 29–50. This point about the importance of King's roots is the key to Wills's essay.

13. Quoted in Lewis, *King,* 236.

14. Ibid., 254.

15. Quoted in David J. Garrow, *The FBI and Martin Luther King, Jr.: From "Solo" to Memphis* (New York, 1981), 217–18.

16. Stephen B. Oates, *Let the Trumpet Sound: The Life of Martin Luther King, Jr.* (New York, 1982), 232.

17. Robert Stepto, *From behind the Veil* (Urbana, Ill., 1979).

18. Bennett effectively makes this point in his biography of King.

19. This positive reading of King's response to the difficulties of his

last two years is emphasized by Manning Marable, "Toward an Understanding of Martin Luther King, Jr.," *From the Grassroots* (Boston, 1980), 51–58, and Taylor Branch, "Uneasy Holiday," *New Republic,* 3 Feb. 1986, 22–27.

20. King, *Chaos or Community,* 66.

21. See Smith and Zepp, *Search for the Beloved Community,* as well as Hanes Walton, *The Political Philosophy of Martin Luther King, Jr.* (Westport, Conn., 1971).

22. King, *Chaos or Community,* 98; Lillian Smith, *The Winner Names the Age* (New York, 1978).

23. Martin Luther King, Jr., *Strength to Love* (London, 1969), 50. The classic work on this subject is Anders Nygren, *Agape and Eros* (London, 1954), and Gene Outka, *Agape: An Ethical Analysis* (New Haven, 1972), is a valuable discussion. In *Search for the Beloved Community* Smith and Zepp claim that King rejected the view that one should love one's enemy only because God loves him or her (pp. 63–66). The passage quoted in the text would call that claim into question.

24. Martin Luther King, Jr., *Stride toward Freedom: The Montgomery Story* (New York, 1958), 107; the second part of the quotation is from Smith and Zepp, *Search for the Beloved Community,* 113.

25. See Smith and Zepp, *Search for the Beloved Community,* 25–26; Martin Luther King, Jr., *Why We Can't Wait* (New York, 1964), 61. See also Sacvan Bercovitch, *The Puritan Origins of the American Self* (New Haven, Conn., 1975), and idem, *The American Jeremiad* (Madison, Wis., 1978), for the "white" origins of this sense of chosenness and the centrality of the jeremiad. For the black origins of similar themes, see Vincent Harding, *There Is a River: The Black Struggle for Freedom in America* (New York, 1983) and V. P. Franklin, *Black Self-Determination* (Westport, Conn., 1984).

26. King, *Why We Can't Wait,* 93.

27. King, *Chaos or Community,* 129.

28. King, *Stride toward Freedom,* 37, 215.

29. King, *Why We Can't Wait,* 30.

30. King, *Chaos or Community,* 44–46, 57.

31. King, *Why We Can't Wait,* 80; idem, *Stride toward Freedom,* 101.

32. King, *Why We Can't Wait,* 39. The visual trope dominates the Sartrean account of interpersonal relationships as explored in *Being and Nothingness.*

33. King, *Why We Can't Wait,* 100.

34. King, *Chaos or Community,* 28.

35. Ibid., 71, 84.

36. Ibid., 102–3, 106, 112.

37. Ibid., 92, 91.

38. King, *Why We Can't Wait,* 81, 94.

39. King's indictment of white southern moderates and his acceptance of the "extremist" label owed much to Lillian Smith, particularly her "The Right Way Is Not a Moderate Way" (1956). A copy of it can be found in

the Martin Luther King, Jr., Papers, Mugar Library, Boston University. It is printed in Smith, *Winner Names the Age*, 67–75.

40. In *Stride toward Freedom* King says "one of the great glories of democracy is the right to protest for right" (p. 62), while Oates records that at Montgomery King said, "One of the great glories of American democracy is that we have the right to protest for rights" (*Let the Trumpet Sound*, 78–79). The voice recording in the Landau film indicates that at Montgomery he said, "The great glory of American democracy is the right to protest for right," while at Memphis he modified it to "The greatness of America is the right to protest for right." There is a difference between protesting for "right" and "a right" or "rights." "Right" is a moral term (that is, "He was right to return the billfold he found") but "a right" is a legal entity (that is, "I have a right to buy alcohol if I am a certain age") that can have a plural: "rights."

41. Hannah Arendt, *The Origins of Totalitarianism*, 2d ed. (Cleveland, 1958), 296. Arendt went on to add that racism foreclosed freedom for black people, less because of its demeaning content than that it rendered all black opinion or action deducible from racial traits. See Stephen J. Whitfield, *Into the Dark* (Philadelphia, 1980), 110–12, for the history of the influence of this notion of a right to have right(s) on Supreme Court decisions in the 1950s and 1960s.

42. My discussion of just and unjust laws focuses on King's account in "Letter from Birmingham Jail" in King, *Why We Can't Wait*, 82–83. The core of "Letter" can be found in idem, "Love, Law and Civil Disobedience," (1961), *Civil Disobedience in America*, ed. by David R. Weber (Ithaca, N.Y., 1978), 212–19. Only in the essay of 1961 does King explicitly acknowledge that natural law thinking is foreign to most people.

43. See John Rawls, *A Theory of Justice* (Cambridge, Mass., 1971), and Ronald Dworkin, *Taking Rights Seriously* (Cambridge, Mass., 1977), for influential liberal theories of civil disobedience. Dworkin challenges the view that the lawbreaker is duty bound to accept the punishment for breaking the law. April Carter, *Direct Action and Liberal Democracy* (London, 1973), is a less theoretically, more historically oriented discussion of the various ways of considering civil disobedience.

44. The notion of political participation as a kind of freedom is central to the civic humanist/republican tradition of politics, the most powerful contemporary exponent of which is Hannah Arendt. My claim about participatory freedom does not depend on the conscious intentions or awareness of the participants in the civil rights movement. Finally, the distinction between assertion and implication roughly parallels the distinction in speech-act theory between locutionary and illocutionary speech-acts.

45. King, *Chaos or Community*, 58.

46. Hannah Arendt, "Civil Disobedience," in *Crises of the Republic* (New York, 1972), 51–102. The material quoted is found on p. 56.

47. See George Kateb, *Hannah Arendt: Politics, Conscience, Evil* (Oxford, 1981), chaps. 1 and 3.

48. King, *Why We Can't Wait*, 38.

49. Ibid., 39.

50. Pat Watters, *Down to Now: Reflections on the Southern Civil Rights Movement* (New York, 1971), 7. Hannah Arendt develops the idea of "public happiness" in *On Revolution* (New York, 1965).

51. Interview with Ella Baker, Civil Rights Documentation Project, Moorland-Spingarn Research Center, Howard University, Washington, D.C., 16.

52. In *Black Self-Determination*, Franklin gets at something like this when he contrasts "political" and "cultural" self-determination (p. 8).

53. Hans Gerth and C. Wright Mills, eds., *From Max Weber* (New York, 1958), 126.

54. See Philip Rieff, *Triumph of the Therapeutic* (New York, 1965) for the original statement of this shift from moral and religious to psychological and therapeutic descriptions of the self.

55. This is an incredibly complicated problem. One way to begin sorting it out might be to distinguish deeply rooted racism, which fills some "need" in an individual and group, from conformist or institutional racism. The question about the morality of racism might be addressed to the latter but not the former version of racism.

56. See Richard Rorty, "Contingency as Community," *London Review of Books* 8 (24 July 1986): 10–14 for an extended discussion of this point.

57. See Reinhold Niebuhr, *Moral Man and Immoral Society* (New York, 1942), chap. 9.

58. Martin Luther King, Jr., *Trumpet of Conscience* (New York, 1968), 15.

59. King, *Chaos or Community*, 126.

60. See David J. Garrow, *Protest at Selma* (New Haven, Conn., 1978). Here it should be stated that King and his associates were quite mindful of this element of danger involved in nonviolent "provocation."

61. See Arendt, *Crises of the Republic*, 53, for a statement from law professor Charles Black to this effect.

62. Hannah Arendt, *The Human Condition* (Garden City, N.Y., 1959), 218.

63. Friedrich Nietzsche, *The Use and Abuse of History* (Indianapolis, Ind., 1957).

64. King, *Strength to Love*, 49.

GEORGE M. HOUSER: "FREEDOM'S STRUGGLE CROSSES OCEANS AND MOUNTAINS: MARTIN LUTHER KING, JR., AND THE LIBERATION STRUGGLES IN AFRICA AND AMERICA"

1. Homer A. Jack wrote a retrospective on the conference in the newsletter *Toward Freedom*, published in Chicago (Mar.–Apr. 1985).

2. Martin Luther King, Jr., "The Wind of Change Is Blowing," *New York Amsterdam News,* 7 July 1962. The article's title came from a phrase in a speech by British Prime Minister Harold Macmillan in Cape Town, South Africa, early in 1960.

3. Quoted by Inez Smith Reid, "Black Americans and Africa," in Mabel M. Smythe, ed., *The Black American Reference Book* (Englewood Cliffs, N.J., 1976), 660.

4. The original name of the organization in Jamaica was the Universal Negro Improvement and Conservation Association and African Communities League.

5. George Padmore, *Pan-Africanism or Communism* (New York, 1971), 87. Padmore points out that many critics claimed the adherents were only half that number.

6. W.E.B. Du Bois, *Dusk to Dawn* (1940; reprint ed., New York, 1968), 277.

7. Padmore, *Pan-Africanism,* 102–3.

8. W.E.B. Du Bois, *The Souls of Black Folk* (Greenwich, Conn., 1953), 23, 16–17.

9. W.E.B. Du Bois, "Little Portraits of Africa," *Crisis* 27 (1924): 274.

10. Ibid., 278.

11. The Congress grew out of a NAACP project to investigate the treatment of black American soldiers at the end of World War I.

12. He was given the title of envoy extraordinary and minister plenipotentiary to the inauguration of President C.D.B. King of Liberia.

13. W.E.B. Du Bois, *The Autobiography of W.E.B. Du Bois: A Soliloquy on Viewing My Life from the Last Decade of Its First Century* (New York, 1968), 291, 344.

14. *Crisis* 36 (1929): 424.

15. Reid, "Black Americans and Africa," 666.

16. Martin Luther King, Jr., "Honoring Dr. Du Bois," *Freedomways* 8 (1968): 104–6, 110.

17. Paul Robeson quoted in *Spotlight on Africa* (newsletter of the Council on African Affairs), 27 Feb. 1952.

18. Hollis R. Lynch, *Black American Radicals and the Liberation of Africa: The Council on African Affairs* (Ithaca, N.Y., 1978), is a helpful source of information.

19. Liberian ambassador to Martin Luther King, Jr., 24 Feb. 1959, Martin Luther King, Jr., Papers, Mugar Library, Boston University.

20. Stokely Carmichael and Charles Hamilton, *Black Power* (New York, 1957), xi.

21. Interview with James Farmer, June 1986.

22. "Let My People Go," in Eduardo Mondlane, ed., *The Struggle for Mozambique* (Harmondsworth, U.K., 1969), 110.

23. King describes this incident in *Where Do We Go from Here: Chaos or Community?* (New York, 1967), chap. 2.

24. "It is not enough to condemn black power," Oct. 1966, Martin

Luther King, Jr., Papers, Martin Luther King, Jr., Center for Nonviolent Social Change, Atlanta, Ga.

25. James Farmer, *Lay Bare the Heart* (New York, 1985), 229. George Breitman, *The Last Year of Malcolm X* (New York, 1967), 43.

26. The text of the Basic Unity Program of the OAAU is to be found in the appendix of Breitman, *Last Year of Malcolm X.*

27. Malcolm X, press conference, Mar. 12, 1964, in *Malcolm X Speaks: Selected Speeches and Statements* (New York, 1966), 21–22.

28. King Papers, King Center. There is no record of the precise date or place of the speech. Martin Luther King, Jr., *Why We Can't Wait* (New York, 1964), 91.

29. The text of the speech is in the files of the American Committee on Africa, which sponsored the meeting (American Committee on Africa archives, Amistad Research Center, Tulane University, New Orleans).

30. *Playboy,* Jan. 1965.

31. See his speech made on the occasion of the golden anniversary of the Urban League, Dec. 1960, in James M. Washington, ed., *A Testament of Hope* (New York, 1986), 146. Similar ideas are also found in his article "The Time for Freedom Has Come," *New York Times Magazine,* 10 Sept. 1961.

32. King, *Why We Can't Wait,* p. 83.

33. King to Tom Mboya, 8 July 1959, King Papers, King Center.

34. From a speech made 24 Nov. 1962, at the American Negro Leadership Conference on Africa, King Papers, King Center; *New York Amsterdam News,* 27 Oct. 1962.

35. Quoted in Stephen B. Oates, *Let the Trumpet Sound: The Life of Martin Luther King, Jr.* (New York, 1982), 118.

36. King, *Where Do We Go from Here?,* 53.

37. Ibid., 171.

38. John B. Morsell to George M. Houser, 13 Jan. 1959.

39. King to Kwame Nkrumah, 17 Apr. 1959, King Papers, Boston University.

40. Ibid., n.d. The notes are in his own handwriting.

41. Quoted in Homer A. Jack, "Conversation in Ghana," *Christian Century,* 10 Apr. 1957. Jack was the representative of the American Committee on Africa at Ghana's independence and spent some time with Dr. King there.

42. From a radio sermon given in Atlanta, Ga., 22 Mar. 1959, King Papers, King Center.

43. See *Declaration of Conscience,* American Committee on Africa archives.

44. See the American Committee on Africa archives. In 1962, American economic ties with South Africa were beginning to grow. Capital investment exceeded $700 million, more than half of all American investment in Africa. Trade had reached $500 million. Twenty years later the United States was South Africa's chief trading partner, and direct and indirect American investments had reached almost $14 billion.

45. King to Albert Luthuli, 8 Dec. 1959, King Papers, Boston University.

46. Rev. James W. King to Martin Luther King, Jr., 25 Mar. 1964, King Papers, King Center.

47. Martin Luther King, Jr., to James King, 6 Apr. 1964, King Papers, King Center.

48. Speeches in the King Papers, King Center.

49. 10 Dec. 1965, American Committee on Africa files.

50. King's letter of 9 Feb. and the response from N. M. Nel, South African vice-counsel, 17 Mar. 1966, are located in the King Papers, King Center.

51. *Cape Times,* 25, 22 Nov. 1965.

52. AMSAC grew out of the first International Congress of Writers and Artists in Paris in 1957. Composed of black intellectuals and professionals, it combined a cultural with a political interest in Africa. It disbanded when the exposé of CIA involvement with a broad spectrum of American organizations also revealed some assistance to AMSAC, to the consternation of most of its membership.

53. *Washington Star,* 27 May 1969.

54. The essence of the reform by the government of Prime Minister John Vorster was to make it possible for South Africa to have a multiracial team for international competition, but with members selected in separate, and racially segregated trials. The prime minister, in announcing the reform, had said there would still be no mixed sports events in South Africa, and on this there would be no compromise, negotiations, or abandonment of principles. See a January 1982 document issued by the United Nations Center against Apartheid, "The International Impact of South Africa's Struggle for Liberation," 21.

55. *New York Times,* 5 Apr. 1985.

JAMES H. CONE: "MARTIN LUTHER KING, JR., AND THE THIRD WORLD"

1. Cited in Coretta Scott King, *My Life with Martin Luther King, Jr.* (New York, 1969), 294.

2. The Ecumenical Association of Third World Theologians (EATWOT) is an organization of Asian, African, Latin American, Caribbean, and U.S. minority Christian scholars and activists. It was founded in Dar es Salaam, Tanzania, in 1976, for the purpose of encouraging persons in each region to work together to broaden their analysis of the sociopolitical and religiocultural structures in their countries and to develop a theology that is accountable to the large numbers of the poor. International conferences have been held in Accra, Ghana (1977), Wennappuwa, Sri Lanka (1979), São Paulo (1980), New Delhi (1981), and Geneva (1983). For an interpretation of EATWOT, see James H. Cone, "Ecumenical Association of Third World Theologians," *Ecumenical Trends* 14 (1985): 119–22; idem, "Black Theology and Third World Theologies," in idem, *My Soul Looks Back* (Maryknoll, N.Y., 1983), chap. 4. See also

Theo Witvliet, *A Place in the Sun: An Introduction to Liberation Theology in the Third World* (Maryknoll, N.Y., 1985). An account of each international conference has been published by Orbis books at Maryknoll, N.Y. See especially those of the Dar es Salaam meeting in Sergio Torres and Virginia Fabella, eds., *The Emergent Gospel: Theology from the Underside of History* (1978), of the New Delhi meeting in Virginia Fabella and Sergio Torres, eds., *Irruption of the Third World: Challenge to Theology* (1983), and the Geneva meeting in idem, eds., *Doing Theology in a Divided World* (1985).

3. The effect of Martin King's life and thought on the Third World is obviously more difficult to evaluate. Scholars have just begun the painstaking task of assessing his impact upon American life and culture. Only with the passage of time, after many of the celebrations honoring him have subsided, will scholars be able to determine more precisely his meaning for America. Even more time will be needed before an adequate assessment can be made of his significance for the Third World. We must be careful not to equate well-meaning birthday celebrations with abiding significance.

4. For the purposes of this essay, I have limited my analysis chiefly to two periods in King's thinking, but it is important to note that I have found three periods in the development of his life and thought from the time of the Montgomery bus boycott (5 Dec. 1955) to his assassination (4 Apr. 1968). The first period is quite brief (the early weeks of the boycott) and is defined by his primary focus on *justice*. The second period (early 1956 to the fall of 1965) focuses primarily on love, with justice and hope interpreted in its light. The third period (1966 to his assassination in 1968) focuses primarily on hope, with love and justice seen from its perspective. The distinctions are not rigid but rather a matter of emphasis in his thinking. In all periods concern for justice, love, and hope is present and the three are intertwined. For an interpretation of the development of King's thinking in terms of the three periods, see James H. Cone, "The Theology of Martin Luther King, Jr.," in *Union Seminary Quarterly Review* 40 (1986): 21–39.

5. See Martin Luther King, Jr., "The Legitimacy of the Struggle in Montgomery," 4 May 1956 (one-page statement), Martin Luther King, Jr., Papers, Martin Luther King, Jr., Center for Nonviolent Social Change, Atlanta, Ga.

6. Idem, "The Birth of a New Age," 7–11 Aug. 1956, 86, King Papers.

7. Ibid. King also used this statement in his first major address at Holt Street Baptist Church, 5 Dec. 1955, and repeated it in several addresses. A tape and a printed copy are in the King Papers.

8. Idem, "Facing the Challenge of a New Age," *Phylon,* Apr. 1957, 26. This is the published version of King's address of 3 Dec. 1956, at the First Annual Institute on Nonviolence and Social Change, Montgomery, Ala. It is essentially the same address that he delivered at the Alpha Phi Alpha convention in August of the same year.

9. See idem, "The Time for Freedom Has Come," *New York Times Magazine,* 10 Sept. 1961.

10. Ibid., 25.

11. For King's interpretation of the impact on him of the independence celebration of Ghana, see especially idem, "Birth of a New Nation," Apr. 1957 (twenty-two-page address), Dexter Avenue Baptist Church; see also Homer A. Jack, "Conversation in Ghana," *Christian Century,* 10 Apr. 1957, 446–48. For King's interpretation of his trip to India, see Martin Luther King, Jr., "My Trip to the Land of Gandhi," *Ebony,* July 1959; idem, "Sermon on Gandhi," 22 Mar. 1959 (eleven-page address), King Papers. See also Swami Vishwananda, "With the Kings in India," a souvenir of Dr. Martin Luther King's visit to India, Feb.–Mar. 1959. Gandhi National Memorial Fund; "Farewell Statement" of King on his departure from New Delhi, 9 Mar. 1959 (one-page statement); "Statement of Dr. King upon Landing at New York City," 18 Mar. 1959 (one-page statement), King Papers.

12. King, "The Time for Freedom," 118.

13. Idem, "Facing the Challenge," 25.

14. Ibid.

15. Ibid.

16. Idem, "Letter from Birmingham City Jail," *The New Leader,* 24 June 1963, 8.

17. Idem; "Pilgrimage to Nonviolence," in Martin Luther King, Jr., *Strength to Love* (1963; reprint ed., Philadelphia, 1981), 154.

18. Idem, *Stride toward Freedom: The Montgomery Story* (New York, 1958), 44.

19. King, *My Life with Martin King,* 183.

20. See especially Martin Luther King's commencement address at Lincoln University, "The American Dream," 6 June 1961, published in the *Negro History Bulletin* 31 (May 1968): 10–15. This address was presented in Lynchburg, Va., 12 Mar. 1961, and is available on tape at the King Center Gift Shop, Atlanta, Ga.

21. Ibid.

22. Idem, "The Acceptance Speech of Martin Luther King, Jr., of the Nobel Peace Prize on Dec. 10, 1964," in the *Negro History Bulletin* 31 (May 1968): 21.

23. See idem, "The Quest for Peace and Justice," 11 Dec. 1964, Oslo, Norway (King's Nobel lecture), King Papers.

24. Ibid., 5.

25. See idem, "Nonviolence: The Only Road to Freedom," *Ebony,* Oct. 1966.

26. Idem, "My Trip to the Land of Gandhi," 86.

27. *"Playboy* Interview: Martin Luther King," a reprint of the January 1965 issue of *Playboy.*

28. Martin Luther King, Jr., "Transforming a Neighborhood into a Brotherhood," 10 Aug. 1967, National Association of Real Estate Brokers, San Francisco, 9, King Papers.

29. Idem, "The Sickness of America," 16 Mar. 1968, Los Angeles (taped address), King Papers.

30. See idem, "Rally Speech," 19 Mar. 1968, Laurel, Miss., 3–4, King Papers.

31. See idem, "Next Stop: The North," *Saturday Review,* 31 Nov. 1965.

32. See idem, *Where Do We Go from Here: Chaos or Community?* (Boston, 1968), 112.

33. For an account of the origin of this theological movement, widely known as "Black Theology," see James H. Cone, *For My People* (Maryknoll, N.Y., 1984).

34. James Bevel, one of King's aides, often spoke of the Chicago slums as a "system of internal colonialism." King adopted the same description for his addresses. See the "Chicago Plan," a statement by Martin Luther King, Jr., 7 Jan. 1966, 3; idem, "European Tour," Mar. 1966, 8, King Papers.

35. Cited in Stephen B. Oates, *Let the Trumpet Sound: The Life of Martin Luther King, Jr.* (New York, 1982), 390.

36. King, *Where Do We Go from Here?,* 133.

37. Ibid.

38. Ibid.

39. Ibid., 167.

40. See note 4 above.

41. See Martin Luther King, Jr., "Thou Fool," 27 Aug. 1967, Mt. Pisgah Missionary Baptist Church, Chicago, 14, King Papers. This sermon includes King's account of his deep crisis of fear during the Montgomery bus boycott, which led to his appropriation of the faith of his early childhood. I think this is the most critical turning point in his life. Although I have always maintained that King's faith, as defined by the black church, was indispensible for understanding his life and thought, David J. Garrow was the first person to identify the "kitchen experience" (as it might be called) as the decisive experience in defining his faith. See especially Garrow's definitive text, *Bearing the Cross: Martin Luther King, Jr., and the Southern Christian Leadership Conference* (New York, 1986). My interpretation of the experience is found in Cone, "Theology of King," 26–28.

42. For an account of the development of King's position on Vietnam, see Adam Fairclough, "Martin Luther King, Jr., and the War in Vietnam," *Phylon* 55 (1984); see also Russell E. Dowdy, "Nonviolence vs. Nonexistence: The Vietnam War and Martin Luther King, Jr." (M.A. thesis, North Carolina State University, Raleigh, 1983). For King's reference to his dream being turned into a nightmare, see especially his "Christmas Sermon on Peace," in *Trumpet of Conscience* (New York, 1968), 75–78.

43. Idem, "Why I Am Opposed to the War in Vietnam," 30 Apr. 1967, Ebenezer Baptist Church, Atlanta, Ga., 8, King Papers.

44. Idem, "A Testament of Hope," reprinted from *Playboy,* Jan. 1969, 4.

45. Idem, "Why I Am Opposed," 6.

46. Idem, "Who Are We?" 5 Feb. 1966, 9, King Papers.

47. Idem, "Why I Am Opposed," 3, 4.

48. Idem, "Standing by the Best in an Evil Time," 6 Aug. 1967, Ebenezer Baptist Church, Atlanta, Ga., 7–8, King Papers.

49. Ibid., 6.

50. Idem, "To Minister to the Valley," 23 Feb. 1968, Ministers' Leadership Training Program, Miami, 13, King Papers.

51. "Beyond Vietnam," 4 Apr. 1967, Riverside Church, New York City, reprinted in 1982 as a pamphlet entitled *Martin Luther King, Jr.: Beyond Vietnam* by Clergy and Laity Concerned, with responses by Robert M. Brown, Vincent Harding, Anne Braden, and C. T. Vivian, 1.

52. This was a point that King repeatedly made.

53. Martin Luther King, Jr., 22 Mar. 1968, Albany, Ga., 7, King Papers.

54. Idem, "Which Way Shall We Go?" 2 Aug. 1967, Louisville, Ky., 15, King Papers.

55. Idem, *Trumpet of Conscience*, 76.

56. Idem, "The Other America," 10 Mar. 1968, address at Local 1199, Hunter College, N.Y., 11, King Papers.

57. Idem, *Stride toward Freedom*, 81.

58. See idem, "Quest for Peace and Justice," 13.

59. For a fuller account of my experience in South Korea, see James H. Cone, "A Black American Perspective on the Asian Search for a Full Humanity," in Virginia Fabella, ed., *Asia's Struggle for Full Humanity* (Maryknoll, N.Y., 1980), 177–90.

60. For accounts of the international celebrations of King's legacy, see Carroll Green, "A Man for All Nations," *American Visions* 1 (1986): 36–37; Martin Luther King, Jr., Federal Holiday Commission, "1986 Report"; see also the Commission's news release, 6 Mar. 1986, King Papers.

61. Statement by Rev. Canon L. John Collins, president of the International Defense and Aid Fund for Southern Africa, in United Nations *International Tribute to Martin Luther King, Jr.* (New York, 1979), 46.

62. Statement by Paul Vomani (Tanzanian ambassador to the United States), ibid., 23.

63. Interview with Tissa Balasuriya in Beijing, China, May 1986. In addition to Balasuriya, other interviews with EATWOT members regarding King's impact on the Third World included José Miguez Bonino (Argentina), Carmen Lora (Peru), Virginia Fabella (Philippines), and Engelbert Mveng (Cameroun). I also interviewed Ms. Zhang Lei, a young Chinese university student who was our interpreter during EATWOT's visit to China, and Ms. Theresa Chu (our guide) of the Canada China Programme. I also have had many conversations with graduate students from the Third World in my class entitled "Martin Luther King, Jr., and Malcolm X" at Union Seminary. My interpretation of King's impact on the Third World has been greatly influenced by these conversations.

64. World Council of Churches, *World Conference on Church and Society: Official Report,* with a description of the conference by M. M. Thomas and Paul Abrecht (Geneva, 1967), 6.

65. Ibid., 41.

66. This sermon is also found in King, *Strength to Love,* 56–66. See Oates's discussion of King's invitation to speak at the WCC meeting in Oates, *Let the Trumpet Sound,* 410.

67. M. M. Thomas, "Awakened Peoples, Developing Nations, and the Dynamics of World Politics," in Harvey Cox, ed., *The Church amid Revolution: A Selection of the Essays Prepared for the World Council of Churches' Geneva Conference on Church and Society* (New York, 1967), 111. This volume is an excellent summary of the revolutionary spirit emerging among Third World Christians.

68. Ibid., 113. See also M. M. Thomas, *Towards a Theology of Contemporary Ecumenism: A Collection of Addresses to Ecumenical Gatherings (1947–1975)* (Madras, 1978). This collection (which includes the preparatory essay quoted here) is quite useful for analyzing the development of radical thinking in the international church meetings among Protestants. Thomas's work on Asia and the Third World is perhaps the most influential by a Protestant theologian in the second half of the twentieth century. He has shown a special interest in King. See his "Basic Approaches to Power—Gandhiji, Andrews, and King," *Religion and Society* 16 (Sept. 1969): 15–25; idem, "Significance of the Critique of Gandhian Presuppositions by Martin Luther King for the Development of a Non-violent Strategy of the Revolution," in Arthur Rich, ed., *Humane Gesellschaft Beitrage zu Ihrer Sozialen Gestaltung* (Zurich, 1970), 319–32.

69. Ibid., 114.

70. Ibid.

71. World Council of Churches, *World Conference on Church and Society,* 6. See also Paul Bock, *In Search of a Responsible World Society: The Social Teachings of the World Council of Churches* (Philadelphia, 1974).

72. See especially "Medellin Documents: Justice, Peace, Family and Demography, Poverty of the Church," in Joseph Gremillion, ed., *The Gospel of Peace and Justice* (Maryknoll, N.Y., 1976), 445–76. See also International Documentation on the Contemporary Church, ed., *When All Else Fails: Christian Arguments on Violent Revolution* (Philadelphia, 1970). Camilo Torres was a well-known Latin American priest who joined the guerrilla movement and was killed in 1966. His writings and death did much to inspire the rise of liberation theology in Latin America. See Camilo Torres, *Revolutionary Writings,* trans. R. Olsen and L. Day (New York, 1969). The classic text on liberation theology in Latin America is Gustavo Gutierrez, *A Theology of Liberation,* trans. Caridad Inda and John Eagleson (Maryknoll, N.Y., 1973). An excellent introduction to this theology is José M. Bonino, *Doing Theology in a Revolutionary Situation* (Philadelphia, 1975). In response to my question regarding King's impact in Latin America during the 1960s and 1970s, Bonino said: "Although Martin King was widely known as the most prominent leader of the black freedom struggle

in the 1960s, his impact on Latin America was not significantly felt during the 1960s because of the powerful presence and enormous influence of Che Guevara and his advocacy of radical change through violent revolution. It was not until the 1970s that Martin King's voice was heard by many Latin Americans. He was best known for his advocacy of radical change through nonviolence, and Don Helder Camara was his most articulate and influential supporter." Bonino gave two major reasons for the turn toward Martin King: (1) "the failure of the guerrilla movements in many Latin American countries (Bolivia, Uruguay, Argentina, etc.), due both to the strength of the military and the lack of support of the masses of the people"; and (2) "the take-over by military regimes in country after country. . . . This forced the people to think of an alternative form to resist persecution and repression. Thus both the idea of nonviolent resistance and the methods of the civil rights movement in the United States were adopted by many groups in Latin America" (interview with José M. Bonino, May 1986).

73. C. S. Banana, "In Search of Human Justice," Martin Luther King Lecture, 22 Oct. 1981, Wesley Theological Seminary, Washington, D.C., 1–2. See also Banana's *Theology of Promise: The Dynamics of Self-Reliance* (Harare, Zimbabwe, 1982), 89–105.

74. See especially Allan Boesak, "Coming in Out of the Wilderness: A Comparative Interpretation of the Ethics of Martin Luther King, Jr., and Malcolm X" (Ph.D. thesis, Theologische Hogeschool der Gereformeerde Kerken, Kampenm, Netherlands, 1976).

75. Idem, *Farewell to Innocence: A Socio-Ethical Study on Black Theology and Black Power* (Maryknoll, N.Y., 1977), 70.

76. Included in the group were Cornel West of Yale University Divinity School and Charles Villa-Vicencio of Cape Town, South Africa. Boesak's similarity to King is found not only in the content of what he says but also in his style of saying it. See especially his address, "Peace in Our Day," 20 Aug. 1983, Cape Town, South Africa, in idem, *Black and Reformed* (Maryknoll, N.Y., 1984), 155–63.

77. See Desmond Tutu's interview under the title, "King Was a Pacifist; I'm Just a Peace-lover," in *USA Today*, 20 Jan. 1986. See also Christopher Whipple, *"Life* Visits Bishop Tutu," *Life* 8 (Nov. 1985), 116.

78. Desmond Tutu, *Hope and Suffering* (Grand Rapids, Mich., 1984), 158.

79. See "Tutu Begs West to Turn on Heat," in *Winnipeg Free Press,* 1 June 1986. To my knowledge, this is the first occasion that Tutu explicitly said that the Church would be justified in condoning violence in South Africa. But he has hinted at it many times with his suggestion that apartheid and nazism are identical.

80. Commenting on white South Africans who failed to express moral outrage regarding the oppression of blacks, Tutu said: "I don't think they get appalled. Shouldn't they have been appalled by sixty-nine people being killed at Sharpeville? Shouldn't they be appalled that many hundreds have been killed? Children are being put in jail. Where is the

moral outrage?" ("*Penthouse* Interview: Bishop Desmond Tutu," *Penthouse,* June 1986, 113).

81. See *Pine Bluff Commercial,* 23 July 1986.

82. Tutu, "*Penthouse* Interview," 114.

83. King, "Facing the Challenge," 34.

84. Cited in Pat Watters, *Down to Now: Reflections on the Southern Civil Rights Movement* (New York, 1971), 366.

85. King, "To Minister to the Valley," 21.

CLAYBORNE CARSON: "RECONSTRUCTING THE KING LEGACY: SCHOLARS AND NATIONAL MYTHS"

The author wishes to thank Penny Russell, Rachel Bagby, Susan Carson, Leslie Harris, Karl Knapper, and other members of the staff of the Martin Luther King, Jr., Papers for their assistance.

1. David J. Garrow, *Bearing the Cross: Martin Luther King, Jr., and the Southern Christian Leadership Conference* (New York, 1986); Taylor Branch, *Parting the Waters: America in the King Years, 1954–63* (New York, 1988).

2. See Lawrence D. Reddick, *Crusader without Violence: A Biography of Martin Luther King, Jr.* (New York, 1959); Lerone Bennett, Jr., *What Manner of Man? A Biography of Martin Luther King, Jr.* (Chicago, 1964); and William R. Miller, *Martin Luther King, Jr.: His Life, Martyrdom, and Meaning for the World* (New York, 1968).

3. August Meier, "On the Role of Martin Luther King," *New Politics* 4 (1965): 1–8; David L. Lewis, *King: A Critical Biography* (New York, 1970).

4. Kenneth L. Smith and Ira G. Zepp, Jr., *Search for the Beloved Community: The Thinking of Martin Luther King, Jr.* (Valley Forge, Pa., 1974); Harold L. DeWolf, "Martin Luther King, Jr., as Theologian," *Journal of the Interdenominational Theological Center* 4 (1977), 1–11; John J. Ansbro, *Martin Luther King, Jr.: The Making of a Mind* (Maryknoll, N.Y., 1982).

5. James P. Hanigan, "Martin Luther King, Jr.: The Shaping of a Mind," *Debate & Understanding* 1 (1977): 190–206, idem, *Martin Luther King, Jr., and the Foundations of Nonviolence* (Lanham, Md., 1984). See also Paul R. Garber, "Black Theology: The Latter Day Legacy of Martin Luther King, Jr.," *Journal of the Interdenominational Theological Center* 2 (1975): 100–113.

6. Lewis V. Baldwin, "Martin Luther King, Jr., The Black Church, and the Black Messianic Vision," *Journal of the Interdenominational Theological Center* 12 (1984–85): 93–108; James H. Cone, "Martin Luther King, Jr., Black Theology—Black Church," *Theology Today* 41 (1984): 409–20; idem, "The Theology of Martin Luther King, Jr.," *Union Seminary Quarterly Review* 40 (1986): 21–39; David J. Garrow, "The Intellectual Development of Martin Luther King, Jr.: Influences and Commentaries," *Union Seminary Quarterly Review* 40 (1986): 5–20.

7. Martin Luther King, Jr., "An Autobiography of Religious Development," Nov. 1950, Martin Luther King, Jr., Papers, Mugar Library, Boston University. In this paper written for a college class, King commented: "I guess I accepted Biblical studies uncritically until I was about twelve years old. But this uncritical attitude could not last long, for it was contrary to the very nature of my being."

8. Aldon D. Morris, *The Origins of the Civil Rights Movement: Black Communities Organizing for Change* (New York, 1984), 10.

9. King described this episode, which occurred on the evening of 27 Jan. 1956, in a remarkable 1966 speech delivered in Chicago. See the discussion in Garrow, *Bearing the Cross*, 56–58, and in Professor Garrow's essay in this volume.

10. See, for example, Hanes Walton, *The Political Philosophy of Martin Luther King, Jr.* (Westport, Conn., 1971).

11. This new orientation is most clearly evident in studies of local movements, such as William H. Chafe, *Civilities and Civil Rights: Greensboro, North Carolina, and the Black Struggle for Equality* (New York, 1980); David R. Colburn, *Racial Change and Community Crisis: St. Augustine, Florida, 1877–1980* (New York, 1985); Robert J. Norrell, *Reaping the Whirlwind: The Civil Rights Movement in Tuskegee* (New York, 1985); John R. Salter, *Jackson, Mississippi: An American Chronicle of Struggle and Schism* (Hicksville, N.Y., 1979). A movement from King-centered biographies to more broadly conceived studies is also evident in the best works on King and the SCLC: Branch, *Parting the Waters;* Adam Fairclough, *To Redeem the Soul of America: The Southern Christian Leadership Conference and Martin Luther King, Jr.* (Athens, Ga., 1987); Garrow, *Bearing the Cross;* Lewis, *King;* and Stephen B. Oates, *Let the Trumpet Sound: The Life of Martin Luther King, Jr.* (New York, 1982).

12. See Clayborne Carson, *In Struggle: SNCC and the Black Awakening of the 1960s* (Cambridge, Mass., 1981); Howard Zinn, *SNCC: The New Abolitionists,* 2d ed. (Boston, 1965).

13. For incisive critiques of psychological analyses of the modern black struggle, see Doug McAdam, *Political Process and the Development of Black Insurgency, 1930–1970* (Chicago, 1982), and Morris, *Origins of the Civil Rights Movement.*

14. "The Drum Major Instinct," 4 Feb. 1968, in James Melvin Washington, ed., *A Testament of Hope: The Essential Writings of Martin Luther King, Jr.* (San Francisco, 1986), 267.

Contributors

MARY FRANCES BERRY is Geraldine R. Segal Professor of American Social Thought and History at the University of Pennsylvania. She is also a member of the United States Commission on Civil Rights.

CLAYBORNE CARSON is professor of history at Stanford University and senior editor and director of the Martin Luther King, Jr., Papers Project at the Martin Luther King, Jr., Center for Nonviolent Social Change and Stanford University.

JAMES H. CONE is Charles A. Briggs Distinguished Professor of Systematic Theology at Union Theological Seminary in New York City.

JOHN HOPE FRANKLIN is James B. Duke Professor of History Emeritus at Duke University.

DAVID J. GARROW is professor of political science at the City College of New York and the CUNY Graduate Center.

SHUN P. GOVENDER is director of the Kairos Center of the Belydende Kring (Confessing Circle) of the Dutch Reformed Churches in Cape Town and is the editor of *Dunamis (Power)*, the Belydende Kring's quarterly theological journal.

VINCENT HARDING is professor of religion and social transformation at the Iliff School of Theology in Denver, Colorado.

LOUIS R. HARLAN is distinguished professor of history at the University of Maryland, College Park.

GEORGE M. HOUSER is executive director emeritus of the American Committee on Africa.

NATHAN I. HUGGINS was W. E. B. Du Bois Professor of History and Afro-American Studies and director of the W. E. B. Du Bois Institute at Harvard University. He died on 5 Dec. 1989.

CORETTA SCOTT KING is founding president and chief executive officer of the Martin Luther King, Jr., Center for Nonviolent Social Change and is a member of the board of directors of SCLC.

RICHARD H. KING is a reader in American Studies at the University of Nottingham.

ALDON D. MORRIS is an associate professor in th :partment of sociology and in the Center for Urban Affairs and Policy Research at Northwestern University, Evanston, Illinois.

ROBERT PARRIS MOSES is currently pursuing a Ph.D. in philosophy at Harvard University and serves as a volunteer teacher in an experimental mathematics program at the Martin Luther King, Jr., School in Cambridge, Massachusetts.

CORNEL WEST is professor of religion and director of the Afro-American Studies Program at Princeton University.

HOWARD ZINN is professor emeritus of political science at Boston University.

Index